THE CLASSICS OF WESTERN SPIRITUALITY

THE CLASSICS OF WESTERN SPIRITUALITY
A Library of the Great Spiritual Masters

George A. Maloney, S.J.—Director, John XXIII Ecumenical Center, Fordham University, Bronx, N.Y.

Bernard McGinn—Professor of Historical Theology and History of Christianity, University of Chicago Divinity School, Chicago, Ill.

John Meyendorff—Professor of Church History, Fordham University, Bronx, N.Y., and Professor of Patristics and Church History, St. Vladimir's Seminary, Tuckahoe, N.Y.

Seyyed Hossein Nasr—Professor of Islamics, Department of Religion, Temple University, Philadelphia, Pa., and Visiting Professor, Harvard University, Cambridge, Mass.

Heiko A. Oberman—Director, Institute fuer Spaetmittelalter und Reformation, Universitaet Tuebingen, West Germany.

Alfonso Ortiz—Professor of Anthropology, University of New Mexico, Albuquerque, N. Mex.; Fellow, The Center for Advanced Study, Stanford, Calif.

Raimundo Panikkar—Professor, Department of Religious Studies, University of California at Santa Barbara, Calif.

Jaroslav Pelikan—Sterling Professor of History and Religious Studies, Yale University, New Haven, Conn.

Fazlar Rahman—Professor of Islamic Thought, Department of Near Eastern Languages and Civilization, University of Chicago, Chicago, Ill.

Annemarie B. Schimmel—Professor of Hindu Muslim Culture, Harvard University, Cambridge, Mass.

Sandra M. Schneiders—Assistant Professor of New Testament Studies and Spirituality, Jesuit School of Theology, Berkeley, Calif.

Huston Smith—Thomas J. Watson Professor of Religion, Adjunct Professor of Philosophy, Syracuse University, Syracuse, N.Y.

John R. Sommerfeldt—Professor of History, University of Dallas, Irving, Texas.

David Steindl-Rast—Monk of Mount Savior Monastery, Pine City, N.Y.

William C. Sturtevant—General Editor, Handbook of North American Indians, Smithsonian Institution, Washington, D.C.

David Tracy—Professor of Theology, University of Chicago Divinity School, Chicago, Ill.

Victor Turner—William B. Kenan Professor in Anthropology, The Center for Advanced Study, University of Virginia, Charlottesville, Va.

Kallistos Ware—Fellow of Pembroke College, Oxford; Spalding Lecturer in Eastern Orthodox Studies, Oxford University, England.

RICHARD ROLLE

THE ENGLISH WRITINGS

TRANSLATED, EDITED, AND INTRODUCED BY
ROSAMUND S. ALLEN

PREFACE BY
VALERIE M. LAGORIO

PAULIST PRESS
NEW YORK • MAHWAH

Cover Art: Courtesy of the Bodleian Library, Oxford, England

The publisher gratefully acknowledges the following: Oxford University Press for permission to use material from *The English Writings of Richard Rolle*, edited by Hope Emily Allen; the Marquess of Bath for permission to use material from *Longleat 29;* the University of California Press for permission to quote from P.H. Theiner, ed. and trans., *The Contra Amatores Mundi of Richard Rolle.* Excerpt from *The Fire of Love and the Mending of Life* by Richard Rolle. Translation copyright © 1981 by M.L. del Mastro. Reprinted by permission of Doubleday, a division of Bantam, Doubleday, Dell publishing Group, Inc.

Library of Congress Cataloging-in-Publication Data

Rolle, Richard, of Hampole, 1290? -1349.
[Selections. 1988]
The English writings / Richard Rolle ; translated, with an introduction and foreword, by Rosamund S. Allen ; preface by Valerie M. Lagorio.
p. cm. — (The Classics of Western spirituality)
Bibliography: p.
Includes index.
ISBN 0-8091-0401-6 : $16.95. ISBN 0-8091-3008-4 (pbk.) : $12.95
1. Christian literature, English (Middle)—Modernized versions.
2. Theology—Middle Ages, 600-1500. 3. Mysticism—England.
I. Allen, Rosamund, 1942- . II. Title. III. Series.
PR2135.A2A65 1988 88-19785
821'.1—dc19 CIP

Published by Paulist Press
997 Macarthur Boulevard
Mahwah, New Jersey 07430

Printed and bound in the United States of America

Contents

Editor of This Volume

ROSAMUND S. ALLEN is a graduate of University College, London, and King's College, London, and is currently Lecturer, Queen Mary College. She is a specialist in Old and Middle English Language, and Old Icelandic. Her publications include, "Notes on Some Textual Cruces in *King Horn*"; " 'Singuler Lufe': Richard Rolle and the Grammar of Spiritual Ascent," in *The Medieval Mystical Tradition in England.*

Author of the Preface

VALERIE M. LAGORIO is professor of English at the University of Iowa. She received the Ph.D. from Stanford University and has taught at the San Francisco College for Women and the University of Missouri. Professor Lagorio's research interests are twofold: the legend of King Arthur and the Holy Grail; and mysticism, medieval and modern, with a special concentration on women mystics. She is the co-author, with Ritamary Bradley, of *The Fourteenth Century English Mystics: A Comprehensive Annotated Bibliography*, and for the past fifteen years has been the editor of *Mystics Quarterly*.

But the soul which is in the third degree of love is like burning fire, and like the nightingale, which loves song and harmony and exhausts itself in its great love.

—*The Form of Living*, Chapter 8

TO THE MEMORY OF CANON JOHN PREEDY
AND
FATHER ALBERT TOMEI
who instructed me in the faith.

Preface

This long-awaited Modern English version of Richard Rolle's Middle English writings not only brings these works into the twentieth century but, thanks to its all-encompassing introduction and notes, pinpoints Rolle as a man and a mystic for all seasons and times.

Earlier criticisms of Rolle's life, drawn largely from the *Officium*, *Miracula*, and autobiographical references in his works, centered on his irregular eremitic lifestyle, the conjectural reasons for his leaving Oxford, the possibility of his attending the Sorbonne, his negative attitudes toward ecclesiastical authority, his misogyny, and his status as a priest or a layman. Additionally, critics had a penchant to classify him as "the Father of English Prose," drawn from E. K. Chambers' seminal study, head of "the School of Richard Rolle," as in the Wells' *Manual of Middle English Writings*, extended to include William of Nassington, and a slightly romanticized sylvan gyrovag, enthusiastically preaching his message of God's love to lady recluses and humble Yorkshire folk. Actually, as Professor Allen shows, relatively little is known about Rolle's life and one must take great care to distinguish fact from hagiographic embellishment (as in the posthumous *Officium* and *Miracula* written to promote his sanctification cause), and to weight judiciously biographical elements in his writings. What emerges from her exploration is a clear portrait of a young man with a dynamic personality, further characterized by unworldliness, which she considers his paramount trait, consistent integrity, warmth and tenderness for his flock, particularly the holy women for whom he served as spiritual director and wrote several of his most inspired works, an autodidact, amplifying his Oxford training by drawing from scriptures—much of his life can be seen as biblical *imitatio*—the Fathers of the Church, and more contemporary theologians. Additionally, he shares common attributes with the other fourteenth-century English mystics: an independence from monastic religious life and a preference for the solitary life; anti-intellectualism, an aversion to abstract speculation, and a predilection for affective piety and the primacy of the will in contemplation; devotion to Christ as God and man, to his passion and to the name of Jesus; strict doctrinal orthodoxy; a freedom from the influence of the Continental mystics; and writing in the vernacular to reach a wider, literate religious and lay audience.

In her *apologia pro sua vita*, Professor Allen also explores Rolle as a mystic who, until relatively recently, was denigrated as one who never achieved the higher reaches of contemplation and experiential union with God, an influential put-down advanced by Dom David Knowles. Even Hope Emily Allen, one of his most energetic and sympathetic critics, felt that his path on the *via mystica* stopped at or before the illuminative stage. Possibly when contrasted with the more restrained and intellectual *Cloud* author and Walter Hilton, Rolle suffered a fate similar to that of Margery Kempe, who was invidiously compared with Julian of Norwich, found very wanting indeed, and consequently dismissed, unfairly, as a mystic. The major criticism levied against Rolle resulted from his use of sensual images of fire, sweetness and song (*calor*, *dulcor*, *canor*) to describe his progress toward union (which he felt, incidentally, he had achieved), but such usage was metaphorical, referring to the spiritual senses. Yet the *Cloud* author and Hilton cautioned against such manifestations of false comfort, not so much directed at Rolle himself, but rather as a warning to those who sought after or equated such literal sensations with mystical experience. Thus they were actually protesting against the possible deleterious effect Rolle could have on his readers and followers. Another major criticism which Professor Allen elucidates is Rolle's claim to a continual union with God, and his delineation of the three degrees of mystical love as insuperable, inseparable, and singular, omitting the fourth stage of "insatiable" love, which refers to the life of contemplation-in-action, whereby the mystic returns to the world as God's instrument for justice and Christian love in the church and in the world—and this is the ultimate extension of the mystical life. Most assuredly Rolle lived this life of mystical social responsibility as a prophet, writer, teacher and spiritual guide, and his great popularity in his own lifetime and afterward, both in England and on the Continent, attests to his zeal and influence.

What is so singularly impressive about Professor Allen's depiction of Rolle is her comprehensive knowledge of his texts, both Latin and English, the context in which they were written, their audience and purpose, and such major influences as scriptures, the Church Fathers, Anselm, Bernard of Clairvaux, the Victorines and Edmund Rich, among others. While she touches on Franciscan influence, she does not consider Rolle's epithet as "the English Bonaventure," an accolade earned by his emphasis on *canor* or song, which, according to William Pollard, coalesces with Rolle's participation in the twin thrusts of Franciscan spirituality, affective piety and ecstatic joy, and his espousal of the cult of the Holy Name, exemplarism and celestial harmony, all fused in the passion of Christ.

Professor Allen's choice of Hope Emily Allen's 1931 anthology of Rolle's English works (supplemented by additions from the *English Psalter*) is a wise one for several reasons. In recent years there have been modern English translations of his major Latin works, such as the *Incendium Amoris* (*Fire of Love*), *Emendatio Vitae* (*Mending of Life*) and the *Contra Amatores Mundi* (*Against the Lovers of the World*), but his English canon has largely remained in its Middle English linguistic cloister until now, despite the fact that it includes three of his greatest and most mature works: *Ego Dormio*, *The Commandment* and *The Form of Living*. Allen's resultant work is a compendium of medieval spiritual writings, which far from archaic relics of an age gone by (although one must admit that *The Bee and the Stork* in the allegorized bestiary tradition is thoroughly medieval), speaks to the problems, needs and aspiration of life today. It offers guidance on reading, meditation and prayer, leading to self-knowledge and contemplation within the Christian sanction, but applicable to the search for meaning in our lives which impels all of us. The variety of this collection is astonishing: The *English Psalter* and commentaries speak to the need for *lectio* or reading as a preliminary step for contemplation; the *Meditations on the Passion* invites the reader to identify with the crucified Christ, not only to instill sorrow for our transgressions, but to exemplify the boundless love of the Savior; the catechetical treatise on the *Ten Commandments*, essential to Christian faith and practice, is supplemented by the moving, exclamatory prayers

Ghostly Gladness and *Desire and Delight*, as well as a series of meditative and ecstatic lyrics; and the three great epistles, addressed to a single person but obviously intended for a wider audience, are knowledgeable and loving guides to the contemplative life. Often I am asked to define Christian mysticism and to recommend a guide to the progressive prayer life of purgation, illumination and contemplative union, and I invariably suggest *The Form of Living* with its clearly demarcated stages of progress, its intense and beautiful language, its lyric ecstasies, and, above all, its sustained and joyful expression of trust, hope and divine love which mark the relationship between God and humankind.

As a medievalist specializing in Christian mysticism and editor of *Mystics Quarterly*, I owe an enormous debt to the Paulist Press's Classics of Western Spirituality Series. Like the present work of Professor Allen, the adaptations are superb, and the introductory material, suggestions for supplemental reading and informative notes enlightening for a wide audience of academics, religious and the general public. Some would argue that these and other devotional and mystical texts should be studied only in the original language, which would limit their audience to researchers and scholars, a restriction with which I do not agree, nor, may I add, would Richard Rolle—hence, his vernacular works. Others hold that only theologians can deal responsibly with these texts, but this overlooks the fact that the great mystics did not write solely for theologians but rather for their "even Christians." Thus the Paulist Press wisely adheres to this dictum of excellence and a broad audience.

With this Rolle volume, and with the forthcoming Modern English edition of Walter Hilton's *Scale of Perfection*, the Paulists will have published the major works of the fourteenth-century English mystics, but there are many other texts such as *A Talking of the Love of God* and the Anselmian *Wooing Group*, Hilton's *On the Mixed Life* and Rolle's *Melos Amoris*, to mention only a few. Can we perhaps hope that the English mystical canon can continue to receive the favorable attention of the Paulist Press, so that, like this present edition, these works can become a part of our spiritual heritage today?

Foreword

About This Volume

It is well over fifty years since Rolle's English writings were published in Heseltine's translation, and the general reader has long been without a generally available modern version of those works which Rolle wrote in Middle English. Much of his most mystical work is in Latin, and even the English works, which he wrote toward the end of his life, are not easy reading today because of the difficulties which his Yorkshire dialect of Middle English presents for all who are not students of the English language. The beauties of Rolle's rhythms and alliterative patterns are inevitably impaired or lost in translation, but his viewpoint remains clear, and it is possible to capture in modern idiom some of the earnest tone of the conscientious teacher; the teaching is the man, and of perennial interest. Rolle's Latin works are now receiving the attention they deserve; they are in the process of being translated, mainly by scholars in North America, and are increasingly the subject of critical attention by theological and literary specialists. Apart from the continuing Fordham University project on Rolle's English *Psalter*, his English works have been in need of thorough re-appraisal, both to determine the exact canon of his English writing and to establish an accurate text. The forthcoming edition of Rolle's works in Middle English by Dr. Ogilvie-Thomson will accomplish this, and time and again while translating I have wished that her volume had already been published. I have used the text of Rolle's *English Writings* edited by Hope Emily

Allen in 1931; this is a selection of Rolle's English work, which I have supplemented from Horstman's first volume of *Yorkshire Writers* (1895) and Bramley's 1881 edition of Rolle's English *Psalter*.

A Note on the Translation

Rolle's Middle English presents his translator with the usual examples of semantic change, often in his case disguised by the fact that religious language has not tended to keep pace with change of meaning in secular usage. When Rolle uses a word like *comforted*, for instance, he means "strengthened," although the liturgy still speaks of the Holy Spirit as "comforter"; for Rolle the *will* is the appetitive faculty of the soul and not mere inclination. He himself translates *gloria* in the psalms as "bliss" and "joy" (although he also uses the adjective *glorious*) rather than "honor" or "praise," but there must be semantic overlap here, since although both *joy* and *glory* were used in the later fourteenth century for the splendor and bliss of heaven, Rolle also uses *joy* to connote the spiritual delight of loving God in this world (e.g. *Form*, Chap. 2). At times Rolle seems to span uneasily the divide between the older language and the newer English made more "refined" by the importation of French loanwords: he uses *tholemodeness* in his Psalm translations but prefers *patience* when writing his letters; I cannot determine whether he made any distinction of meaning between the two. Only occasionally is it possible to retain Rolle's alliterative phrases and rhythms; once or twice, where modern English affords an alliterative collocation not available to Rolle, I have used this to translate a phrase which did not alliterate in the original; this, I felt, was in keeping with Rolle's own style and reflects a tendency to alliterative phrasing still current in English ("careless driving kills," "believers' baptism," etc.). Where possible I try to avoid using polysyllables and latinate words; Rolle's vocabulary was, in its time, up-to-date, but many of our theological and philosophical words did not enter the language until a hundred years after his time (*conscientious*, *perception*, *donation*), and it seems that Rolle would have avoided them had they been available—his aim seems to have been to write simply, probably so that his reader(s) could manage to follow without the assistance of a trained cleric. Therefore I have tended to use simple words such as *just*, *good*, *knowing*, *seeing*, *giving*. Especially in the case of the verbal nouns, I have tried to keep to Rolle's pattern of using runs of words ending in *-ing;*

the device echoes something of the urgency of his message and matches his own dictum that activity is important. I have also retained Rolle's *burning* in preference to *ardor*, *ardent*, mainly because the connotations of domesticity and familiarity in the native word are an important aspect of Rolle's meaning. I keep *degrees* (properly *steps* or *stages*) of love because Rolle's "three degrees of love" are so famous that any other rendering would have been confusing.

A real problem for the translator is posed by *love*. Rolle's habitual spelling for our words *love/loving* was probably *luf*, *lufand;* in northern manuscripts, *love* should mean "praise," but scribes probably often confused the two, especially where context does not indicate which is meant. I have tried to translate "praise" wherever the southernized manuscript Longleat 29 uses this word, but this itself may often be merely scribal.

One archaism I have kept: the form *Jesu*, still heard in hymns and sometimes prayers, was regular in Middle English, especially in second person address, where it derived from the Old French oblique form. Although *Jesu* occurred in the earlier Bible translations and in the *Prayer Book*, it was not used in the Douay and Authorized Version translations, but its presence in hymns has led us to associate this form with intimacy and perhaps personal fervor, and I retain it in the *Meditations* where Rolle addresses Christ directly, but use "Jesus (Christ)," even where Rolle uses *J(h)esu*, in the third-person references.

The most difficult Middle English word to translate is *alas:* it is simply not modern style to give vent to dismay in this form; I retain it in the *Lyrics*, but use a circumlocution elsewhere.

Symbols Used in the Text

- [ ] The square bracket signals a reading adopted from a manuscript other than that used for the main body of the text, as indicated in the headnote for each item.
- ( ) Parentheses mark words supplied for idiomatic Modern English style.

Dictionaries

The dictionaries used in the preparation of this translation were: *The Middle English Dictionary*, ed. H. Kurath and S. M. Kuhn (Ann Arbor, 1954) for A through P (*MED*), and for the remainder of the alphabet, *The Oxford English Dictionary*, ed. James A. H. Murray, corrected re-issue of *A New English Dictionary on Historical Principles* (Oxford, 1933), (*OED*).

Except for his *Psalter*, Rolle's works are not well-covered by either of these dictionaries, and frequently his use of a word or sense predates the earliest dated entry by some twenty to fifty years.

Abbreviations

The following abbreviated titles are used in the Notes to the Introduction and Notes to the Translated Text:

WA: Hope Emily Allen, *Writings Ascribed to Richard Rolle, Hermit of Hampole, and Materials for his Biography*, The Modern Language Association of America, Monograph Series III, New York: D. Heath and Company, 1927.

EW: Hope Emily Allen, *The English Writings of Richard Rolle, Hermit of Hampole*, Oxford: Clarendon Press, 1931, repr. 1963.

YW I: C. Horstman, *Yorkshire Writers: Richard Rolle of Hampole and his followers*, Library of Early English Writers, Vol. I, London: Swan Sonnenschein, 1895.

YW II: C. Horstman, *Yorkshire Writers: Richard Rolle of Hampole and his Followers*, Vol. II, London, Swan Sonnenschein, 1896.

Acknowledgments

I am deeply indebted to Dr. Ogilvie-Thomson, who supplied advice freely, gave a copy of her 1959 article and permission to consult her D. Phil. thesis on the contents of MS Longleat 29, and has kindly allowed me to use the format of Longleat 29, rather than that of MS CUL Dd V 64 as printed by Hope Allen, for the *Lyrics*.

The encouragement and help of Professor Valerie Lagorio, who first suggested this volume, must be gratefully recorded. My thanks are also extended to two former students, Marianne Williamson, who read much of the translation in typescript and gave suggestions for improvement, and Simon Forrest who typed the translations.

My final debt of gratitude is to my husband and daughter, Stephan and Veronica Sulyak, for whom my many absences (and even more trying presence) during the preparation of this work caused many extra domestic duties and many sacrifices.

Introduction:
Richard Rolle: c1300–1349

His Personality and Life

"*Frater meus insanit:* My brother's gone mad."[1]

"She knew that he was loyal to his promise, and he had promised her that as long as he was alive in the body she would never again suffer such anguish."[2]

These two very different reactions to Richard Rolle's vocation as a hermit in rural Yorkshire in the early fourteenth century are recorded in the Office of lessons and antiphons which was drawn up in the 1380s in preparation for his canonization. In fact Rolle was never officially canonized, but inspired a flourishing cult, especially in the north of England, for nearly two hundred years. Both of these recorded reactions relate, significantly, to his relationships with women. Rolle's English works translated in this volume were probably all prepared for the spiritual guidance and for the devotions of women. Rolle himself seems to have been acutely aware of the female sex, as a source of temptation in his youth, but later as the object of quite tender concern.

Yet the dismayed outcry of his sister: "My brother's gone mad," was not unprovoked, and his response to her shriek (we do not even know her name) was to drive her away from him with threats (Office, Lesson I). When the call of his vocation conflicted with family or personal interests, Rolle could be severe (on himself as much as others) to the point of violence, and this is sometimes apparent in his writing. The occasion of his sister's outburst is recounted in the first Lesson of the Office of "Saint Richard of Hampole."

> During the long vacation from Oxford University, probably in his fifth year there, Rolle had asked his favorite sister for two of her tunics, a gray and a white, and, trustingly, she had brought them to him, as arranged, in a little wood near their home. There, he had vandalized both garments, ripping the sleeves from the gray and the buttons from the white tunic, and had then scandalized his sister by dressing up in them, wearing the white next to his skin and the now sleeveless gray tunic over it, completing the ensemble with his father's rain-hood as a cowl.[3]

Rolle was making a desperate bid to try his vocation as a hermit, attempting a homemade version of the traditional hermit's habit. He seems to have retained these colors even after patrons were found who could give him more orthodox clothing, since this is how he was dressed when, after death, he appeared in a vision to a sick woman.[4] This touching account of Rolle's "clothing" must have been supplied either by Rolle himself (and if so, probably to one of his female acquaintances, since the details of the clothing are so specific) or, more likely, by the sister.

The other comment quoted at the head of this section must also have been supplied to those compiling Rolle's Office by the person concerned. She was Margaret Kirk(e)by, an enclosed recluse, who had suffered a severe seizure which left her unable to speak or move. Rolle, summoned to her cell, had held her during another, apparently epileptic, attack, and when it was over had remarked genially: "Even if you had been the devil, I would have held you!" He had then promised her that she would never suffer another such attack while he was alive.[5] She did have another attack, the Office claims it was some years later,[6] but in fact it must have been just five months after, on September 29, 1349, and a messenger whom she had dispatched from East Layton, on the Durham border, all the way down to Hampole near Doncaster, brought back the information that Richard had died at the very moment of her spasm. She suffered no further attacks for the rest of her long life and died about 1405.[7] Margaret is of interest since the finest of Rolle's English works, *The Form of Living*, was written for her.

The tone of Margaret's report of Rolle's promise to her is serene, reflecting a deep and fruitful friendship. Richard Rolle was a man who inspired deep affection in those who knew him, and a loyal following of friends, particularly from the peasant class, after his death. The miracles recorded in the readings in the Office for the Octave of his feast, the week following the proposed feast-day itself, show Rolle's intervention in curing children who had choked, drowned or been suffocated, whose mothers must have been the intercessories with "saint" Richard, but cures of people of both sexes, especially those suffering from deafness, are recorded.[8] The cult of Richard seems to have begun in the 1380s when a man called Roger was instructed in a series of visions by Rolle.[9] Roger was "inflamed with a spirit of holy devotion" and in gratitude attempted to build a tomb for Rolle; he was rescued by the "saint's" miraculous intervention when the cart in which he was carrying the materials for the tomb overturned, nearly crushing him by depositing two enormous stones on him.[10] Rolle's cult was still flourishing in the early sixteenth century; perhaps only the change of religion prevented his final canonization: his popularity among the unlearned was undiminished.[11]

Yet despite the popular following his personality seems to have inspired, and despite the fact that many very high-ranking layfolk and clerics in the fifteenth and sixteenth centuries owned his books,[12] Rolle himself writes of his many enemies and of the way in which those who had supported him had now become his greatest opponents.[13] His manner with the desperately ill Margaret was gentle and reassuring, and his extant letters to her and to other women whom he advised are understanding, intimate in tone and encouraging, as can be seen in *Ego Dormio*, *The Commandment* and *The Form of Living* in this volume. There must have been much advice on the same lines which Rolle gave orally to those seeking his help. Nevertheless Rolle did also write some of the most critical comments on the female sex to have come out of the notoriously antifeminist Middle Ages.[14]

The enigma posed by the contrasting images we have of Rolle, given in the Office itself in the records of his sister and Margaret Kirkby, and reflected in his writings and, apparently, his reputation, is not easily resolved. The Office is not accurate in the details of Rolle's life and gives very little information at all between the initial stages of Rolle's conversion and the final months of his life. Hope Allen conjectures many attendant details and circumstances for the few details we glean from the Office and Rolle's own work; while these hypothetical details are very illuminating for the life and attitudes of Rolle's times, they have no more certain status than surmise in many cases, despite her subsequent assumption of many of her guesses as fact. Nor is Rolle's own writing necessarily as biographical as we might assume. He often writes in the first person where he is in fact talking generally, using himself as an "Everyman" figure, or reliving the experiences of the Psalmist, the prophet or Christ himself in his own person, along the lines suggested first by St. Paul: "Always, wherever we may be, we carry with us in our body the death of Jesus, so that the life of Jesus, too, may always be seen in our body" (2 Cor 4:10). Rolle was deeply imbued with biblical texts and their glosses and is often writing more generally than his apparently idiosyncratic imagery and subjective tone might imply.

The only details in Richard's biography which can really be substantiated with some degree of certainty are those contained in Lessons I, II and III and Lesson VIII in the Office; these have been investigated by Hope Allen, and further filled out by Frances Comper and Geraldine Hodgson.[15] Colophons to his works were supplied by fifteenth-century scribes, often as far away as the south of England or even Bohemia, and may or may not depend on reliable sources.[16]

Rolle was born at "Thornton, near Pickering," which probably means Thornton le Dale in the North Riding of Yorkshire. His birth is likely to have been about 1300, although some scholars put it at 1290 or soon after.[17] His father William was probably a family retainer, or former retainer, of John de Dalton, himself perhaps the younger son of Sir Richard Dalton of Bispham in Lancashire; John had come east in the service of Thomas, Earl of Lancaster, whom he served, dishonestly it seems, in the capacity of constable of Pickering Castle and keeper of Pickering Forest from about 1306 to 1322.[18] In 1322, John suffered the inevitable eclipse which followed Lancaster's rebellion and execution: his estates at Pickering and his private manor at Foulbridge were confiscated and he himself imprisoned, although he soon secured his release through the good offices of a near neighbor, Henry de Percy, and was able to buy land at Kirkby Misperton and Knapton in the East Riding in 1323.[19] Dalton was never knighted—his title remained esquire—and his mismanagement of the forest estates involved wastage of timber, harassment and impoverishment of the poor folk living in its boundaries, false acquisition of land and manors, opposing the king and besieging the king's representative, Piers Gaveston, at Scarborough Castle.[20] Much of this was done under Lancaster's leadership, although the wrongful appropriation of land is Dalton's own malfeasance. Yet this worldly and extortionate man is named in Lesson II as Rolle's first patron after he left university.

The first lesson recounts that Rolle's parents provided for his schooling. This would be difficult but not impossible even if they were serfs, as a probable ancestor of Rolle in 1160, one Ricardus Rollevillein, certainly may have been.[21] Entries under the name William Rolle of Yafforth, where Rolle's family might have moved, in the Lay Subsidy rolls for 1327 and 1333 indicate payments of subsidy of 9d. and 2s.,[22] making William (perhaps Rolle's father or brother) a small householder, probably a tenant farmer; if the family was able to move from Thornton, a village at the foot of the moors, into the district of Richmondshire forty miles away, they must have been freeholders; serfs and villeins would not be allowed to move, except to other estates of their overlord, and Dalton does not seem to have owned any in Yafforth. Rolle's parents did not have means to send him to university, since the Office states that his expenses there, in board, maintenance and tuition fees, were paid by Thomas de Neville, the fifth son of Ralph, first Lord of Raby, who became archdeacon of Durham and gained many other benefices in his very lucrative church career; he may also have been a professor of civil law in 1327.[23] Neville was probably little older than Rolle and perhaps hoped to have Richard's support, once he had graduated as *magister*, in the growing administrative duties deriving from Neville's various properties and prebends, or perhaps there was a political motive behind sponsoring a young lad from the Yorkshire countryside, as there may have been in Dalton's case.[24]

Rolle's patron and family alike must have been disappointed when Rolle, in his nineteenth year, failed to return to Oxford after the long vacation in which he took up his calling as a hermit by seizing his sister's tunics (pp. 9–10, above). He would have been up at Oxford since the age of about 14 or 13 and would have been expected to reach his M.A. at the age of 21 or soon after.[25] Without his degree he could not proceed to major orders, could not preach, nor teach, and was thus disqualified from holding a benefice and so supporting himself and assisting his family, and from holding any major bureaucratic office beyond acting as an accountant on some small country estate. This would certainly not have interested him anyway; the Office

(Lesson I) recounts his interest in theology and biblical studies rather than in philosophy or secular studies. Oxford was more noted for the last two, so Rolle's university career may have been a disappointment to him in his turn.

After his bizarre attempt to gain his sister's support in trying his eremetical vocation, Rolle left home at once. We hear no more of his family, although he was living in Richmondshire in the 1340s and may have been reconciled to them eventually. He fled in his gray-and-white tunics from their probable new home in Yafforth, near Northallerton, to the old family home of Thornton, probably his own birthplace, forty miles to the east in the East Riding. He may have been looking for solitude: the area round Pickering was wild (and dangerous, under Dalton) in those times. He would also have wished, being underage, to get well away from parental influence: Lesson III recounts his extreme reluctance to admit his identity in case he was forced to return home. But Rolle's immediate need, when he left his astounded sister in that summer wood, would have been to find himself a patron, and he must have thought that Dalton, his father's former squire,[26] would be suitable. Possibly the unworldly young man had not even realized Dalton's reputation for unfair dealing.

Lesson II describes, in quasi-miraculous style, how on August 14th Dalton's wife discovered Richard praying in her seat in a certain church and refused to allow her sons to turn him out, not wishing to disturb his deep devotions. It describes how the following day Rolle donned a surplice and, unbidden, sang the office of Matins and assisted at the Mass of the Feast of the Assumption, and, obtaining permission from the officiating priest, was allowed to preach a sermon of such "virtue and power" that all present were moved to tears. This is romantic hagiography. How Rolle, unordained, obtained permission without diocesan licence to preach is a puzzle; it must have been the first and last sermon of his life. It is strange, therefore, that we are not told its text and theme; some embroidery of fact has probably taken place here.[27] Sitting in the seat of the lady of the manor was probably not a sign of arrogance or spiritual rapture: Rolle probably wished to make contact with the squire's family as quickly as he could and chose this way; he can hardly have sat in the manorial pew by mistake, as the Office suggests, since medieval churches had very little seating (apart from stone seating round the walls) and he probably picked the only seat in the church. This church was not necessarily that at Pickering (although the "multitude" of the congregation mentioned in the Office makes that likely), but could have been the small church at Snainton, near the Dalton's manor of Foulbridge, an old Templar holding which had not been cultivated since the Conquest;[28] it was a mile east of Yedingham Priory which, one manuscript claims, was the convent where lived the nun to whom *Ego Dormio* was addressed.[29]

After Mass Dalton invited Rolle to his house for the main meal of the day, probably taken sometime about late morning. When the meal was ready, Lesson III recounts, Rolle could not be found. He was eventually located in a certain "broken-down old house" or "room"; Hope Allen conjectures that if "house" is meant, this could be the ruined Templar building.[30] He was persuaded to join the feast, ate in silence, tried to retire before the trestle tables on which the meal was served were taken down (a signal for dancing to begin) and was then detained by Dalton and asked details of himself. This is extraordinary. The Office explains the event by alluding to Christ's advice to choose the lowest position at feasts (Lk 14:10). If this was Rolle's motive, a foretaste of his later tendency to model himself on the scriptures, then it was gauchely done. The medieval feast, especially on a church festival such as this, the Assumption of Our Lady, was an art form in itself: it comprised music, several elaborately prepared courses of food, witty conversation, entertainment by jesters, acrobats, storytellers, actors, comic turns and animal acts. A self-willed man like Dalton could have interpreted Rolle's total taciturnity as a gross insult, especially as he had placed the young man above his own two sons, themselves scholars from Oxford, at the table. The seating of guests at feasts was a matter of elaborate and exact protocol.

Dalton, who had already been informed of Rolle's identity by his sons who had recognized him the day before in the church, showed amazing forbearance. Having wrung from Rolle the grudging admission that "perhaps he might be the son of William Rolle," he proceeded to house the young man in a cell in his house and to provide him with a proper habit and with food instead of sending him back to his father in Richmondshire.

Why did Rolle behave so strangely? Why did the Office devote three- and one-half readings from the liturgy for Rolle's hoped-for feast day to such strangely unworldly behavior? Del Mastro surmises that this was a discreet compromise by the aspirant hermit, who wished to withdraw from the world and so unexpectedly found himself the center of attention at the kind of feast he most wanted to avoid.[31] This is possible; it is less likely that Rolle was being deliberately uncooperative because he despised worldly pleasure or scorned Dalton for his reputation: he describes in his Latin writings how he was censured for joining in at banquets while living with the Daltons and for not living abstemiously.[32] It may be that Rolle was too nervous or socially inexperienced to know how to behave with propriety at a feast. The Office dwells on these events because they show how very untypical of his time (and by inference, how saintly) Rolle was: churchmen were regularly invited to feasts in medieval times; abbots and priors, living more as country gentlemen than devout religious, entertained at their own feasts, while bishops held feasts on a scale as lavish as those of the nobility. Because Rolle had himself referred to detractors who accused him of worldliness, the compilers of the Office must have felt it important to give extensive coverage to the details of his first encounter with the Daltons, drawn perhaps from some old family retainer who recollected the events of sixty years before (probably not very accurately), in order to refute the charge.

Rolle was presumably housed at Dalton's main residence at Pickering rather than the summer residence of Foulbridge.[33] The Office says that he remained under Dalton's patronage "for a long time," so that it must have been there that he experienced his initial mystical manifestations and suffered his only recorded major temptation. This is quoted in Lesson VII of the Office from the account Rolle himself gave in his *Comment on the Canticles.* He thought that he was being visited late one night by a beautiful young lady whom he knew and who was fond of him. When she sat down, to his amazement, on his bed, he tried to get up to make the sign of the cross and found she held him back. This made him suspect a diabolical visitation, and he managed to pray mentally: "O Jesus, how precious is your blood," making the sign of the cross on his breast with one finger, at which the infernal vision disappeared.[34] This detail was probably selected for the Office from Rolle's writing because it initiated his famous devotion to the Holy Name, by his own account, and because it shows Rolle as a man strong against temptation, in true saintly mold. Very interestingly, it also matches the account Rolle gives in *The Form of Living* (Chap. 2) of the woman tempted by a devil, who showed her a false image of the Virgin Mary, a tale Rolle took, directly or indirectly, from Cassian. In *The Form* Rolle connects such experiences with the initial stages of conversion, as must have been his own situation.

After its lengthy account of how Rolle embraced the life of a hermit, the Office is very silent on his subsequent mode and place of living. The initial account is lengthy because Rolle's procedure was irregular: he should have sought permission for his life as a hermit from the bishop[35] and given proof of his ability to maintain himself, either by working a plot of land or by undertaking some public work, such as tending a road, ferry, bridge or hospital, or being endowed in a hermitage well away from the community. The long narrative is an *apologia pro vita eius;* in Lesson VIII there is an apologetic account of Rolle's reasons for changing his cell(s) later in life. Rolle did not conform, even to the standard model of a hermit.

While Lessons IV, V, VII and IX are devoted to Rolle's spirituality, mainly by extensive quotation from his works, Lessons VI and VIII continue, in anecdotal form, to describe the man himself. Lesson VI furnishes two anecdotes, doubtless drawn from eyewitnesses, which probably come from his time at the Dalton's. In one we hear how the lady of the house visited his cell after dinner, with a bevy of guests, and cajoled him into conversing with them; he continued to instruct them for two hours, while at the same time continuing to write, on a completely different topic and presumably in Latin. The other recounts how when Rolle was at prayer, his cloak was once removed, darned and replaced without his being in the least aware of the operation. These "signs of sanctity" in reality prove little more than a prodigious ability to concentrate. Another, even more naive report, is given in Lesson VIII of Rolle's intervention when a "certain lady" lay dying and was troubled by spirits. Because Rolle had given much help to those who were disturbed by malignant forces, he was sent for when all attempts to allay the spirits with holy water and prayers had failed. Rolle succeeded, but at great cost: his own cell was troubled by demons for a long time after, and made uninhabitable. The account further embellishes the story by describing the burnt tracks of ox-hooves which could be seen in the rushes covering the floor. Hope Allen surmises that the lady in question was not Dalton's wife but Lady de Percy, a near neighbor at Foulbridge.[36] There is no proof of this; the event might have occurred after Rolle left Dalton. It seems to be recorded in the Latin work, probably of Rolle's middle years, called *Contra Amatores Mundi*

(Chap. 6). There Rolle describes how, not long before the time of writing, a certain prominent woman, who with her husband had maintained him "for many years" went the way of all flesh, and he experienced "such horror (which) flew about my heart and my flesh that it was terrifying for me to enter my cell, which I did with pleasure before . . . and until the time that the body was put into the ground, the terror did not leave me; afterwards it vanished completely, but only little by little."[37] Rolle explains there that he was not afraid of the corpse, nor of death, nor of devils. The terror was nameless, and the more unbearable for that reason.

The Office (Lesson VIII) then announces that Rolle took himself to "other parts" after this terrifying experience, justifying "frequent changes of abode" as necessary in cases of persecution, local difficulties or the harassment of evil men, but without explaining which of these Rolle claimed as his reason.[38] It seems that Rolle had long since left the Dalton's at the time of the death-terror; Dalton's downfall and imprisonment took place in 1322, and Rolle was probably only at his house for about three years. In his *Judica Me Deus*, probably a very early work, he explains how he was disturbed "because of the people gathering in the harvest," by which he means all the produce of the outlying farms whose tenant farmers brought produce to the barns on Dalton's manor from Whitsun until the annual livestock cull at Martinmas (November 11).[39] Rolle then declares that he prefers to remain in one place which is convenient winter and summer alike and announces that "he" did not care for Rolle, and may take "another."[40] Rolle archly hints that there is another reason why he left, which he will never divulge.[41] In *Melos Amoris* he claims that his patron, presumably Dalton, left him cold and gave him filthy rags to wear while he feasted on the fat of the land, but this cannot have been Rolle's reason for leaving either.[42]

Whatever the reason for Rolle's change, he was very defensive on the subject, adverting to it again in the *Melos*. The first change must have come early; *Judica Me Deus* is a set of four tracts, mainly taken from a contemporary, William of Pagula, or Paull, near Kingston-on-Hull, who completed the work by 1327, but the autobiographical account is contained in the first part, "Judica A," which is not drawn from the source and could date from 1322 or even before.[43] Whatever Rolle's reason for leaving Dalton, he was spared the confusion and dangers of Dalton's disgrace after the 1322 uprising.

The Office (Lesson VIII) then narrates, in what is already an over-long lesson,[44] the account of Rolle's healing of Margaret which is alluded to above. This account Hope Allen thinks is likely to be "veracious" because it is hard to see why the strange details in the story should have been fabricated.[45] After Richard had been sent for, from his cell twelve miles away (an authentic-sounding reference) he arrived to find her unable to speak at all. Since an anchoress could not admit a male visitor to her guest parlor, he remained outside her cell and in this way they ate a meal; she fell asleep then, so the narrative runs, with her head on his shoulder. It was at this moment that she had her seizure and seemed likely to smash the window in her convulsion, but was suddenly able to speak again, crying "*Gloria tibi, Domine.*" Richard completed the compline hymn which she had begun and advised her to use her restored power of speech for spiritual good. The incident was repeated a little while later, and she became apparently insane, but Richard held her and then made her the promise that she would not suffer again in this way in his life.[46] The subsequent account, in which she learned of his death after a further seizure, Hope Allen dismissed as a memory disturbed by the horrors of the Black Death, which was raging in Yorkshire in 1349, although beginning to abate by mid-Autumn, when Rolle died. It certainly sounds like a pious fantasy, with the requisite element of the supernatural in it for a saint's life, but this can hardly be said of the account in which Margaret sleeps on Richard's shoulder. This does not belong in a lectio for Matins; not only does it make the reading far too long and provide material for possible scandal, but it is sentimental in tone and excessive in detail. Hope Allen assumes some disruption here, material originally planned for the readings of the octave having been displaced by additional evidence in the form of increasing *miracula* occurring at the shrine, which were inserted into the octave readings.[47] Even so, the story of Margaret is inappropriate, although it might conceivably be suitable in a more lengthy saint's life. It looks as if the Office was not more than a preliminary draft, recording for future use the depositions of many eyewitnesses who were aging by the 1380s and whose testimony was in danger of being lost to posterity. This, if anything, increases the value of these reminiscences, not as historical truth, necessarily, but as impressions made on contemporaries by the personality of Richard, showing where he matched the contemporary image of "a saint," and where he fulfilled their needs and assisted them in real difficulties. His unworldliness seems to have impressed them deeply; since his message in all his writings was the vital necessity of freeing oneself from the snares of worldliness, he seems to have been a man of consistent integrity whose life reinforced the theme of his already powerful writing. The more touching or puzzling details are more valuable for modern readers; they modify the somewhat stern image which much of his Latin writing gives and support the impression we gain from the English works, written largely for women, that he was a man of tenderness and concern, especially for the weak, neglected and the poor, who were the most loyal devotees of his cult. In reality it seems that Richard was not an enemy of all women, but was deeply resentful of the frivolities, the extravagance and superciliousness of women of the gentry and nobility; in fact, he is equally scathing about the ideals of upper-class males, with their knightly ethos and obsession with martial prowess:

> Some make proud vanity or empty honour their god, for the sake of which they exalt themselves, endure hardship, undergo need, give and take wounds, kill and are killed. Some make silver and gold their god, some castles and manors, some land holdings and villas, some hounds and dogs, some a strong horse, some a beautiful woman, and some their bellies. Others make sexual pleasure their god; and all of these are lost along with their gods (*Contra Amatores Mundi*, trans. Theiner, p. 181).

Rolle is reacting against the salient idealisms of his time: courtly love, chivalry and the upward mobility of the developing middle class. He has a distinctly Franciscan aversion to materialism, and there are elements of Franciscan devotion in his writing too. Like Francis he left family and friends and seems to have suffered a certain degree of physical deprivation, although while he lived with the Dalton's his frustrations, stemming from interruption and noise, were his chief penance. His life was socially and financially insecure, dependent as he was on benefactors for food and shelter, and exposed to scandal if their immoral lifestyle caused legal reprisals in the community, as happened to Dalton after Rolle had left his household. Rolle claims in *Melos Amoris* that his critics said he was not living a penitential life because he ate with the household and slept under their roof;[48] this conflicts with the Vienna MS which describes his life of extreme abstinence in total enclosure. It is possible, as Hope Allen suggests, that he did enter full enclosure late in life.[49] His comments in *The*

Form of Living[50] and in *Incendium Amoris* that fervent devotion is more important than all ascetic extremes imaginable seems more consistent with his own practice and with spiritual maturity.

Richard was not an anchorite in his early career. A total recluse, male or female (although women more commonly took up this profession, like Margaret Kirkby herself) would be totally confined to one house. There she would be "enclosed" in a formal ceremony in which a bishop read the service of the dead over her, indicating that she was "dead to the world," and made an impression with sealing-wax on the door of her house—she was never to emerge except to be buried. In fact, Margaret herself did move from her first place of enclosure at East Layton, three miles from the Durham border, to Ainderby near the Great North Road and about eight miles south of Yafforth, where Rolle's parents may have lived.[51] She did not move until 1357, and the Office is wrong in implying that she was at Ainderby prior to being cured by Richard; she moved some seven years after his death, as Clay discovered in her researches on recluses,[52] because she could not see the high altar through the window of her cell. A cell would normally have one window in the church wall against which the anchorholds were built, in addition to one giving on to the outside world, like the one through which Margaret had communed with Richard. Margaret moved yet again, to Hampole, where she had probably begun her religious life as a Cistercian nun before becoming an anchoress.[53] Her final move, probably after the miracles began at Richard's tomb, may have been because of age and infirmity (although she was to live for another twenty years, it appears)[54] or perhaps to superintend the growing cult of "saint" Richard. But such moves were very unusual indeed for recluses. Rolle, not being an enclosed anchorite, at least at the start of his career, was not required to remain in one place. The Office is very incomplete in its account of Rolle's middle years, implying by omission that he moved from Dalton's home directly to Richmondshire, where he was twelve miles from Margaret, in the far north of the county. This is misleading: Clay's discovery that Margaret was not enclosed at East Layton until December 12, 1348, means that "some years" cannot have elapsed between Margaret's cure in April on Maundy Thursday and Richard's death in September, although this is the wording of Lesson VIII. It also means that wherever Richard was between 1321/2 and 1349, no specific allusion to the period is contained in the Office. He could have wandered from patron to patron within Richmondshire; it was an enormous area covering the west part of the modern North Riding, parts of modern Lancashire, Westmorland and Durham.[55] He could have remained the entire time near or with his family at Yafforth, which is almost exactly twelve miles from East Layton; we simply do not know.

It might in fact have been expedient for Rolle to move about the country for the sake of security. Yorkshire in his time was subject to frequent Scottish raids, which themselves would have made Margaret's enclosure on the Durham border dangerous. Convents were frequently disrupted as a result of such attacks, and their inmates had to be rehoused in other, safer, houses such as Hampole in the far south of the West Riding, near Doncaster, to the detriment of the religious tone of these convents generally. Besides this, Yorkshire was an important focus of English political life; Parliament was often held at York in this period, and the insurrection of the Duke of Lancaster in 1322, in which Dalton, his adherent, was penalized, was part of the general movement to oust Edward II and replace him with his Queen Isabella and her lover Mortimer. Dalton was later approached for support for the exiled king but cannot have responded since he was pardoned by Mortimer for any suspected connivance with royalist supporters.[56] The gentry of the time were likely to be tenants of one of the great noble families and being associated with the wrong leader at the wrong time could produce catastrophic repercussions. Hope Allen suggests that Margaret Kirkby may have received support from the Scropes of Masham and the FitzHughs of Ravensworth, families powerful enough to withstand the troubled times, but there is no real evidence of this, and no proof that Richard himself had their support.[57]

Because of this lack of evidence of Rolle's movements between the time when he left Dalton and the last months of his life, some scholars are inclined to accept as genuine the entries in three manuscripts in Paris which are assumed to be accurate copies of medieval registers of students at the Sorbonne in the period just before and after 1320. These MSS, *Bibliothèque de l'Arsenal* MS 1021 and 1022 and MS 1288 record the presence at the Sorbonne of Ricardus de Hampole. In the two former manuscripts, seventeenth-century copies of supposedly medieval material, he is entered as having been recorded in the prior's register in 1326, after being admitted in 1320, with a note that he died in 1349 among the sisters of Hampole near Doncaster in Yorkshire; in the third manuscript his name appears seventh among a list of ten visiting scholars at the university in the years 1315–20. This last manuscript seems to be a collection of material assembled by Hémére, librarian at the Sorbonne from 1638–46, for a history of his institution.[58] Arnould does not accept the authenticity of these documents;[59] of recent writers on Rolle, Marzac is inclined to accept the evidence,[60] as is Riehle;[61] Hope Allen is more sceptical than Noetinger, writing in the earlier years of this century, who felt that Rolle's theological knowledge was too accurate to be consistent with his having left Oxford, not itself a theological center, at eighteen.[62] Allen speculates that he cannot have remained at the Sorbonne throughout the period from 1320–26 and surmises two separate visits on the two extreme dates. It seems unlikely that Rolle would find a sponsor to finance studies abroad,[63] but Allen observes that poor scholars, who were very numerous at the theological school of the Sorbonne, were financed by the institution as well as by patrons. Rolle's style, in both his Latin and his English works, which are different in presentation and manner, seems to be the result of self-teaching rather than a systematic indoctrination in the methods of scholastic theology. He seems to have used models for his English writing, which he used intelligently and sensitively, developing his own style by gradual mastery and constant application. The same may well be true of his Latin works. Rolle deliberately avoids the appeals to authority and the display of learning which were the hallmarks of contemporary scholarship; he uses the Bible as his prime authority—in this he was deeply versed—and rarely cites, even where he uses, the doctors of the church or later theologians. This would only be the method of someone who was deliberately forgetting all that he had been taught.

The Office devotes the remainder of the coverage to Rolle's spiritual life and to the posthumous miracles (in the lessons for the Octave). The date of Rolle's death, Michaelmas 1349, is recorded in too many colophons in manuscripts of his work to be doubtful. The only remaining detail of interest supplied by the Office, not found elsewhere, is Rolle's family surname. Elsewhere he is Richard hermit, saint Richard, or Richard of Hampole, a name which could only have been applied to him after his death, unless he was indeed resident at Hampole for a number of years before 1349. This factor makes the supposed register entries for the Sorbonne suspicious, since he would certainly not have had the title Hampole in the 1320s. Rolle's function at Hampole is not clear; he was not the nuns' official confessor, who was a Franciscan, and would not have had ecclesiastical sanction for this, since it is most unlikely that he ever received ordination, despite one apparent reference to priesthood.[64] He was not at the Sorbonne for the requisite seven years for achieving the baccalaureate, even supposing he was there for the six years some assume, and his name appears nowhere in the lists of those who were ordained in the York or Durham dioceses in the relevant years. The Office declares (but at the head of Lesson VIII, as if this pre-dated his acquaintance with Margaret and hence with Hampole, where she had been a nun) that Rolle was in the habit of charitably advising recluses and those troubled in spirit. He seems to have practiced the kind of role nowadays taken by student and marriage guidance counsellors, and no doubt, to judge from his quiet and humorous command of Margaret's crisis, he did this efficiently and inspired confidence.

We do not know whether Rolle died of plague or not. He was buried at first in the nuns' cemetery, where Roger was attempting to build him a tomb when his cart overturned. Later records of people making offerings of candles at his shrine show that he was moved first to the chancel and then to his own chapel. His cult was still flourishing among the local people at the time of the Dissolution of monasteries; Hampole, which of course had benefitted financially from the offerings at his shrine, and was no longer able to support more than a limited number of nuns,[65] was dissolved on November 19, 1539, and the buildings seem eventually to have become the barn and house of a farmstead. The shrine and priory disappeared except for a few stones and fragments of early English architecture.

There is one other named friend of Rolle, William Stopes,[66] to whom the late Latin epistle *Emendatio Vitae* was possibly addressed. Stopes seems to have acted as Rolle's literary executor.

Rolle himself furnished four further anecdotes about himself, in chapter 12 of his *Incendium Amoris*, one of a series of autobiographical passages from that work which circulated independently of the whole work and must have had much interest for contemporaries. These anecdotes also relate to Rolle's relationships with women and are often cited as evidence of his antifeminism. I think it is possible to see them as evidence of a certain impish sense of fun, which both caused the incidents in the first place, as youthful pranks which rather misfired, and led to his recording them many years after, as a joke against himself. In the first of these anecdotes he criticized a woman for her ornamented headgear (she told him he ought not to be aware of such things), in a second he complimented a woman on her chest measurements (she said it was no affair of his what size they were), and in a third he seems to have been involved in a mild piece of roughhouse which involved brandishing a stick at her. Her comment, "Calm down, brother!" suggests she interpreted the game as mildly erotic or suggestive. But these rebukes, which Rolle observes were all quite justified, are nothing compared with his final anecdote, where a lady put him down with the highly emasculating retort: "You're just a pretty face; the act is quite beyond you." To all this, Rolle contents himself, as if in pique, with the observation that it's best to avoid women altogether rather than face their immoderate love or scorn. This looks like typical medieval antifeminism, but I detect in the whole passage a certain wry humor, which would match Rolle's observation to Margaret that he would have held her, even if she had been the devil. There is an element of self-caricature here not unlike Chaucer's, three or four decades later.

Rolle's Mystic Experience

Rolle spent about thirty-one years living as a hermit, writing, advising and directing those who needed spiritual guidance. During the first six of those years he experienced special spiritual graces. Later he attempted to describe them, but seems to have refrained from talking of his special gifts at first for fear their intensity would wane; for this reason, he avoided the customary ecclesiastical interrogation of those claiming suprasensual experiences.[67]

It may not have been until the early 1330s that Rolle began to write of his mystic life. His most concerted attempt at self-analysis is found in Chapter 15 of *Incendium Amoris*, written, like all his works up to the last ten or twelve years of his life, in the Latin in which he had been trained in grammar school and university. This chapter is essential for understanding Rolle's own attitude to his vocation; together with Chapters 1 and 12 of the same work, it circulated independently of the rest of *Incendium*. Part of the prologue to the same work, also a biographical passage, was quoted in Lesson V of the Office. Rolle's contemporaries must have recognized that Rolle's experience colored all his writing and was essential for appreciating his spirituality.

In Chapter 15 of the *Incendium* Rolle describes his spiritual progress in terms of four seminal images: the open door, heat, song and sweetness. Each of the images records a stage in attaining that familiarity with God which the classic terminology of mysticism terms *unio;* for Rolle this state of union is expressed in the image of the medieval feast in the scented warmth of joyful conviviality, with sweet strains of music and all that is delectable to the taste and soft to the touch, and with the glorious vision of the beloved presiding lord constantly present and ever undimmed. To Rolle this final total attainment of "his settle" (seat) in heaven is only possible after death, but mystic ecstasy makes it perceptible in part, and frequently he will deploy *synaesthesia*, the simultaneous appeal to several senses at once, in a poetically ingenious attempt to convey the hints which ecstasy affords of that total fulfillment of all awareness called heaven.

This image is ancient; Rolle has merely made it medieval by re-envisaging it in feudal terms: God is the superior lord whose gracious condescension allows him to become a friend. The Epistle to the Hebrews has the traditional image of returning to the homeland:

> What you have come to is Mount Zion, and the city of the living God, the heavenly Jerusalem where the millions of angels have gathered for the festival with the whole Church in which everyone is a "first-born son" and a citizen of heaven (Heb 12:22–3).

The New Testament allegory of homecoming as a representation of death and reunion with Christ seems to amalgamate the image of the land promised to Moses in the desert, and the yearning to return to Israel after the Exile, with the Greco-Roman image of a homeland from which the soul was exiled by being born into this life. Both were given new stimulus by the neo-platonist Augustine and the stoic Boethius; the former (at least) Rolle had read. The return to Jerusalem theme was adopted thirty years after Rolle by Walter Hilton in Part II of the *Scale of Perfection*.

Rolle's writings in both Latin and English are shot through by this highlighting image of home, and usually he mingles different aspects of the total image in order to convey the impression of more than mere physical sense-perception, as in "resonant banquets" (*Melos Amoris*, Chap. 7) or "the soul's resonant rejoicing will be visibly resplendent" (*Incendium*, Chap. 34).

What Rolle describes in Chapter 15 of *Incendium* is an attempt to use the imagery of entry into the city/hall, of fire, sweetness and song, as a systematic account of the gradations of spiritual life. He describes, with the time-lapses, his gradual initiation. After he had begun his life in religion, two years and eight or nine months elapsed before he experienced any sense of enlightenment. This would correspond to the phase normally termed the purgative way in the mystic terminology which Bonaventure outlined in *De Triplici Via*.[68] At this point Rolle experienced what he called "the opening of the door of heaven (allowing the eye of my heart to contemplate heavenly things)" (*IA*, Chap. 15, trans. del Mastro). During the next eleven months "the door remained open"; that is, he experienced what mystic theology terms the illuminative stage, and then, after a further nine months and three weeks, Rolle was granted "the infusion and perception of the celestial or spiritual sound which belongs to the canticle of divine praise" (del Mastro). We are not told where he was living at these various stages; Hope Allen's conjectures are pure surmise; clearly Rolle did not regard it as relevant to say where he was domiciled; he did think it important to state that he was seated in a chapel (the same one) when the second and third stages occurred. He had probably left the Daltons by then.

Imagery of heat, fire, music, sweetness, touch and sexual union are very common in the writings of all mystics in the Judaeo-Christian tradition; they figure very markedly in the writings of the Rhineland mystics, who were Rolle's near contemporaries, in the thirteenth and fourteenth centuries.[69] Rolle's imagery, especially in his great poem-treatise the *Melos Amoris*, is a lyrical outpouring of his love for Jesus. It is not, however, meant to correspond to literal sense-impression. There was a very ancient mode of spiritual analysis, deriving from Origen, in the third century, which allocated sense receptors to the soul on analogy with those of the body.[70] The soul is frequently spoken of in medieval theology as having ears, eyes, a tongue and sense of touch, and this is not mere metaphor but an attempt to express the ineffable. More than that, these modes or acts of perception are (the language) "in which the mystical experience itself takes place."[71] The case is not merely that there is no language for recording an experience which is outside time and space, since all language operates in linear sequence of ordered parts of speech, but there is also no medium for the finite human intellect to experience the ineffable. Therefore, so the theory of spiritual senses runs, the soul must be allowed the impression of "experiencing a supernatural object which reveals itself as if it were present in some concrete manner."[72]

This is what Rolle is attempting to convey when he describes his gifts of heat (*calor*) and song (*canor*) in Chapter 15. In both cases he was sitting in a chapel in meditation. Rolle always preferred to be seated for meditation: "And I have loved to sit . . . simply because I knew that I loved God more effectively, and the consolation of love lasted longer (with me) than walking or standing or kneeling" (*Form of Living*, Ch. 10) On the first occasion,

> Suddenly I experienced within myself an unaccustomed and joyous burning ardor.

On the second occasion, nearly ten months later, he was singing the psalms in the evening before supper when

> I jumped as if at the ringing, or rather, the playing of stringed instruments above me (trans. del Mastro).

The language here seems traditionally metaphorical [Ps 41:5]. But Rolle causes confusion in the Prologue to *Incendium Amoris* when he makes his famous declaration:

> I frequently felt my chest to see if this burning might have some external cause . . . just as when a finger is placed in the fire it experiences physical burning, so the soul set on fire by love in the way I have described feels the more real burning desire (*Incendium*, Prologue, trans. del Mastro).

Rolle is still speaking in this quasi-literal vein in the last work he ever wrote, *The Form of Living:*

> He or she who is in this (third) degree of love can as easily feel the fire of love burning in their soul as you can feel your finger burn if you put it in the fire (Chap. 8).

What Rolle is attempting to explain is that the intensity of spiritual "sensation" is as keen (even perhaps painfully so?) as the most intense physical sense-impression. He is not suggesting that physical manifestations accompanied his intimations of God. It is important to stress this, because he was misunderstood in his own era, at least by Margery Kempe in the early fifteenth century, and by those whose mistaken notions Walter Hilton and the *Cloud* author were attempting to correct in the 1370s and 1380s.[73] What is more significant still is the underestimation Rolle has suffered in the twentieth century. Hope Allen, his most assiduous researcher, can yet dismiss Rolle as "the simplest possible type of mystic,"[74] declaring that his was no true apocalypse. Others, reading only his English works, relegate him to the rank of the illuminative mystics only, denying that he achieved full union.[75] This is perhaps because of his honest admission:

> But there are others who say . . . that they have seen heavenly things clearly. Let them speak thus who have known this phenomenon: I have not experienced it, and do not expect to experience it as long as I remain in the flesh. Even Paul, who was caught up to the third heaven, did not say that he saw God or those in heaven face to face (*Contra Amatores Mundi*, Chap. 5, trans. Theiner).

This, however, is orthodox theology; those who are accorded the rank of the greatest mystics did not claim to know God as he is, nor to be united to God in his essence.

Certainly Riehle, a critic who has made a detailed recent study of the language of the medieval mystics of Germany and England, and in particular of the imagery of Rolle's Latin works, is convinced that Rolle was "imbued with a very intense mystical experience."[76] In fact, when Rolle writes of his mystic experience his language is redolent of the transports of total ecstasy:

> For this fervent, loving soul is continually suffering thirst, until the pleasure of eternal sweetness appears to her; meanwhile, as long as her earthly state does not interfere, a certain sweet gift flows into the pure mind, and, as if drunk with strong wine, she melts completely into the pleasure of the Creator (*Contra Amatores*, Chap. 3, trans. Theiner).

> Inebriate my spirit with the burning wine of your sweetest love, so that, forgetting all evils and all limited sights, illusions and images, I may exult, embracing you alone, and I may rejoice in God my Jesus (*Emendatio Vitae*, Chap. 11, trans. del Mastro).

Rolle's imagery at times anticipates that of later English mystics such as Hilton or, here, the *Cloud* author:

> And so we are snatched upward from here in an abundance of joy; for indeed the mind touched by heavenly sweetness does not cease to climb upwards. It strives to penetrate the layers of clouds; it is not afraid to lift itself above the starry heavens. It seeks a place among the choirs of angels; it desires to look upon its own most dearly beloved. Wherefore, the nearer one lifts himself to his beloved in the royal court of heaven, the more sweetly he must burn with the fire of eternal love; there surely he is inflamed and consumed; he is illuminated by the splendor of Christ's godhead (*Contra Amatores*, Chap. 2, trans. Theiner).

Here the affective tone ("beloved," "inflamed," "sweetly," "joy") are typical of Rolle; the kinesthetic imagery of movement and ascent is especially common in *The Cloud of Unknowing*, but Rolle too speaks frequently of "running" to the embrace of the beloved, or of "climbing" or being "raised" to heaven.

Other common images in the terminology of union among the mystics are also frequent in Rolle, again indicating that the full transports of mystic rapture into union were not unknown to him. Rolle, like the Rhineland mystics, uses imagery of melting, drunkenness, ravishing, annihilation and sexual climax when attempting to convey this ineffable state:

> A certain sweet gift flows into the pure mind, and, as if drunk with strong wine, she melts completely into the pleasure of the Creator (*Contra Amatores*, Chap. 3, trans. Theiner).

> A man . . . changed into that other glory, naturally by the grace of Christ . . . would melt completely in eternal love (*Contra Amatores*, Chap. 5).

> The very fervour of their sweet love ravishes them (contemplatives) with the sight of their Beloved. Flowering through this loving flame into all virtue they rejoice in their maker. Their mind is changed and passes into lasting melody. From now on their meditations become song (*Incendium*, Chap. 5, trans. Wolters).

> Little wonder when a man is first made a true contemplative, and tastes the sweetness and then feels the warmth, that he almost dies through excess of love. He is held tight in the embrace of eternal love, *almost as though* it were physical (*Incendium*, Chap. 19, trans. Wolters).

Here Rolle has remembered to qualify the sensual metaphor by *quasi—as if* in the body. This was not sufficient to deter Margery Kempe of Lynne, who "saw" the Holy Ghost seated on a white cushion (Bk I, Chap. 86) and was able to "feel" Christ's toes "in the sight of her soul" (Bk I, Chap. 85).

Another objection to Rolle's attainment of full union is his apparent claim to a permanent state of union with God. No other mystic has claimed this, although Ruysbroeck seems to have been able to achieve the grace of very prolonged ecstasy in extreme old age. Rolle's claim is not, however, to continuous union, but continual; once he had attained the gift of song the way was continually prepared for further experience of mystic union, but sleep inevitably obtruded, and other demands of the body.[77]

The "dark" or desolation of spirit which succeeds the ecstasy of union is certainly not unknown to Rolle, although he does not use this image for the loss. Instead he uses the image of the closed door:

> My soul pants for you; my whole being is athirst for you. Yet you will not show yourself to me; you look away; you bar the door, shun me, pass me over; You even laugh at my innocent sufferings (*Incendium*, Chap. 2, trans. Wolters).

Even more poignant is the inability of the physical body to bear the force of the spiritual contact it sustains:

> My soul, devoted to you, O God, desires to see You. It cries out to You from far away. In you it burns. It languishes from love of you. O unfailing love, you have completely conquered me! O sweetness and beauty everlasting, you have wounded my heart, and now, conquered and wounded, I succumb. I am scarcely alive, for I die in the face of joy, because in my corruptible flesh I am not strong enough to carry the sweetness of such great majesty. For my whole heart, fixed in desire for Jesus, is transformed into the fire of love, and is absorbed into another shape and glory (*Emendatio Vitae*, Chap. 12, trans. del Mastro).

> Gazing on heaven so that I may be raised to salvation and may indeed behold him for whom I yearn for so long, "I languish with love" [Cant. 2:5]. Set on fire, I linger in heavenly savours. I am consumed by fire within, I recognise my beloved, the heavenly flames blaze within my soul and I do not desire anything save Christ, my desire, so devotedly am I entranced by divine sweetness (*Melos Amoris*, Chap. 55).

> And when I die, disease will not have been the cause, nor will adversity dare to hurl me downwards, for love will open the door of the elect, firmly locked to all sinners, and to those who boorishly are precipitated down far from the King's majesty, because rising from the failing flesh I shall attain the continuous association craved by my burning heart, and the assembly will harmonise their melodies aloud as I am led forward to the presence of the presiding father. May the Beloved command that I, rejoicing in my moving from the world do not relinquish the melody, nor, then dying, have any terror, because I am languishing with love (*Melos Amoris*, Chap. 55).

It is for this reason that Rolle yearns for death: death alone will bring the complete and uninterrupted vision of God, total union; all Rolle's work, in Latin and English, prose and canticles, echoes with the yearning cry for physical annihilation so that spiritual perfection may be achieved:

> Here now is a soul perfectly loving Christ and shining and burning agreeably in the invisible fire, and from this point it pants to pass out "from the body of this death" (Rom 7:24) and to be joined with the citizens above in the vision of God's face, from where it addresses others living in the church: "support me with flowers, comfort me with apples, for I languish with love" [Cant. 2:5] (*Melos Amoris*, Chap. 53).

> Then Jesus is all your desire, all your delight, all your joy, all your consolation, all your strength, so that your song will always be about him, and in him all your rest (*Ego Dormio*).

Rolle's Poetic Skill: His Instruction of Others

Rolle's aim in writing his experiences and opinions was instruction. He made many different attempts, using different techniques, and two languages, to communicate his mysticism to others, trying "to find a language which is capable of transmitting (its) intensity as far as is possible, so that the wish for a similar experience will be awakened in the reader."[78] It must be admitted, however, that Rolle succeeds better in Latin in conveying the intensity and transcendental aspect of his spiritual life than he does in his later English works. He had been trained to write Latin and must have felt more confidence in that medium; the sources he worked with were also mainly in that language, affording him models of style and structure, and, above all, his major source book, the Vulgate Bible, was in Latin. There were accepted methods of writing about matters of profundity or complexity in that language which English was as yet ill-equipped to match. As Riehle notes, "the beauty of his Latin language and imagery far surpasses that of his English texts."[79] In spite of this, Rolle himself created a standard of writing in English, using those models which were available to him (see page 52) and, as a result, has been styled (not quite deservedly) the first master of English prose; it is true, however, that he was very widely read in the fourteenth and fifteenth centuries, more so even than Chaucer,[80] and must have exerted a strong stylistic influence as a result.

We must acknowledge Rolle's boldness in selecting English as his alternative to Latin. Much of the devotional writing of the previous three or four generations had been in Anglo-Norman, the dialect of French spoken in the British Isles from 1066 until the later fourteenth century among the upper classes. Written Anglo-Norman enjoyed a heyday between the mid-twelfth and the mid-thirteenth centuries, and was especially common for devotional, recreational and business matters, being used in the Law courts until the eighteenth century. In choosing English Rolle may have been deliberately aiming at a readership among the gentry and freeholders, like his own family. Even if he did not speak it at home, he must have learned Anglo-Norman at university, where it was permitted at the dinner-table and often used for general conversation (although Latin was preferred), where English was forbidden. It does not seem likely that it was a language barrier which prevented Rolle from communicating with the Daltons at his first meal with them; in all probability they spoke English themselves. Although Rolle's disciple Margaret seems to have been from the Le Boteler (Butler) family of Skelbroke, near Hampole, and may therefore have known Anglo-Norman, being of gentle stock, he wrote to her in English, perhaps also aiming at a wider audience.

There can be no doubt that Rolle wished to instruct and to reach as wide an audience as he could. This is stated in the Office, and at the beginning of most of his major Latin works:

> Yet wonderful and beyond measure useful was the work of this saintly man in holy exhortations, whereby he converted many to God, and in

> his sweet writings, both treatises and little books (*libellis*) composed for the edification of his neighbours, which all sound like sweetest music in the hearts of the devout (Office, Lesson VI).

> Therefore, I offer this book for consideration not by philosophers, not by the worldly-wise, not by great theologians ensnared in infinite questionings, but by the unsophisticated and the untaught, who are trying to love God rather than to know many things. For he is known in doing and in loving, not in arguing. . . . I am rousing everyone here to love (*universos excito ad amorem*) (*Incendium*, Prologue, trans. del Mastro).

But, as Rolle must have realized, the untaught would not know Latin, and would need an interpreter before the secrets of Rolle's *Fire of Love* could be manifest to them.[81]

The audience of *Melos Amoris* must have been more "lettered": this work is not only in Latin of a very daring and inventive kind, but makes freer use of scriptural quotation than *Incendium Amoris*, in addition to the *postillae*, elaboration of biblical texts, which form the backbone of its structure. Yet *Melos* is also supposedly written for the information of "all":

> I speak plainly: I do not fear those who are testing me, for such men will be slaughtered in the whirlwind. I do not know how to keep silent, so much does love constrain me [cf. II Cor 5:14] that all should know how adept I am in crying aloud in song and receiving the melodious fire of heaven, since I have loved to absent myself from the torment of the wealthy, and live sitting in holy solitude, singing and fervent, but rejoicing immensely (*Melos*, Chap. 1).

Despite the apparent self-satisfaction of this last quotation, Hope Allen is not justified in speaking of "the audacious self-confidence" of Rolle's Latin writings.[82] Rolle's works are all instructive, but only the last four he wrote, the Latin *Emendatio Vitae* and the three English epistles, *Ego Dormio*, *The Commandment* and *The Form of Living*, explicitly give advice. For each of them he had a specific recipient in mind (and perhaps a wider audience as well): *Emendatio Vitae* may have been addressed to William Stopes, possibly later Rolle's literary executor, *Ego Dormio* and *The Commandment* are said in one manuscript to be for nuns of Yedingham and Hampole respectively, while *The Form of Living*, on reliable authority, was for Margaret Kirk(e)by.

In each of these works he addresses a single recipient, *tu* or *thou*, the tone is more intimate, and hence more attractive to the modern reader. Because he is writing to a familiar acquaintance, Rolle has no need to prove himself or introduce his special gifts, hence Hope Allen's remark that "the author seems modest and not assertive."[83] But this subdued style only rarely breaks into lyrical poetry, and even impassioned prose is not nearly as frequent in these last four works, except at the close, as in the *Incendium* and *Melos*. In the latter, especially, Rolle uses alliterative Latin verse of the type commonly used in Middle English alliterative poetry, to express his song of love, his *melos*. Even where he retains prose as his medium, it often becomes impassioned, and as his affective piety intensifies, so his language becomes more inventive, and his style more alliterative:

> Ex quo enim sancto amore mens mea incensa est, positus sum in langore videnti maiestatem tuam, paupertatis proinde portior effectus, despicio dignitatem terrae, nec curo de ullo honore. Gloria enim mea amicitia est (*Incendium*, Chap. 42). (For from this holy love my spirit has been enkindled; I have been placed in the languor of seeing Your majesty, just as, made the bearer of poverty, I despise the dignity of earth and do not care about any honour. For my friendship is glory) [trans. del Mastro].

In these jubilant hymns of praise, which he breaks into in *Melos*, *Incendium*, *Emendatio*, *Ego Dormio* and *The Form*, Rolle deserts prose as he attempts to match the upsurge of his spirit in soaring poetry. In the Latin hymns we see him at his most inventive. There he displays a verbal facility which is astounding in its poetic vigor and its capacity to evoke in the uninitiated reader a powerful impression of the transports of mystic rapture. The rhythmic repetition of the alliterative phrases resembles much mystic writing; use of rhythm, balance and rhyme seem to be means of conveying the sense of total calm and proportion in the being which mystic consciousness evokes. The adornment of the style by means of such devices was accepted in medieval rhetoric as a valid method of indicating the seriousness, the dignity of the topic. Rolle's audience would not have found such ornateness of verbal patterning with such "difficult" metaphoric use of language at all recherché or attention-seeking;[84] Rolle's *Melos* is "the musical vocalization of a truth discerned by the enlightened eye through the window made in the firmament itself where eternal truth is celebrated in angelic song. . . . Thought has been turned into song."[85] It is most certainly not barbarous, nor would it have caused outrage for Rolle's readers: so difficult a piece for the copyist would hardly have been reproduced at least twelve times, were that the case, and the ten extant complete manuscripts probably represent only a fraction of the original total.

Although Rolle's Latin works show formal and verbal brilliance and innovation, he seems less daring in his English writing, and the lyric pieces there can seem almost banal, especially so (regrettably) in translation. Rolle's English is very simple; instead of deploying the rich resources of language in order to vary his expression with the enormous fecundity of his Latin alliteration, he uses rhyme to achieve the effect of balance and proportion so important in mystical writing, and his rhymes tend to be of the simplest. In fact, he frequently uses monosyllables, both in the body of the line and in the rhymes; very often he uses medial as well as end-rhymes, a device he probably derived from other writers of Latin; he uses it himself in his Latin poem to the Blessed Virgin, probably a very early piece:

Puella pulcherima prostravit ludentem
Fronsque serenissima facit hunc languentem.
Crines auro similes carpunt conquerentem;
Gene preamabiles solantur sedentem.[86]

Far from revealing "no sense of poetic form,"[87] such "doubled rhyme" shows Rolle's consciousness that words addressed to Christ or his mother, or written about them, must be as dignified and resplendent as possible. Even in his prose he constantly has recourse to the rhetorical device of *similiter desinens*, words ending with an identical grammatical inflection, or *similiter cadens*, where the sound is the same but the grammatical function is different:

> In hoc statu vel gradu amoris est amor castus, sanctus, voluntarius, amatum pro seipso amans et se totum in amato figens, nihil extra ipsum querens, de ipso contentus, flagrans, aestuans, vehemens, illum in se ligans, impetuosus miro modo, omnem modum excedens, ad solum amatum se extendens, cuncta alia contempnens et obliviscens, in amato iubilans, ipsum cogitans, ipsum incessanter reminiscens, ascendens in desiderio, ruens in dilectio, pergens in amplexibus, absortus in osculis, totus liquefactus in igne amoris (*Emendatio Vitae*, Chap. 11,

quoted in John Clark, "Richard Rolle: A Reassessment," *Downside Review* 101, p. 126).

(In this state or degree of love, love is chaste, holy and willing, loving his Beloved for His own sake, not for His gifts, and fixing himself totally in love, he seeks nothing outside Him, contented by Him. Burning and blazing fiercely, binding Him within himself, impetuous, ardent in a wonderful manner, exceeding all measure, stretching himself out to the Beloved alone, he holds all other things in contempt. Forgetting them, rejoicing in the Beloved, thinking of Him, remembering Him unceasingly, rising up in desire, falling down in delight, going on in embraces, he is overcome [lit. absorbed, swallowed up] in kisses and entirely melted in the fire of love) (trans. del Mastro).

This device also occurs in the English works:

The swetnes of hym in this degre es swa comfortand and lastand in his lufe, sa byrnand and gladand, that he or scho that es in this degre mai als wele fele the fyre of lufe byrnand in thaire saule als thou may fele thi fynger byrn, if thou putt it in the fyre . . . than thi saule es Jhesu lufand, Jhesu thynkand, Jhesu desirand, anly in the covayties of hym anedande, til hym syngand, of hym byrnand, in hym restand (*The Form of Living*, Allen, *EW*, p. 105).

Yet such devices are less frequent in the English work: the rhetoric and rhymes are simpler, and the tone of the lyrics more petitionary and less ecstatic than in the Latin. Part of the explanation for this is, as Riehle says, Rolle's greater confidence stemming from his formal training in Latin.[88] But in part, I think, the simpler diction of the English works is a deliberate ploy of Rolle's. He is writing for those who are indeed "untaught," women, for the most part, who do not know Latin, who might be confused by verbal artistry if it were too elaborate or frequent, and who cannot even easily read English if the words are too long or the vocabulary too Latinate. Rolle does not avoid French words, for though fairly new in the language (some are recorded for the first time in his works),[89] these would be familiar to his readers, who would speak, or at least be able to understand Anglo-Norman. Even more than the intimacy of tone and the concern expressed about the diet and clothing of his readers, Rolle's concern to find simple expressions which they could comprehend marks him preeminently as a teacher. In this he resembles another devout Yorkshireman five hundred years later, Patrick Brontë, father of the famous Brontë sisters, who also wrote devotional pieces in simple words for the instruction of his rural parishioners. The English lyrics, both those inserted in the prose writing and those which circulated separately, are not the ecstatic reaching out to capture the divine *melos*, "dispersing meaning to the frontiers of unmeaning"[90] of his Latin lyrical passages, but meditational poems, devices to induce the state of mind capable of receiving the mystic song. For Rolle the experience of rapture and the instruction of others so that they might receive it are inseparable.

Toward the end of his life Rolle attempted to schematize the levels of mystic contemplation which he had identified into a mystic progression of the kind outlined by Bonaventura, whose threefold progression from meditation through prayer to contemplation became classic in mystical studies. At first Rolle tried to categorize his own experience of *calor*, *dulcor* and *canor* into a systematic progress, preceded by alienation from the world, making a fourfold system. In the *Melos Amoris*, probably a work of the mid to late 1330s, Rolle outlines this scheme:

> First they (the saints who migrate from Babylon to Jerusalem) renounce all they possess; then, eager for heavenly things alone, they are set alight in love of the Creator; third, now they have already tasted the uncreated sweetness, they are enkindled by great eagerness to be part of the angelic choirs . . . ; fourthly, because of the greatness of their joy and the enormous love with which they are filled, they receive into themselves the celestial sound, and are shadowed by divine harmony, and flee into solitude lest they should be hindered from that spiritual song (Original quoted by Allen, *WA*, p. 84).

Later, however, Rolle must have read Richard of St. Victor's *Four Steps of Passionate Love.* In this highly emotive, not to say erotic twelfth-century work, the earlier Richard, drawing on the newly evolving cult of *fine amour*, secular, "courtly" love, forms an analogy between four stages of sexual passion, culminating in total obsession, and four stages of divine passion, culminating in a fourth stage in which the lover of God returns to the world after his encounter with the Absolute and, totally oblivious to all pain and mental humiliation, yearns only to express his divine passion among his fellow men. He called this ultimate stage *insatiabilis*—insatiable—for love can never do enough to retain the experience of God and is in a sense desolate for him. But Rolle seems to ignore this stage and does not use this term. The other three stages of Richard of St. Victor's system, *insuperable*, *inseparable* and *singular*, figure in three of Rolle's late works. They are outlined in *The Commandment* and *The Form* in his English works, and in the Latin *Emendatio Vitae:*

> Indeed there are three steps of the love of Christ; on them he who is chosen may advance from one to the other toward love. The first step is called "insuperable," the second is called "inseparable" and the third is called "singular." Then indeed love is "insuperable" when it can be overcome by no other affection, and when it freely rejects all impediments for the sake of him. . . . Love is, in truth, "inseparable" when the spirit, already set ablaze by the most vehement love and clinging to Christ by inseparable thought, at no moment indeed allows Christ to recede from his memory, but, as if he were tied to Him in heart, he thinks of Him and he sighs for him. . . . Love ascends to the "singular" stage, therefore, when it excludes every consolation except the one which is in Jesus, and when nothing besides Jesus can satisfy it. In this step the established soul loves One—Him alone (*Emendatio Vitae*, Chap. 11, trans. del Mastro).

In Rolle's English work *Ego Dormio* three degrees are mentioned but not titled, and seem in fact to correspond to three states of life—secular, active religious and contemplative religious.

It looks as if Rolle came upon Richard of St. Victor's *Four Steps* late in his career, although he knew other works by both Richard and Hugh of St. Victor earlier in his life. He is modifying his earlier schema, for under this system all his mystical experience belongs in the third category, *singular* love, at least according to his *Ego Dormio* and *Form*. Why Rolle should have omitted the fourth stage, "insatiable," is not clear. It has been surmised that he would not have found it relevant to his "gentle" type of mysticism;[91] this does not seem to square with the fierce imagery of burning and the passionate ardor of the *Melos*, however. Moreover, as has been shown above, the desolation of the insatiable degree was known to Rolle. It was, less plausibly, suggested by Hope Allen that Rolle preferred triads,[92] and in this instance would have modified the Victorine scheme to accommodate the triple scheme of St. Gregory. The answer may lie in the degree of spiritual development of the two recipients of the English works, a nun of Hampole (probably), and Margaret Kirkby, and of William Stopes, to whom *Emendatio Vitae* was perhaps written. If they were all three in the earlier stages of development, they would not need to be confused by the spiritual desolation of the insatiable degree.

In most of Rolle's writing there is one aid to devotion which all can follow, no matter how little their degree of proficiency, and that is his devotion to the "name" of Jesus. As outlined above, he himself derived his devotion to Jesus from his early experience of temptation in which he was rescued by an ejaculatory prayer to the Precious Blood. He did not initiate this devotion, and did not introduce it to England, but must have been instrumental in its steady growth in popularity which actually survived the change of religion in the sixteenth century. Rolle's expressions of this devotion were sometimes exuberant and are modified by corrections supplied by Hilton, who, with the *Cloud* author, redefined several "gray" areas which Rolle's enthusiasm had sketched in too vaguely as his mystic ardor carried him forward too fast to explain his experience clearly. Rolle explains clearly enough in Chapter 9 of *The Form* and in the concluding section of *The Commandment* that he means "Jesus" as salvation. Even in the *Psalter Commentary* he will continually introduce this theme: Ps 9:10 "You are refuge of poor men, not of rich who love other things beside you, for the former hope in you, not in the world nor in any man; all who have known your name, that is to say, they who have felt in their soul the sweetness of the love of Jesus, and know it by proof, not those who know it by looking at it in books or by reciting it. For you did not forsake those who were seeking you and nothing besides you: [if] you allow them to be in ill-health or in difficulties, you do not abandon them, but in so much do you appoint for them a greater joy" (Bramley, p. 32).

The directive in Chapter 9 of *The Form* to "greet Mary frequently," coupled with the tenderly sympathetic handling of Mary's role at the crucifixion in the two *Meditations on the Passion* shows that Rolle did not abandon his devotion to the Virgin after his early hymn in her praise, the *Canticum Amoris*, in favor of devotion to the Holy Name, as Hope Allen has claimed.[93] Rolle's sensitive, almost feminine spirituality would never have been guilty of neglect of the mother of God. His induction into the vocation of hermit took place on her feast day, and presumably his only sermon was preached in her honor. The text "your name is oil poured out" furnishes Rolle with the pretext for a two-paragraph panegyric on Mary as the vessel from which the oil was poured in the *Comment on the Canticles*, the very text where Rolle discusses the beginning of his devotion to the Holy Name.[94]

Rolle's Latin and English Writings

Rolle's career as a writer must have covered about two decades, but we have no certain dating within that period for the majority of his works.[95] The earliest works must have been his *Canticum Amoris*, a Latin rhyming and alliterative poem to the Blessed Virgin, and *Judica Me Deus*, the first part of which may antedate 1322. The latest piece to come from his pen was probably the English *The Form of Living*, which must have been written in the autumn of 1348 at the earliest and was probably written within a few months of Rolle's death in September 1349; it is addressed to Margaret Kirkby, who entered her enclosure as a recluse on December 12, 1348, and is a guide for her life as an anchorite. Within those limits we have a very considerable body of undated material, in most cases almost certainly attributable to Rolle. These works, both the Latin and the English, are often classified into commentaries, treatises and epistles, but in fact each of his works contains some measure of each of these forms, in varying proportions.

The works classified as commentaries include a *Commentary on the Readings in the Office of the Dead taken from Job;* a *Commentary on the Canticles* (covering the first two-and-a-half verses of *The Song of Songs*); two *Commentaries on the Psalter*, one in Latin, which may be early, and an English commentary, with translation of the Latin Psalms into English, which may have been written for Margaret Kirkby, and hence may date from the later 1330s; a separate, longer, Latin *Treatise on Psalm 20;* a commentary on the Lamentations of Jeremiah (*Super Threnos*); a *Commentary on the Apocalypse*, covering the first six chapters of the Book of Revelations; and others on the Lord's Prayer, the Magnificat and the Apostles' Creed; similar to these is the English explication of the Ten Commandments included in this set of translations; a comment on Proverbs 31:10, *Super Mulierem Fortem* and another on a single verse, Psalm 88:2, *De Dei Misericordia*, although the latter was possibly written by John Waldeby in the later fourteenth century.

The technique deployed in these works of commentary is the time-honored one, demonstrated by Augustine in his *Comment on Psalm 41*, of working systematically through the text supplying interpretations. These comprise varying combinations of four possible modes of reading: the literal or historical, the allegorical or typological, the moral (tropological) and the anagogical.[96] The second mode, when interpreting Old Testament texts, normally involves the identification of leading characters in the Old Testament with Christ and the resolution of prophetic or obscure passages in the Old Testament by the revelation of the New. The anagogical method of interpretation normally relates the meaning of a given passage to the future rewards and joys of heaven; in Rolle's case this level of interpretation includes information of mystical knowledge of divine matters imparted in this life, rather than making reference to the state of the soul after death:

> *You will be hated by all men on account of my name* (Mt 24:9). Thus truly the lover of Christ, relinquishing the empty and fallible spoils of this world, longs continually for the celestial riches, and, suffering joyfully the adversities of the present life, tastes untiringly those eternal delights (Exposition of Ps 21:8 in *Treatise on The Twentieth (Vulg.) Psalm*, trans. Boenig).

In commenting on holy scripture Rolle felt himself to be inspired by God: "*Divinitus didici quod dico:* By inspiration I have learned what I am saying" (*Melos Amoris*);[97] this was the aspect of his mystical gift which was reserved for his fellowmen, and he exerted himself conscientiously to make it available to them. The psalm commentaries must have involved immense labor, especially the English Psalter, where Rolle seems to have consulted modernized versions of the Anglo-Saxon Psalter glosses in order to provide his translation of the psalms.[98] Rolle's main concern in his commentaries was with that aspect of interpretation which covered the soul's relationship with God. In the Psalters his comments tend to be on the moral level, covering the problems of the individual, and on the typological, dealing with Christ's experiences as man and his appeal to each Christian:

> Ps 58:1 (Ps 59) "*Rescue me from my enemies, my God, and deliver me from what is rising within me.*" Comment: Christ and his lovers, like someone surrounded by enemies, cry out saying: "Rescue me from my enemies"; our enemies are the devil and his angels, which do not cease each day to rise against us, desiring to deceive our weakness, which is surrounded by temptations, and evil enticement and many different stirrings (Bramley, p. 207).

There are, however, many original mystical interpretations in both psalter commentaries:

> Ps 38:14 (Ps 39) "*My heart grew hot within me, and fire shall burn in my thinking.*" That is, my heart really grew hot with the fire of the love of Christ, [so] that my thought was entirely taken up into the joy of God; and in my thinking, that is, in meditating on Christ and on heaven, the fire of perfect love shall burn, so that I feel the burning in my heart (Bramley, p. 143).

Rolle's English Psalter commentary is not a translation of his Latin commentary but a separate piece of labor. Often he gives different interpretations in the two works, such as in Psalm 20, where the Latin Psalter, like the longer Treatise on the Twentieth Psalm, interprets the psalm in relation to the individual soul, whereas the English Psalter relates the psalm to Christ.[99] Both Psalters ultimately depend on the *catena* of Peter the Lombard, but Rolle makes considerable original additions. Selections from the English Psalter are included in this volume.

The commentaries on scripture supply the novice with some of his training in the techniques of *lectio*, the reading of the Bible and the fathers, which was a preliminary to meditation and prayer. This was the traditional training used in the cloisters where the system had been perfected, and where, incidentally, it had fostered the development of mystical theology. Rolle's interpretations will all have been based on sound learning, but he rarely displays his sources and authorities; for Rolle, the Bible itself was the one authority needed.

Apart from the Psalter, Rolle did not write scriptural commentary in English. This must be because in England, where nuns were not taught Latin, as they were in the convents in Europe; such close scriptural meditation was not possible, for the Bible was still only issued for authorized use in Latin. The readers of Rolle's English works would have been nuns and lay brothers, and perhaps the pious laity; his Latin commentaries must have been accessible only to those in orders or those who, like himself, and like William Langland two or three decades later, never completed their university studies but took from them an intimate knowledge of Latin.[100]

Two of the Latin commentaries, the study of the *Canticles* and that of *Psalm 20*, approach the sermon in their technique, developing one specific text or idea rather than progressing through a longer passage elucidating each verse in turn. Rolle is not known to have delivered more than one sermon, and that apparently extempore, but at the start of his career he seems to have thought that preaching and pastoral counselling might form part of his vocation.[101] Certainly one very early work, *Judica Me Deus*, covers this part of the priestly vocation, concluding with a sample sermon, on the topic of Judgment, the theme of many of Rolle's "mini-orations" in his later works. *Judica Me* is a translation of a pastoral manual written by a fellow Yorkshireman, and contemporary of Rolle, William of Pagula, or Paull, in Holderness. Pagula's manual, based on a new type of pastoral instruction begun in the late thirteenth century, was the first example of this new trend in England; it was titled the *Oculus Sacerdotalis* and *Pars Oculi*, that portion of it which Rolle used for part B2 of *Judica* was not completed until after 1326, although the source for *Judica* B1 and B3, the *Dextera Pars* of Pagula's work, was written between 1320 and 1326.[102] Rolle was absolutely up to date in his own pastoral theology and concerned that ordained clergy should be so too, for he addresses the work to a friend who is already a parish priest; this man's name and living are unknown. The so-called *Judica* A might date from 1322 or earlier, but is unlikely to have circulated before the remainder of the work; it is Rolle's personal apologia for having changed cells as a hermit, followed by an earnest exhortation to his friend to avoid punishment after death by austere living, recommending solitude, and insisting on self-analysis rather than the judgment of others. Its tone is "warm and human."[103]

But early in his career Rolle must have realized that his own vocation was not to be preaching. Accordingly, he uses his written tracts, letters and commentaries to preach the message of love and repentance which he was not licensed to preach orally, utilizing the opportunity afforded there for direct address, both forceful and coaxing as necessary. He also completed a range of material which covered the requirements of those preparing for contemplation: reading, meditation, prayer.

Closely akin to the biblical commentaries, and covering the next requirement, meditation, are the two English *Meditations on the Passion* included among these translations from Rolle's English work. Here Rolle comments on a syncretic version of the passion of Christ drawn from all four gospel narratives. His aim is not now to elucidate the narrative but to induce in the reader introspective meditation on the torture endured by Christ on account of the reader's own sin;

Rolle aims to make the reader *feel* the events described. Rolle is rarely purely scholastic. The nearest he approaches to the methods of presentation and the citations of authorities of medieval scholarship are *Judica Me Deus* and *Job*. Even there his aim is not to inform for its own sake, but to persuade readers to inform themselves, first by informing their consciences and then by subjecting themselves to minute self-analysis. In the *Meditations* his method represents the next stage in the road to mystic enlightenment: novices must now reflect on the relevance of the scriptures to themselves and to their relationship with God; this proves to be a painfully intimate relationship, centered on the suffering and death of the Beloved.

Because the *Meditations* supply an essential discipline for the purgative stage of mystic growth, they do not contain mystical material. These are to be the tears of sorrow which precede the song of joy, the *jubilus*. In *Contra Amatores Mundi* Rolle explains that weeping was important to him in the early stages of his spiritual growth,[104] and the *Meditations* are certainly lachrymose. For a modern reader they seem gruesome, even morbid, but this tone of sentimental penitence lies at the core of the affective piety of Rolle's age.

After meditation comes prayer, and the prayers which Rolle supplies for guidance are of two kinds: examples of his own prayers, and samples which he offers for his students. To the first category belong those lyrical passages in the prose, and the separate English Lyrics, together with his early *Canticum Amoris*. Of the latter type are the prayer-songs in *Ego Dormio* and *The Form of Living*, written to inspire love-longing in the heart of the disciple:[105]

> Among other aspirations and songs you may in your longing sing this in your heart to your Lord Jesus, when you desire his coming and your leaving:
> When will you come to comfort me and bring me out of care? etc. (*The Form of Living*, Chap. 8).

If we find Rolle's lyrics unformed, unpoetical or (in the case of the Latin lyrics in *Melos Amoris*) barbarous, as Hope Allen did,[106] then one justified corrective is Geoffrey Shepherd's observation: "Roughness and irregularity are the dynamics of vibrant utterance."[107] We must also remember that Rolle has been called an "oral" poet on several occasions.[108] He may have aimed deliberately at an unformed style in his English poetry and in the non-metrical alliterative prose in the *Melos* and *Incendium* in an attempt to match the spontaneity and fervor of actual inspired prayer. He also uses regular features of formal verse, end-rhyme and medial rhyme, alliteration and repetition, and regular meter is often used, in addition to irregular alliterative prose, in the *Melos Amoris;*[109] the incantatory effect of these formal devices may also be designed to suggest inspiration. Rolle does not use the formal *cursus* of much medieval prose, both vernacular and Latin;[110] this is unlikely to be the result of his having left university early, or of not noticing it in his reading, but is probably a further reflection of his desire for spontaneity: he prefers to suggest the effects of poetic utterance rather than learned prose and to give the impression of speaking aloud to a congregation of those who needed to hear his message. Being denied actual pulpit oratory, he developed an oratorical style in which he can sound all the stops between the comminatory and the coaxing:

> O what deceived wretches are the lovers of this world! Not only do they, because they hold no hope for future joys, subject themselves to every sort of impiety, but also they add malice to their iniquity by despising humble men and the servants of Christ (*Contra Amatores Mundi*, Chap. 4, trans. Theiner).

> Why do you blunder, malicious one? You rant in vain, unfortunate creature, rotting in darkness, for the Trinity directed me, and gave me what I am instructing you (*Melos*, Chap. 38).

> O young men, you who have been thus far deceived, learn now to love. But from now on, love rather Him whom you have not loved before. Come with me; hear of delight; desire to love; but taste of eternal love, which gives life, and not of temporal love, which kills (*Contra Amatores*, Chap. 3, trans. Theiner).

The three great works of Rolle's middle period, *Contra Amatores Mundi*, *Incendium Amoris* and *Melos Amoris* are, therefore, not so much treatises as "addresses." All three contain lyrical prayer to Christ or God and appeal to readers of varying classes and ages and of both sexes, the elect, the conscientious and the degenerate. Rolle even supplies dramatic passages in which the damned bewail their mismanaged life on this earth. In addition these works are bound together by scriptural allusion. The very fabric of the expression is scriptural quotation and allusion, and all three also contain some explication of biblical texts, of Psalm 3:4 and Psalm 22:5, for example, in *Incendium* Chapter 36, and of Psalm 138:12 in *Contra Amatores Mundi*. *Melos Amoris*, meanwhile, takes for its structural principle the *postilla*, a commentary on a biblical text: "it is a discursive, but attractive, series of postills on the nature of divine love;"[111] "ordinarily a postill on the text forms the chapter or several chapters, and these postills, strung together loosely at times, form the *Melos*."[112] In this work, very many of the texts are taken from the Song of Songs, which had already been the subject of a separate commentary by Rolle. As Alford has shown, Rolle continued the techniques of his commentary writing in his more discursive works.[113] In these he uses three traditional medieval commentary methods: *association* with another relevant passage of scripture, *substitution* of a word or phrase in the text under consideration by another which explains the meaning, and *amplification* of the text by the addition of explanatory matter. It is especially this last device which is used in the longer works; one cannot call them "more original" than the commentaries proper, for their fabric is composed of biblical quotes, allusions and idioms:

> *Moreover, all things, however he works them out will be made manifest after this life.* (cf. Is 40:5: The glory of the Lord will be revealed; Rom 2:5: his righteous judgement will be revealed). *All the ways of the Lord are agreeable judgements.* (cf. Ps 98:9: he will judge the world in righteousness). *That is to say, they are true and just.* (cf. Ps 119:142: and your law is true; Rv 15:3: Just and true are your ways). *He neither damns this man apart from wondrous justice, nor chooses that man for life without great mercy, which is also just.* (cf Ps 46:8: think of God's marvels, the astounding things he has done in the world; Acts 15:12: all the signs and wonders God had worked through them. Jn 15:16: you did not choose me, but I chose you; Is 56:4: who choose what pleases me (God); Ps 89 (Vulg. 88) espec. v. 14). *Just so, we ought to consider that "the abyss, like a garment, is His clothing"* Ps 103:6) (*Incendium Amoris*, Chap. 30).

The relationship between God's mercy and his wonders, and the abyss which "clothes" him is obscure; the clue is furnished by the first part of Psalm 46, which is a point of reference for the wonders of God. Psalm 46 begins: "God is our shelter, our strength, ever ready to help in time of trouble, so that we shall not be afraid when the earth gives way, when mountains tumble into the depths of the sea" (Ps 46:2), an eschatological vision which returns us to the opening image of the manifestation of all things "after this life."

Such thought associations by means of image and context rather than logical progression of ideas form the substance of Rolle's exposition. We can tease out the connections by means of a Bible concordance; Rolle simply knew the Bible in minute detail, not merely as a source of handy texts, but as a spiritual language. His favorite books seem to have been the Psalms, which he would pray as part of his daily office, the Song of Songs, *locus classicus* of all mystical writing (see page 54), and other poetic books in the Old Testament, such as Job and the prophets, particularly Lamentations, and, of course, the gospels and epistles of the New Testament, together with the Apocalypse. It is perhaps significant that he not only quoted them frequently, but supplied separate commentaries on many of them. Rolle did not write commentaries on the epistles, but imitated these more indirectly by composing his own letters to augment the more general exhortations of the longer Latin works, mentioned above.

Rolle's four letters are all addressed to single recipients: "I am writing this especially to you (sg.)" (*Ego Dormio*). All the letters contain very similar material. Much of *Emendatio Vitae* appears in *The Form*, but not its ecstatic eleventh chapter, part of which had already appeared in *Melos Amoris.* In three of the four letters the three degrees of love are discussed. Rolle even repeats details like the loving song of the nightingale which continues until death: this appears in chapter 8 of *The Form of Living*, at the end of a long career of citation; this symbol had already been used in the *Incendium* and *Melos* and, if the work is Rolle's, in the Commentary on Psalm 88:2, *De Dei Misericordia.*[114]

Because Rolle repeats himself so much, it is difficult to decide the order of the composition of these four last epistles; probably *Emendatio Vitae* precedes *The Form*, and it is likely that *Ego Dormio* and *The Commandment* precede *Emendatio*, but judgment is subjective and depends largely on the degree of "maturity" in the tone. Despite the repetitions each work of Rolle's must really be assessed on its own merits since *a priori* judgments about order of composition may mislead us into identifying "facts" about his development, change of attitudes or of audience which cannot be verified. The habit of self-repetition led Hope Allen to decide that *Melos Amoris* was an early work which Rolle then proceeded to pillage in his later writings. She then inferred that the style and method of the *Melos* had been abandoned by Rolle in favor of more prosaic statement, and further extrapolated from this inference that *Melos* must have caused scandal for the young Rolle. There is no firm evidence for any of this, and Arnould suggests that the more extensive coverage of topics such as Rolle's vocation, and the question of a fixed abode, with the respective merits of conventual and eremetical lifestyles given in *Melos* points rather to a later date for *Melos* than *Canticles*, where the same points are made, and possibly than *Contra Amatores*, which Allen puts into the middle period.[115] Another repetition in *Melos* involves material from the very early *Judica*. It looks as if *Melos Amoris*, far from being an early experiment, may be the culmination of a life's effort at communicating the "song" of mystic love, and it could even be that it postdates *Emendatio*, which also carries duplicate material in Chapter 11.[116]

Part of Hope Allen's dating is based on the fact that in "four" texts Rolle refers to himself as *iuvenis*, young man. One of the accepted meanings of this word in Latin is "one in the prime of life," that is, up to age 40,[117] but Allen rejects this meaning in Rolle's usage and would identify the four works where Rolle calls himself "young" as early; these are: *Judica Me*, *Canticum Amoris*, *Job* and *Melos*. There are two objections to this interpretation. One is that Rolle in fact refers to himself as "young" in *Contra Amatores:* "I too am a young lover . . . my beloved is Uncreated Wisdom" (*Contra Amatores*, trans. Theiner: *Quoniam adhuc et ego iuvenis amator . . . hec est dilecta mea sapiencia increata*). The other is that Rolle seems not to use "youth" literally; it was an ideal age, the age of our resurrection, thirty-two years and three months, as he (traditionally) asserts in *Judica B3*.[118] Moreover "youth" or "boy" was a term with specific mystic connotations in spiritual writing, as in the old Latin rendering of Psalm 67:29: *Ibi beniamin adulescentulus: in mentis excessu*. In Rolle's English Psalter this is: "There beniamyn yong child: in out passyng of thoght"; his comment continues: "There in the wells is Benjamin, that is son of the right hand, that is, a contemplative soul; 'young child,' that is, in new life of charity, not old in sin; 'in the passing out of thought' from himself into contemplation of God." Admittedly, *adulescentulus* is younger than *iuvenis*, but at the conclusion of *Melos* Rolle calls himself *puer*, "boy."[119] Rolle gives similar interpretation to the young maidens, *adulescentulae*, in *Canticles:*

> Maidens—not old women or girls—indeed are right because they are strong and powerful and know divine love. Maidens therefore should

love; they should rejoice in eternal love (*Comment on Canticles*, trans. Boenig, pp. 107–8).

Psalm 42:5, the former opening of the liturgy of the Mass, also uses "youth" as a term for spiritual vigor: *Introibo ad altare Dei, ad Deum qui laetificat juventutem meam* (Septuagint; Jer. Bible: "to the God of my joy").

This non-literal use of the word *youth* throws into prominence the whole question of "autobiography" in Rolle. When he writes of his solitary life, his preference for sitting for contemplation, and the fire of his love for God, we may be sure that he is writing from his own viewpoint. When, however, he writes of detractors, of hardships, of malicious criticism and of the temptations of life (apart from the specific account of his own temptation given in *Canticles*), we must not assume that he is writing simply of himself. Hope Allen herself observed in Rolle's *Comment on Job* that "it is often hard to draw the line between what is autobiography and what is interpretation of the texts,"[120] but she then assumes that Rolle would have envisaged the sufferings of forlorn and tormented Job "in terms that he feels are suitable to his own state." Alford provides a *caveat* to this by reminding us that "the value and intensity" of any persecution Rolle may have experienced came from its corroboration of the experience of biblical heroes; his life received validity from its similarity to the great figures of the past. "The longer he looked into it, the more his own identity merged with the reflection, until he was himself Job, and David and Paul."[121] Perhaps even this reappraisal places too much emphasis on Rolle's subjectivity. Vandenbroucke goes even further in his study of the diction of *Melos Amoris;* where Rolle uses numerous periphrases for his main topics, Christ, the devil, love and the lover, angels, devils, song, heat and sweetness, he observes drily that in all this welter of transposed expression, "Rolle parle le plus souvent de lui-meme";[122] the greatest number of verbal substitutions are said to be replacements of the first person pronoun.

In fact it seems here that the evidence has been stood on its head. When Rolle uses periphrases like "lover of the Creator," "most ardent lover," "the yearner," "young man," "the poor man," "humble man," "the holy man in solitude," "the praying man," "the sitter, singer, meditator"[123] he is not speaking *per se* of Richard Rolle, but of "everyman who desires to serve God in the best way"; all people, in other words, should see themselves as Job, David, Paul, and, above all, as Christ, whom they typify. Rolle himself observes that the lover yearns to become like the Beloved, and it is his aim to lead all his readers to this condition. Admittedly Rolle's point of view remains intransigently hostile to the world and its riches, and wholly in favor of total spiritual poverty and simplicity, because "Christ, as an example for man, led a poor man's life while He was on his pilgrimage, because He knew that those people who abound in riches and delights would enter the kingdom of Heaven with difficulty" (*Emendatio Vitae*, Chap. 3, trans. del Mastro). Rolle's view is one-sided in that he considers poverty and solitude to be the only effective way of finding the love of God for certain, but he is not praising himself for having adopted that life. He is attempting to persuade the reader to stand alongside himself and view human life from his perspective, and his use of periphrases aids that end by giving a quasi-objective stance.

Rolle is not arrogantly self-absorbed; his wish to turn others to his way of life is perhaps a kind of arrogance, but an arrogance on God's behalf, not his own. The nine "steps of humility" in chapter 9 of *Incendium*, culminating in "recognising one's weaknesses" and "judging oneself inferior to everyone else" are not the mark of an arrogant man; in *Melos* he declares specifically that he does not wish to be considered proud or boastful for retiring from the comfort of riches. Yet the fact remains that Rolle's view of life is basically polarized into love of God versus love of the world. This is the title of *Liber de Amore Dei contra Amatores Mundi*, and it forms a constant theme throughout his work. Antithesis is the essence of his rhetoric, and his doctrine, the opposition of *caritas* and *cupiditas*, forms the backbone of his structural method and is carried over into his style of writing. Some have detected a note of "asperity" in this uncompromising stance and the accompanying extreme rejection of "the lovers of the world," an asperity which reflects "some of the as yet unresolved tensions in Rolle's own soul,"[124] which is not present in the latest works. This may be so, or it may be that the note of quiet confidence in the last letters reflects Rolle's final discovery of close friends for whom he was yearning in *Incendium* chapter 39, and his assurance that those to whom he was writing were not in need of sharp chastisement. Whatever the explanation, the writings which conclude this volume show Rolle at his most benign and most persuasive; it is helpful to consider these personal letters as a reflection of the real Rolle, able at last to talk frankly to those who indeed have adopted his way of life, and able to lay aside the sustained drama of his oratory for the quiet tone of intimate discourse.

Sources and Influences

Many writers both patristic and contemporary must have shaped Rolle's spirituality, informing his mystical experiences themselves and coloring his attempts to communicate them. There can be no doubt that Rolle was learned, and that somehow he maintained his access to written texts after he left Oxford. His use of Pagula's *Oculus Sacerdotalis*, possibly while it was still in progress, and certainly within six or seven years of its completion is evidence of this. Even with this work, however, we cannot be certain that he knew its author's name, or that he saw all of it; he refers to his sources for *Judica Me*, largely the *Dextera Pars* and the *Pars Oculi* of *Oculus Sacerdotalis*, as "the early fathers" of the Church;[125] there is, however, some truth in this, since Pagula used Fribourg's *summa* of pastoral theology.[126] In this way Rolle might have indirect contact with much scholastic learning. In chapter 6 of *The Form* he draws heavily on Hugh of Strasbourg's *Compendium theologicae veritatis* where Hugh himself is using Julianus Pomerius's *De Vita Contemplativa*. Like many other religious writers of his time, Rolle probably used a *florilegium*, a compendium of quotations from the fathers, rather than complete texts of Cassian, Augustine, Cassiodorus, Gregory, Bernard, Bonaventure and James of Milan where he quotes them. He names very few of these. One to whom he is indirectly indebted for the tone of much of his work, and from whom he takes part of a lyric in *Ego Dormio*, is Anselm, whom he cites in *Melos* only to disagree with him on the merits of the conventual life, without acknowledging his deep debt to Anselm's far-reaching devotional innovations. Rolle possibly did know of Gregory the Great's attempts to combine the pastoral and contemplative lives, especially since this may have been his own aim at the start of his career as a hermit.

Where Rolle obtained his books is not clear. If he were really on bad terms with the regular clergy, he cannot have borrowed books from Rievaulx or Bylands abbeys, and his strictures against the parochial clergy make it seem unlikely that he would have been on book-loaning terms with them either, but much of Rolle's criticism of those in orders may have been general and not particular, and his claims of persecution are largely his way of striking a "biblical" pose.

Rolle rarely cites his authorities: he rejected the contemporary scholastic technique of displaying knowledge by citing other scholars with every assertion; this was learning for learning's sake. He preferred the empirical approach, which may itself have nurtured a spirit of independence in his readers, and perhaps prepared the ground for the Hussite and Lollard movements, both of which used his Latin and English works, although it must be emphasized that Rolle himself remained orthodox in his theology.

The chief influences on Rolle were Anselm (1033–1109) and Bernard of Clairvaux (1090–1153). The prayers and meditations which Anselm sent to Matilda of Tuscany in 1104 began a new spiritual movement of affective piety centering on "compunction" in Western Christianity. Anselm's prayers to Christ and the saints, to be used for personal not liturgical devotions, form "a distinct break with the past."[127] They are written in language "as ardent as it is controlled and refined,"[128] in rhymed and alliterative prose which challenges a personal response of a deeply emotional kind. In earlier centuries extracts from the psalms had been used for private devotions; by the eleventh century other short prayers had been composed, but from Anselm's time there was a focus on the individual soul, and a growing tendency to use unexpected imagery and daring theology.

> And you, Jesus, are you not also a mother?
> Are you not the mother who, like a hen,
> gathers her chickens under her wings?
> Truly, Lord, you are a mother. [Anselm, *Prayer to St. Paul*, trans. Benedicta Ward]

Rolle echoes the following passage from the *Meditation on the Dread of Judgement* (Meditation to Stir up Fear):

> Jesus, Jesus, for your name's sake be to me what your name promises. Jesus, Jesus, forget how in my pride I angered you, and look on me in my wretchedness imploring you. Sweet name, lovable name, name of good hope and consolation to sinners! For what is "Jesus" but "Saviour"? So, therefore, Jesus, for your own sake be to me a "Jesus" (trans. Colledge).[129]

Like Rolle, Anselm experienced a mystic inspiration, providing a solution which enabled him to write the *Proslogion*, and like Rolle, he was praying in church. But, significantly, Anselm was singing Matins in choir whereas Rolle was reciting the office in solitude when he received the gifts of *calor* and *canor*. The techniques of Anselm's prayers, requiring withdrawal, self-examination and compunction, are similar to Rolle's prescriptions for preparing for mystic joy, but Rolle, two hundred years later, represents the new, non-monastic age of the fourteenth-century saints, many of whom were not in orders, but were laypeople.

The chief resemblance between Anselm and Rolle lies not so much in their appeal to the emotions, for after Anselm this is common to most spiritual writers, but in their common love of the Bible and its idiom. Many of the similarities of imagery which seem to link Rolle with Augustine or Gregory, for instance, really derive from their common love and intimate knowledge of the Bible. Rolle makes a short extract from Bernard's *Sermons on the Canticles* in chapter 9 of *The Form*, where he also echoes his own *Comment on the Canticles*. Already in Rolle's time the continental mystics were also using the Song of Songs, and Hilton did so after Rolle. Much similarity in their celebration of divine love stems from this common source. As Liegey has observed: "It seems hazardous to try to trace to any source the symbols of pilgrimage, betrothal, fire, song, light, sweetness, ascent, mountains, and wounds, for all of these seem common property to all who aspire to enter the Holy City."[130] For example:

> The season of glad songs has come, 2:12;
> In his longed-for shade I am seated and his
> fruit is sweet to my taste, 2:3;
> let me hear your voice, for your voice is sweet, 2:14;
> the flash of (love) is a flash of fire,
> a flame of Yahweh himself, 8:6.

In writing of God as fire, Rolle is deploying the most ancient symbol of all, used from Exodus 3:2 to Acts 2:3 and Revelation 1:14. What is distinctive in Rolle's use is perhaps the emphasis he places on the mutual love of Christ and the soul by means of his handling of the commonplace imagery: fire and sweetness are *pervading* influences; one cannot contain fire, its heat will radiate outwards, and sweet scents diffuse over a wide area, so that it is impossible to make distinction, except in degree, between the source of the heat and of the scent and the surroundings which have been influenced by them. As Rolle says in chapter 10 of *The Form:*

> We must strive to clothe ourselves in love, as iron or as charcoal do in fire. . . . The charcoal is so imbued with fire that the whole is fire,

an image Rolle derived from Bernard's *De Diligendo Deo* (see *Form*, note 59). Fire and scent are therefore not simply powerful metaphors for mystic love, but are very evocative of the interactive force of that love with its source; God and the soul become one in their submission to mutual love.

More effective still in suggesting this mutual love, because it points up the active and voluntary response of the soul, far removed from quietism, is Rolle's own characteristic image of *song*. He hears a symphony of song in which he too can participate (*Incendium*, Chap. 15), a shared harmony, one song with many voices. The image is also important in showing that Rolle did indeed recognize that a relationship with other souls, beatified and angelic, was essential. He was a solitary in this life because he could not live with others ("I fled to solitude because I could not live in harmony with people; they frequently hinder me from my joy," *Incendium*, Chap. 27), and probably Rolle was not temperamentally suited to communal life, in monastery or marriage.[131] Yet he realized that earthly solitude is merely a temporary penance; his vision of heaven emphasized the importance of communal praise and enjoyment in the form of the banquet image.

As has already been seen, Rolle derived several passages, directly or indirectly, from Bernard's *Sermons on the Canticles* and *De Diligendo Deo*. Apart from these borrowings, Rolle derived from St. Bernard and the school of writing which he inspired an intense spiritual consciousness of the immanent presence of God. This is epitomized in the hymn *Iesu Dulcis Memoria*, for long attributed to Bernard himself, which Rolle draws on frequently, and from which he derives his own devotion to the Holy Name. A strong emphasis on personal intimacy between the Christian and Christ, founded on the allegorical interpretation of the Song of Songs, is the hallmark of later medieval spirituality, a further development of Anselm's passionate personal appeal to Christ and the saints. Rolle's most significant debt to Bernard lies in Bernard's analogy between carnal and divine love in his study of the Song of Songs.[132] This "brautmystik" informs the Rhineland mystics to a high degree and is very marked in Rolle, especially in *Melos*. There is just possibly a connection between the Rhineland mystics and the English. Riehle would like to posit the

Franciscan Rudolf of Biberach's *De Septem Itineribus Aeternitatis* as a missing link between Thomas Gallus and the *Cloud*-author,[133] while Rolle could have heard of Eckhart's teaching if he were at the Sorbonne in the 1320s, for Eckhart had been there earlier in the century, while Rolle and Suso, who also had a devotion to the name of Jesus, were contemporaries. Most similarities, however, probably lie chiefly in shared use of the Bible as source.

Within the native tradition of English spirituality, Rolle had important predecessors in the twelfth and thirteenth centuries. Notable among these was another northerner, Aelred of Rievaulx (1109–1167), who wrote the *Mirror of Love* (*Speculum Caritatis*) at Bernard's instigation.[134] Aelred, echoing St Augustine, poses just that contrast between *caritas* and *cupiditas* which we find dominant in Rolle's thinking, but which Rolle, like Augustine himself, probably took from St. Paul, e.g. from 1 Corinthians 13:4–8 or Galatians 5:22–24 and Romans 1:29–32 or Galatians 5:19–22. There is one concept which Rolle takes from Aelred (or from Bernard, who was Aelred's source), and this is the term "deification," the soul's capacity for reformation until it regains the image of God lost through original sin.[135] The total rejection of the world and its civilization, which Rolle insists on, is another point of similarity between him and the great Cistercians, Bernard and Aelred.

In seeking solitude, a greater loneliness than the Cistercians in their "deserts" could know, Rolle had many precedents, especially in England, which was renowned for hermits and recluses in the middle ages.[136] Among these was Godrich of Finchale, near Durham, who became a hermit some time before 1128 after spending sixteen years travelling as a merchant, and died in 1170, and Wulfric of Haselbury, who entered an anchorite's cell near Haselbury Plucknett in Somerset some time before 1125, where he lived till his death in 1155; whereas Godrich was self-educated, Wulfric had been a parish priest. Godrich had first served another hermit, Aelfric, near Durham, and a namesake of his was adviser and spiritual father to Christina of Markyate, herself a recluse, in the twelfth century.[137] Many hermits like these must have attracted followers, as Margaret Kirkby seems to have found support from Rolle two hundred years later.

For such anchorites and especially the women among them, several "guides" or "rules" were written, including one by Aelred, *De Institutione Inclusarum*. The *Ancrene Riwle*, probably written just after

1200, was written originally for three young ladies of noble birth but was soon adapted for a larger community and borrowed for other rules, such as the early thirteenth-century *Dublin Rule*. Some time between 1140 and 1215 a priest named Robert, writing a rule for an anchorite named Hugh, claimed to have translated much of the contents from English works, which, if this is accurate, must have been precursors of *Ancrene Riwle*.[138] Aelred's *De Institutione* includes a series of meditations on the life of Christ, and this technique is advised in *Ancrene Riwle* also:

> See how He stands before the judgment seat, head bowed, eyes cast down, face calm, saying little, ready for insults, prepared for blows. Now I know that you can endure no more, you cannot bear to watch how his delicate back is torn with scourges, his face slapped, his adorable head crowned with thorns (Aelred, quoted in Colledge, *Mediaeval Mystics of England*, Intro., p. 34).

> For the moment, my dear sisters, give your thoughts to this: on the day that your dear Spouse, the Lord so worthy of love, the Saviour from heaven, Jesu, God, who is the Son of God, the ruler of all the world, was thus let blood, what was he given to drink? During that blood-letting, which was so painful and so bitter, those for whose sake He bled brought Him no gift of wine, or ale or water. Even though he said "I thirst" while He was bleeding on the cross, yet they brought Him only bitter gall. When was any other man being let blood given such poor fare? (*Ancrene Riwle*, Custody of the Senses, trans. Salu, p. 50).

In the fifty or so years between Aelred's *De Institutione* and *Ancrene Riwle* a stronger note of affective piety developed; during the 150 years between this version of Christ's death and Rolle's two *Meditations* the increase in emotional fervor is considerable. Both versions emphasize that Christ suffered in each of his senses, but Rolle's account is very much more detailed and horrific.

During the twelfth century there also developed a greater interest in mystical theology, partly resulting from the re-availability of pseudo-Dionysius's works through John Sarrazin's revisions of Eriugena's translations of pseudo-Dionysius, and partly because of the wide circulation of the works of Hugh of St. Victor (d. 1141) and the Irishman (or Scot) Richard of St. Victor (d. 1173). Both had independently systematized spiritual knowledge. Hugh isolated four steps of preparation for infused contemplation: study, prayer, meditation and works; contemplation itself he considered a foretaste of blessedness. Richard's work was a development of Hugh's, and a powerful influence on English mysticism, especially on Hilton and the *Cloud*-author; his *Benjamin Maior*, *Benjamin Minor* and *Four Steps of Passionate Love* were probably all known to Rolle. A thirteenth-century English mystic, Edmund Rich, was influenced by the Victorines during his study in Paris before 1200 and returned to Oxford with a master's degree to lecture on Aristotelian logic. His *Mirror of Holy Church* was written when he was Archbishop of Canterbury and became known during his exile in France. It, too, is a guide for the Benedictine novices at Christ Church, Canterbury, but although it is simply written, it is the product of a more highly trained mind than Rolle's. The all-important distinction between this and Rolle's letters of spiritual direction is that Rich wrote in French. Another difference is that Rich taught the *via negativa* deriving from pseudo-Dionysius: "Put every corporeal image outside your heart and let your naked intention fly up above all human reasoning," where contemplative initiates, such as Rich himself, would find "great sweetness and great secrets."[139] Rich was much quoted in the ensuing centuries, and was translated into English and Latin; in that way Rolle could have picked up Rich's version of the concept of deification: "God became man to make man God," a concept Langland wanted preached more widely; Bishop Grosseteste was also teaching it about 1250 at Lincoln.

Such was the context of Rolle's mystical writing and works of spiritual direction. He had many examples to follow in Latin, in England and abroad, but added his own particular contribution to mystical writing.

Rolle's Uniqueness and Contribution to the Tradition of Western Mysticism

Rolle was the first English mystic to write in English rather than Latin, the language of learning, or the socially acceptable language, French. There had been other works in English of an emotive piety before his time, notably the poetic prose of *The Wooing of Our Lord*, another meditation piece, in rhymed and alliterative prose, focusing on Christ's humanity and death, and other related works. These, like Thomas of Hales's English verse *Love-Rune*, probably written about

1250, were written for women and were strongly influenced by *Ancrene Riwle*, not itself mystical, but with many appeals to affective piety, as was shown above. *The Wooing* is partly mystical, and based in part on *Iesu Dulcis Memoria*, together with allusions to the Song of Songs in the kissing and embracing of the soul in the seclusion of Christ's chamber (lines 572–77).[140] Rolle must have known works like *The Wooing*, which reflects a similar emotionalism:

> O, how they are forcing iron nails now through your lovely hands into the hard cross, through your noble feet. O, now from those hands and from those feet, so beautiful, streams the blood, so pitifully. O now they are offering my beloved, who says he is thirsty, the sourest of all drinks, vinegar, mingled with gall, which is the bitterest of all things, a drink so harmful in bloodletting, so sour and so bitter (*The Wooing of Our Lord*, lines 511–22).

In addition, in the thirteenth century English was used for works of moral instruction, like the Essex *Vices and Virtues* or apocryphal narrative like the *History of the Holy Rood Tree*.

When Rolle began writing in English, some time in the late 1330s, he had models available for the various types of English he was to use. Yet he found a model for his first work, the *Psalter*, in a far older work, which Everett surmised was an updated version of the Anglo-Saxon Psalter glosses; this may also have provided guidelines for another psalter version, preceding Rolle's: the rhymed *Surtees Psalter*. Like Rolle's, it makes some errors of translation:

> I am fain of those (sc. things) that said *are* to me:
> "In house of the Lord go shall we" (Ps. 121).[141]

Rolle also makes the same error in rendering the perfect passive.

This survival of Old English texts, especially sermons and other works for instructing the laity, is in contrast to the use of French for entertainment and business purposes, and Latin for record-keeping and learning. From 1150 to 1250, when French was the dominant language of secular works in England, French culture was dominant in Europe and the cult of "refined" (courtly) love, celebrated in song and narrative, was the chief subject of these works. Rolle himself was profoundly touched by the cult even as he rejected its implications of irresponsible sexuality; he claimed that he tried to avoid hearing the songs of profane love whenever he was among people, but he used the rhymed lyric form in which it was written for his own love-songs, to Jesus.[142]

English prose, too, was influenced by French, notably by the new style of preaching in Paris, where Maurice de Sully had been preaching, between 1168 and 1175, a new type of more structured and more vivacious sermon. His sermons themselves were translated into the English of Kent in the early thirteenth century and strongly influenced the style and method of *Ancrene Riwle* about the same time.[143] The witty, conversational syntax of *Ancrene Riwle* and its modulated rhythms are very different from the polished and cadenced prose of Aelfric (fl. 990) which had up to then influenced English, while the citation of authorities and use of logical argument make the new prose both scholarly and intimate, even where it translates the Latin of Bernard or Hugh of St. Victor.[144] Rolle did not follow the new model in its logical presentation and learned authorities; the rhetoric of the Bible provides the logic of his writing. But he clearly learned from *Ancrene Riwle* how to convey the rhythms of spoken English in written form. Since he had only been taught Latin grammar and construction, he must have had to teach himself English from available models like this:

> You, my dear sisters, are following Our Lady, and not the cackling Eve; therefore an anchoress, whatever she is, should be as silent as possible. She should not have the characteristics of a hen, which, when it has laid, can do nothing but cackle (*Ancrene Riwle*, Custody of the Senses, trans. Salu).

> In every case, the better you are, and the less conversation you have with people, the greater is your joy in God's presence. Oh, what sort of greatness is it, to be worth praise and not to be praised. And what sort of misery it is to have the name and the outward garb of a holy life and not to be so, but to conceal pride, anger or malice under the clothing of children of Christ (Rolle, *The Form of Living*, Chapter 1).

Ancrene Riwle was adapted for a larger community in about 1230 (*Ancrene Wisse*), translated into French and Latin, revised in the late fourteenth century and used for a set of sermons in the fifteenth. Like Rolle's own work in the later fourteenth century, it was anthologized in extract. Rolle himself exercised a similar powerful influence on later Middle English prose. He was read by the learned and the wealthy, including the Provincial of the Friars Minor, Lord Scrope of Masham, and John Newton, treasurer of York Cathedral.[145] Much personal use was made of Rolle's work in private devotion, often in extracts from his prose and verse,[146] and his Latin works were frequently translated into English, especially the passage on the Holy Name (*Oleum Effusum*) from the *Canticles.* Misyn translated his *Emendatio* (there were six other independent translations of it) and *Incendium Amoris* in the mid-fifteenth century, and his works were printed regularly from 1483, when his *Job* was the ninth book to be printed at Oxford, to the seventeenth century, when *Emendatio* was published in de la Bigne's edition as one of the tools of the Counter-Reformation.

Although Rolle had his detractors, who were refuted by the hermit Thomas Basset about 1400, and seems to have been misread by Margery Kempe and those whom Hilton and the *Cloud*-author warn against expecting tangible, physical effects in meditation, he was an influential force in his own time and for long afterward, both in England and on the continent. His English works, written for novices in the contemplative art, do not carry us to the heights of his Latin works but are significant landmarks in the development of English prose and in the method of instructing others in the spiritual life; in both respects they formed the groundwork for later writers like Hilton and the *Cloud*-author.

Conclusion: Rolle Today

There are features of Rolle's spirituality which are inescapably medieval, such as his emphasis on the pains of hell, the snares of the devil and the temptations of the female sex. His strictures against women are largely biblical, like so much else in Rolle; they originate from texts like 1 Corinthians 11:7–10 and 1 Corinthians 14:34–5 and are noticeably absent from his English works. His intransigent attitude to lax clerics and self-satisfied monks—again, in his Latin writing—is no more than a historical detail; such criticism was frequently justified in his time, and he was writing in the hope of effecting the much-needed reforms.

The modern reader is likely to find Rolle's condemnations of the Jews at the Crucifixion even more distasteful than his antifeminism. St. Augustine typifies the dualistic attitude to Jews throughout the middle ages, in which Jews are seen both as the chosen people to whom God's revelation was first made and as the killers of Christ (*City of God* 4:34). Chaucer's Prioress and Parson both speak of the "cursed Jewes." Unless he did study in Paris, Rolle would never have seen a Jew: they were banished in 1290 by an act of King Edward I in Council, after repeated injustices: fines, imprisonment and burning of synagogues and homes being among the least. Rolle might have heard local legends of the terrible night before Passover in 1190 when one hundred and fifty Jews in York burned to death after taking sanctuary in York castle, rather than face butchery. He could have seen the allegorical painting in York Minster, executed about ten years before his birth, in which Synagogua is shown with crown falling from her head to symbolize the passing of the Old Law; such depictions, balanced by a contrastive portrait of Holy Church in triumph, were common. In the years after Rolle's death, Jews were tortured and massacred all over Europe, accused of causing the plague. By comparison, Rolle's allusions are mild: true, he lays blame for all Christ's tortures on the Jews, omitting the Romans, but he does not often use opprobrious terms for the Jews, apart from the uncertain reading "hell-hounds," and in fact concludes with the self-accusation that he was 'one of those guilty' of Christ's death, and caused all of Mary's sorrow.

Rolle's rejection of materialism, extreme though it was, is important for us today, and so too is his depiction of the overwhelming joy of mystic union:

> O may Eternal Love totally envelop our "interior man" (Ephes. 3:16), inflaming him with His sweetly flowing fire. May Love introduce him to a completely new glory and transform him into a true likeness to His own nature, as it were deifying him, so that the spiritual substance may be completely absorbed by the uncreated fire and the resounding joy, may remain unyielding among temptations, firm in tribulations. . . . When his "love is perfectly ordained" (Song 2:4) and his coordination is brimful of love, then "all his heart, all his soul, all his strength" will press on to love God and will not cease to wish for spiritual and physical benefit for "his neighbour as for himself" (Mark 12:30–31) [*Melos Amoris*, Chap. 50].

Rolle resembles other fourteenth-century mystics in being a layman, but he does not share their extremes of psycho-physical rapture, with trances and levitation; many of the fourteenth-century female saints, in their highly emotional piety, have recently been termed "sado-masochistic."[147] Rolle was not a social man and may have had a somewhat excitable temperament, but he was not a tormented personality, and in the works which he wrote in English for his women disciples he reveals himself a courteous and considerate teacher whose self-fulfillment in that rôle was an essential part of his vocation as a contemplative.

The English Psalter and Commentary

Rolle wrote two commentaries on the whole 150 psalms, an earlier one in Latin, which may belong to the very early period after he left Oxford, and this English version which is much later, perhaps from the early or mid 1330s. The commentary is basically traditional, deriving in the main from that of Peter Lombard (c. 1100–1160) as Middendorff proved, but Rolle includes personal interpretations in his two psalter commentaries, sometimes similar or identical in each, sometimes adding or omitting points in the English version. In MS Bodley Laud 286 there is a metrical preface to the English Psalter which claims that it was written for "Merget Kyrkby," which is not impossible. This metrical preface also notes the now established fact that Rolle's Psalter was adapted in the later fourteenth century by the Lollards, who inserted heretical matter; two "Lollard" versions have been identified. Rolle's English *Psalter* is not markedly mystical but does make reference to song and to burning love. Hope Allen selected psalms which had apparently personal application, to persecution (Psalms 3, 12 and 56), to the fire of love (Psalms 3 and 12) and song (Psalm 56), with two "lyrical" passages, one in Psalm 56, and the other verse 2 of Psalm 61. To these I have added six further psalms or parts of psalms, selected to illustrate Rolle's translation style (e.g. Psalm 102), which was, as his Prologue explains, literal in both word and word-order, and to show the allegorical approach which is also seen in his *Bee and the Stork* (Psalms 102 and 103). His Prologue identifies the three types of hymn which occur in the psalms: hymns of praise, of thanksgiving and of entreaty; modern bible commentary makes exactly the same distinctions. A marked difference, however, from modern Psalm interpretation lies in Rolle's comment on the point of view present in the psalms: that of Christ, as God and as man; of the elect; or, finally, of the hypocritical. It is important to bear in mind that Rolle did not pray the psalms solely as personal prayers; some earlier criticism of the *Psalter* sees his commentary as having largely autobiographical reference. To illustrate these types of psalm and commentary, I have selected Psalm 131:1–10 because of its christological interpretation; Psalm 102 because this is the voice of the individual soul (i.e. the voice of Everyman); Psalm 121 as part of a hymn of thanksgiving; Psalm 150 because of the musical allegory; and the opening of Psalm 118 for its comment on psalmody and as a prayer of praise from the elect.

For nearly two hundred years Rolle's *Psalter* was the only authorized translation of the Bible into English; it did not need diocesan permission for its use. The consequent popularity of the work is attested by the twenty or so extant manuscripts, only one of which, that of University College, Oxford, forms the basis for Bramley's 1884 edition, with some comparison with eleven others. There are three types of interpolated versions; not all the additions are obviously Lollard. The *Psalter* is the subject of a 1922 London University thesis by Dorothy Everett and is currently being edited by a team of scholars at Fordham University.

Rolle's Latin verses for the Psalter are not taken from his source for the commentary, Peter Lombard, but from Jerome's Gallican Psalter, and from the Old-Latin version which preceded it; both differ from modern versions and it was not possible to substitute these; I have included the Authorized/New International/Jerusalem version numbering in brackets to make comparison with more familiar renderings easier.

Sources: Allen, *EW*, pp. 4–16; Bramley, pp. 357–8, 362–4, 410–11, 439–40, 449–51 and 492–3.

Prologue

A great fullness of spiritual comfort and joy in God comes into the hearts of those who recite or devoutly intone the psalms as an act of praise to Jesus Christ. They drop sweetness in men's souls and pour delight into their thoughts and kindle their wills with the fire of love, making them hot and burning within, and beautiful and lovely in Christ's eyes. And those who persevere in their devotion he raises up to the life of meditation and, on many occasions, he exalts them to the melody and celebrations of heaven.[1] The song of the psalms chases away devils, stirs up angels to help us; it drives out and destroys discontent and resentment in the soul and makes a peace between body and soul; it brings desire of heaven and contempt for earthly things.[2] Indeed, this radiant book is a choice song in God's presence, like a lamp brightening our life, health for a sick heart, honey to a bitter soul, a high mark of honor among spiritual people, a voicing of private virtues, which forces down the proud to humility and makes kings bow in reverence to poor men, nurturing children with gentleness. In the psalms there is such great beauty of meaning and of medicine from the words that this book is called "a garden enclosed," a sealed fountain, a paradise full of apples. Now see: with wholesome instruction it brings agitated and tempestuous souls into a fair and peaceful way of life, now warning them to repent of sin with tears, now promising joy for the virtuous, now threatening hell for the wicked. The song which gives delight to hearts and instructs the soul has become a sound of singing: with angels whom we cannot hear we mingle words of praising, so that anyone would be right to reckon himself exiled from true life if he does not in this way experience the delightfulness of this gift of wonderful sweetness, which never grows sour with the corruptions of this world, but is everlasting in its own superlative quality, and is always increasing in the grace of purest softness.[3] All the pleasures and delights of earthly loves vanish away and at last disappear to nothing, but the longer this gift persists, the greater it is, and is greatest of all, quite the opposite of cursed human love affairs, when love is most perfected.

This book is called The Psalter, a name which it takes from a musical instrument known in Hebrew as *nablum*, the Greek form is *psaltery*,[4] derived from *psalm*, and in English its meaning is "to touch"; and this consists of ten strings, and gives out sound from the upper part when it is touched by hand.[5] In the same way, this book gives instruction on keeping the Ten Commandments and on acting, not for the sake of earthly things, but on behalf of heaven, which is the part above. And so we emit sound from our superior natures at the touch of our hands when everything which we intend to do is for the love of God. Moreover, this book is subdivided into three sets of fifty psalms, in which are symbolized three phases of progress in the faith of a Christian man: the first covers the penitential way of life, the second covers virtuous living, the third deals with praise of eternal life.[6] The first fifty conclude with *Have mercy on me, O God*, the second with *I will sing of mercy and judgment unto thee, O Lord*, and the third closes with the words *Let everything that has breath praise the Lord*.[7] This book of the Holy Scriptures is the one most used in the services of holy church because it is the epitome of the divine writings. This is because it incorporates what all the other books treat at length, in other words, the teaching of the Old Testament and of the New. In it are described the rewards of good people, the punishments of the wicked, the discipline of penance, development in virtuous living, the perfection of the devout which ascends toward heaven, the lifestyle of men of action,[8] the spiritual meditation of the contemplative orders, and the joy of mystic contemplation of the highest degree which can occur in humankind while one is living and sensing within the body, and in addition, what sin strips away from one's soul and what penance restores to it. There is no need to enumerate each significance here since, by God's grace, you, my reader,[9] will find them explained at the passages where they occur. This portion of scripture is called the book of Christ's hymns. A hymn is "the praising of God with song." There are three properties to a hymn: the praising of God, the rejoicing of heart or mind, the affectionate desiring of God's love. Song is the great happiness of thinking of everlasting things and of eternal joy breaking out in the sound of praising. So it is most appropriately termed "the book of hymns" because it teaches us to love God with a cheerful mood and with rejoicing and tenderness in the soul, praising not only in the heart but with the voice also, and showing the way to those who are inexperienced.

The subject matter of this book is Christ and his spouse, in other words, holy church, or, the soul of every virtuous person. The intention is to reform to Christ in newness of life those who are corrupted by Adam's sin. The method of instruction is as follows: in some places the psalmist speaks of Christ in his divinity, in other places in his humanity, in others again by using the voice of Christ's servants. Likewise, he speaks of holy church in three ways: at times in the person of perfect people, sometimes in the person of imperfect people, sometimes that of wicked men, who remain within the church in body but not in mind, in name but not in deed, in a count of heads but not by a reckoning of merit.[10]

In this work I shall not be using learned expression but the easiest and commonest words in English which approximate most closely to the Latin, so that those who do not know Latin can acquire many Latin words from the English. In the translation I follow the letter as much as I am able to, and where I cannot find an exactly equivalent English word, I follow the sense, so that those who are going to read it need have no fear of not understanding. In the explanation

I follow the holy doctors of the church since it could be that it will come into the hands of someone malicious who has no idea how he ought to interpret the work, and who will declare that I did not know what I was saying, and in this way will cause grave harm to himself and to others by despising a work which is beneficial both for himself and for others.[11]

Psalm 3 (3)

(1) *Domine quid multiplicati sunt qui tribulant me; multi insurgunt adversum me.* "Lord, to what end are they numerous who afflict me? Many rise against me." The voice of the soul of a Christian speaking to Christ because of persecution by enemies, spiritual and physical. "Lord, to what end," that is, is it for their disgrace or mine? If I overcome them, it is my crown; if they overcome me, it is my damnation. "Multiplied are those who afflict me," that is, immorality and physical desires against which every just man fights throughout his life here; bad men do not fight at all except against God, and against him they make themselves opponents, and make a truce with sin. "Many," that is, devils and devils' agents, "rise against me" to put me down and bring me as far from spiritual love as they are.

(2) *Multi dicunt animae meae, non est salus ipsi in deo eius.* "Many say to my soul, there is no salvation for it in its God."[12] This saying is about the devil and about many sins which lie in wait to bring people to despair, as one might say "you have sinned greatly and it is hard to leave the urges of your body and the pleasures of the world. Go ahead and lead your life as you want to, because God will not save your soul." These are liars, and they are saying this in order to trick you, because God's mercy is always ready for all who abandon sin, and this the prophet demonstrates in the words

(3) *Tu autem domine susceptor meus es; gloria mea et exaltans caput meum.* "But you, Lord, are my uptaker, my joy and raising my head." In that way they were talking to deceive me, but you take me up into your grace, so that I have not agreed with their saying, and, accordingly, "you are my joy," that is, I rejoice in you and seek your respect alone, not the frivolity nor the praise of men. And you are "raising my head" from earthly love in the contemplation and love of heaven, so that I am not cast down by whatever trial or temptation occurs, since

(4) *Voce mea ad dominum clamavi et exaudivit me de monte sancto suo.*

"With my voice I called out to our Lord, and he heard me from his holy hill." The voice of the heart, in other words, a great yearning for God's love, is sounding in Christ's presence. His prayer he terms "calling" because the force of the fire of love is in his soul, making his prayer pierce heaven. And so he heard him from his holy hill, that is, of his justice, because it is just in God's eyes to assist the man who is in agony because of his love.

(5) *Ego dormivi et soporatus sum, et exurrexi quia dominus suscepit me.* "I slept and am saturated with sleep[13] and I rose because our Lord took me up." What was he doing? "I slept," in other words, I took my rest at first, in sinful living and in lethargy.

"And I am saturated" in my sin
Long lying therein,

and then "I rose" from death to life, from laziness to exercise in the service of God, and this not on my own initiative but because my Lord took me to penance and inspired my heart to hate sin, and therefore

(6) *Non timebo millia populi circumdantis me.* (7) *Exurge, domine, salvum me fac, deus meus.* "I shall not fear thousands of people surrounding me. Rise, Lord, make me safe, my God." This "thousand people" is all the devils of hell and their temptations and all immoral habits which surround people to deceive them and separate them from God. But all these the man whom God has lifted up need not fear. And that it may happen, "rise Lord" he says, that is, make me rise perfectly into your love and "make me safe, my God" because love protects from the fear of all things.

(7) *Quoniam tu percussisti omnes adversantes mihi sine causa. Dentes peccatorum contrivisti.* "For you have struck all those opposing me without reason. The teeth of the sinful you broke completely." You will save me, and you will strike the devil and all his agents in damnation. "Without reason," he says, because no one has any reason to harm a just man who is not harming anyone. Therefore no one can be excused for damaging a good man by words or actions, because all are bound to help him in his need, and to love him in his goodness. "The teeth of the sinful" are the grinding teeth of malicious slanderers, and the deceptive words of flatterers, whom Christ will completely destroy in their actions, because then they will not know how to speak evil against just men, nor good of evil men whom they now

flatter out of timidity or currying favor, but then they shall lose those teeth and burn because of them in the fire of hell.

(8) *Domini est salus et super populum tuum benedictio tua.* "Of the Lord is salvation, and on your people your blessing." Believe what is spoken, and put your faith in Christ and not in yourself, since salvation is only from him, and he will not save any except his lovers. And, Lord, "on your people," that is, on each one of us, be your blessing, so that it may bring us to your love, and so to endless life in heaven.

Psalm 12 (13)

(1) *Usquequo domine oblivisceris me in finem? Usquequo avertis faciem tuam a me?* "How long, Lord, do you forget me in the end? How long do you turn your face from me?" The voice of holy men, who crave and yearn for the coming of Jesus Christ, so that they might live with him in joy, and complaining of delay, they say, "Lord, how long do you forget me in the end" whom I crave to have and hold, that is, "how long are you holding me from the sight of Jesus Christ, who is the right conclusion of my endeavor?" And "how long do you turn your face from me?" that is, "when will you give me perfect knowledge of you?" These words no one can utter honestly except a perfect man or woman who has summoned together all the desires of his or her soul and fastened them to Jesus Christ with the nail of love, so that one hour of one day would seem too long to stay away from him, since they long continually for him.[14] But those who do not love in this way have no longing for his arrival, because their conscience tells them that they have not loved him as they should have done.

(2) *Quam diu ponam consilia in anima mea, dolorem in corde meo per diem?* "How long shall I adopt advice in my soul, sorrow in my heart by day?" Still the longing of a pure soul is being revealed. "How long shall I adopt advice in my heart about various things?" Great ardor of the suffering man is noticed here, as if to say "How long shall I be in adversity?" because people have no need of advice except in adversity. But I am in agony, and misery, in my soul from delay, "by day," that is, continually, while my life lasts, since when we crave for something and that thing is postponed, the misery of yearning increases. And since no one in this world lives without temptation, however perfect he is, he says,

(2) *Usquequo exaltabitur inimicus meus super me?* (3) *Respice et ex-*

audi me, domine deus meus. "How long shall my enemy be raised above me? Look and hear me, Lord, my God." He calls the devil and physical habit his enemy, which is raised above him, while God allows him to have power to tempt him or torture him. But that I may be released from that enemy, you, whose looking is assistance, look, and hear me in this.

(3) *Illumina oculos meos ne umquam obdormiam in morte,* (4) *ne quando dicat inimicus meus praevalui adversus eum.* "Enlighten my eyes, so that I may not at any time sleep in death, lest at some time my enemy may say, 'I had the upper hand over him.' Enlighten with your love the eyes of my heart so that I may not sleep in death," in other words, so that my eyes may not be closed by the pleasures of sin. We sleep, then, in death, when the light of God's love is entombed and extinguished in us, and we take our delight in physical gratification or in any other mortal sin. "Lest my enemy," that is, the devil, may say "I had the upper hand over him." He makes an attack on us, and boasts to God, to get us damned if he can conquer us in any temptation.

(4) *Qui tribulant me exultabunt si motus fuero;* (5) *ego autem in misericordia tua speravi.* "Those who harass me will be glad if I were to be moved; but in your mercy I trusted." The devils who tempt us night and day have no happiness at all unless they can disturb us in our constancy of mind, and make us fall into sin. They harass me so as to disturb me, and then, after being disturbed, lie in wait for me when I fall so that they can make a mockery of me because of it. But, Lord, I trusted in your mercy to remain standing and not to give any attention to their disturbance, any more than a giant does at the wrestling of a puny opponent.

(5) *Exultabit cor meum in salutari tuo;* (6) *cantabo domino quia bona tribuit mihi et psallam nomini domini altissimi.* "My heart shall rejoice in your health; I shall sing to our Lord who gave good things to me, and I shall sing to the name of the Lord most high." You shall not only make me bright and burning in love on my own account,[15] but also will see to it that my enemy is not able to rejoice, since if he is conquered he will experience misery. And my heart will rejoice in "your health," that is, in Jesus,[16] whom I behold in my mind and to whom I sing in gladness of soul. When all the powers of my heart are raised to the sound of heaven, then I can sing with joy and with the miraculous calling out which is part of contemplative life,[17] for he gave me good things in spirit so in that manner I could sing praises

to him; and I shall sing to his honor with the works which are part of the active life, or, to put it another way, "I shall thank him in thought and deed with joy."

Psalm 56 (57)

(1) *Miserere mei deus, miserere mei, quoniam in te confidit anima mea.* "Have mercy on me, God, have mercy on me, for my soul is trusting in you." Have mercy on me that I may arise out of all sins, have mercy on me that I may be steadfast to endure torment, because my soul trusts in you, not in itself, and desires your love.[18]

(1) *Et in umbra alarum tuarum sperabo donec transeat iniquitas.* "And in the shadow of your wings I shall hope, until wickedness is over." That is, in the concealment and cooling of your goodness and your pity, "I shall hope to be saved from torrid vices, till wickedness pass," that is, is utterly completed at the end of time, for always until then distressing evils will not be lacking.

(2) *Clamabo ad deum altissimum, deum qui benefecit mihi.* "I shall cry to God most high, to God who did good to me." I shall not be idle, I shall call out with all the force of my heart to God most high, because I am compelled to call out. But I have proved his goodness, because he did well to me, hearing me calling.

(3) *Misit de caelo et liberavit me, dedit in opprobrium conculcantes me.* "He sent down from heaven and he set me free, and delivered to scorn those who were treading me underfoot." He sent his Son from heaven, and through him delivered me from the devil's prison, and he delivered to the censure of unending torture those "treading me down," that is, the devil and his agents, who torture just men.

(3) *Misit deus misericordiam suam et veritatem suam* (4) *et eripuit animam meam de medio catulorum leonum. Dormivi conturbatus.* "God sent his mercy and his truth, and he took out my soul from the midst of the lion's cubs, and I sleep a troubled sleep." "God sent mercy" to my soul, forgiving my sin, and "his truth," punishing me mercifully, and so "he took out my soul" which was bound with the bonds of sin, "from the midst of the lions' cubs," that is, from the common life of worldly lovers, which are the devil's cubs. Among them, "I slept," that is, I rested in iniquity, in impurity and sin. But I was "troubled" by them, that is, tortured, making me leave them more quickly and hasten to God.

(4) *Filii hominum dentes eorum arma et sagittae et lingua eorum gladius acutus.* "Sons of men, their teeth are armor and arrows, the tongue of them are sharp sword."[19] "Sons of men" in other words, inveterate in malice, "the teeth of them," that is, their bitings and backbitings are "armor" with which they defend themselves against God, and "arrows" with which they wound others, and "their tongue," that is, their poisonous speech, is a sharp sword killing souls.

(5) *Exaltare super caelos, deus, et in omnem terram gloria tua.* "May your glory, God, be exalted above the heavens, and above all the earth." That is, reveal yourself, Christ, above all the angels in power, and over all the earth may the glory of your praise be spread.

(6) *Laquem paraverunt pedibus meis et incurvaverunt animam meam.* "They prepared a snare for my feet and they made my soul crooked." That is, they set the snare of damnation for the affective part of my soul in the form of physical pleasure, and "they made my soul crooked," that is, they intended to drag it from loving God down into the earth.

(6) *Foderunt ante faciem meam foveam, et inciderunt in eam.* "They dug a pit before my face, and they fell into it." That is, they made assiduous preparations so that I should know physical desire, so they could capture me with it, a deep pit for all who follow its lure, and "they fell into it," that is, they harmed themselves, not me, because I understood that all the joy of this world is only like a flower of the field.

(7) *Paratum cor meum, deus, paratum cor meum. Cantabo et psalmum dicam.* "My heart is ready, God, ready is my heart. I shall sing and I shall recite a psalm." They prepared pits and snares for me, but "my heart is ready, God," to perform your commands, my heart is ready to endure extreme suffering for love of you. I shall sing to your praise in spiritual joy, "and I shall recite a psalm," displaying good works for your honor, because

(8) *Exurge gloria mea, exurge psalterium et cithara.* "Let my joy arise, let psaltery and harp arise."[20] That is, may Jesus, who is my joy, make me rise in the joy of the song of praising you, in the happiness of loving you, and that this may happen, "let the psaltery arise," that is, gladness of mind in the contemplative life, and "the harp," that is, purification of all faults with submissiveness in extreme trouble, and so "I shall arise in the dawning," that is, with joy at the general resurrection.

Jesu, you be my joy, all melody and sweetness,
And teach me to sing
The song of your praising.[21]

(9) *Confitebor tibi in populis, domine, et psalmum dicam tibi in gentibus.* "I shall confess to you, Lord, among the people, and a psalm I shall recite to you among men." That is, I shall praise you in converting the people and offering to you works of heaven among the people,

Whilst I sing in sounds most rare
The delight of praising you.

(10) *Quoniam magnificata est usque ad caelos misericordia tua, et usque ad nubes veritas tua.* "For worshipped to the heavens is your mercy, and to the clouds your righteousness." When men, who were rogues, through God's mercy, are to become equal to the angels in the resurrection, then God's mercy "is worshipped to the heavens," and since the knowledge of God's righteousness, which is perfected in the angels, descends to men, his righteousness goes up to the clouds.

(11) *Exaltare super caelos deus, et super omnem terram gloria tua.* "May you be elevated above the heavens, God, and above all the earth your glory." He repeats what he said before, strengthening our faith.[22]

Psalm 61:2 (62:2)[23]

Nam et ipse deus meus et salutaris meus: susceptor meus, non movebor. "For and he my God and my healing, my uptaker. I shall no more be moved." He certainly is my salvation, since he is my God through grace, and my healing, that is my buyer, and my taker-up from the toiling of this world to joy; therefore I shall never more be moved from him because

I know no better weal[24]
Than in my heart to feel
The love of his loving;[25]
Of all it is the best
Jesus to hold firmest
And crave no other thing.[26]

Psalm 102:1–5 (103)

This psalm (v.5) may be compared to *The Bee and the Stork* (p. 127).

(1) *Benedic anima mea domino, et omnia quae intra me sunt nomini sancto eius.* "My soul bless the Lord, and all that is within me his holy name."[27] In this psalm a true soul speaks to itself, urging the love of God for all his goodness, so that every thought and every force and ability should bless "his holy name." It is very apparent that great sweetness and joy are in that soul.

(2) *Benedic anima mea domino, et noli oblivisci omnes retributiones eius.* "My soul bless the Lord, and do not desire to forget all his repayments." In other words, let there be no sinful pleasure in your sight, but repugnance of sin, and God's forgiveness. Think that, however many sins you have, God's requitals are twice as numerous. Twice he recommends his soul to give blessing because he wants our soul to be constantly meditating and praising God.

(3) *Qui propitietur omnibus iniquitatibus tuis, qui sanat omnes infirmitates tuas.* "Who has mercy on your wickedness, who heals all your sicknesses." That is, he forgives your sin, and after forgiveness he heals your soul so that it cannot again be seized by bodily desires, but eventually he heals all men completely.

(4) *Qui redimit de interitu vitam tuam, qui coronat te in misericordia et miserationibus.* "Who redeems[28] your life from the death, who crowns you in mercy and in 'mercyings.' "[29] With the price of his blood he bought you from hell and if you overcome your enemies, he crowns you in heaven, and this only through his mercy.

(5) *Qui replet in bonis desiderium tuum; renovabitur ut aquilae iuventus tua.* "Who fulfills your desiring with good things; renewed like the eagle's will be your youth." After the crown there remains nothing except the fulfillment of your desires in the endless joy which you yearned for, and that will occur when "your youth is renewed like the eagle's." When the eagle is troubled by great age, his beak grows so enormous that he cannot open his mouth to take food, but then he strikes his beak against a stone and gets off the husk, and then he goes to his food and becomes young again.[30] In the same way, Christ removes our old age of sin and mortality from us, which prevents us eating our bread in heaven, and renews us in himself.

Psalm 103:11–24 (104:10–23)

(10) *Qui emittis fontes in convallibus; inter medium montium pertransibunt aquae.* "You who send springs in joined valleys, between the midst of the hills the waters shall pass." That is, he sends waters of grace in those who are meek in body and soul, and waters of learning shall flow, that is, run together from eminent preachers, and from the water,

(11) *Potabunt omnes bestiae agri; expectabunt onagri in siti sua.* "shall drink all the beasts of the field; onagers must wait in their thirst." The beasts of the field are sinful men who have turned to Christ; onagers are wild asses: these are the proud Jews who refuse now to drink of the wholesome waters of Christian men, and wait for the final end of this world.

(12) *Super ea volucres caeli habitabunt, de medio petrarum dabunt voces.* "On those the birds of the air will dwell, from the midst of the stones they shall give voice." On those wells which I mentioned, spiritual men will dwell, who rejoice in the brilliance of God's love and give voice to good teaching "from the midst of stones," that is, from the authorities of devout men.

(13) *Rigans montes de superioribus suis, de fructu operum tuorum satiabitur terra.* "Wetting hills from his upper regions, from the fruit of his works the earth shall be filled." That is, God moistens apostles and contemplative men with his highest secrets, for from his fruit which he imparts to all good men, his lovers are made replete.

(14) *Producens foenum iumentis, et herbam servituti hominum.* "Bringing forth hay for animals and grass for the service of men." The earth brings forth despicable desires for beasts, that is, for beast-like men, who live in physical pleasure, and grass, that is bodily sustenance, for men who live righteously, as men ought to.

(14) *Ut educens panem de terra,* (15) *et vinum laetificet cor hominis.* "That you may lead forth bread from the earth, and let wine gladden the heart of man." The bread of God's word is brought out of the preacher, and wine, that is, the hot drink of Christ's love, gladdens our heart and carries it in ecstasy from earth to heaven.

(15) *Ut exhilaret faciem in oleo, et panis cor hominis confirmet.* "That he may make his face well-cheered with oil, and let bread make strong the heart of man." That is, that man should encourage his thought in the grace of the Holy Spirit, and that the bread of right-

eousness should make strong his heart in charity by this bread and wine.

(16) *Saturabuntur ligna campi et cedri libani quas plantavit,* (17) *illic passeres nidificabunt.* "Filled to overflowing will be the trees of the field, and the cedars of Lebanon which he planted, there the sparrows shall make their nest." That is, humble people, and powerful men of the world, whom God established in the faith, in them, in other words, sparrows, namely poor devout men, "will make their nests," or to put it another way, they are to receive bodily sustenance from them; for that reason God has given them the wealth of this world.

(17) *Herodii domus dux est eorum;* (18) *montes excelsi cervis, petra refugium herenaciis.* "The house of the gerfalcon is their leader; high hills for the harts, the stone is a fleeing-place for hedgehogs." As if to say: although these sparrows have bodily assistance from rich men, Christ, that is, "the leader of the gerfalcons" or the cruellest men, does not desert them if they come; he is the leader of the sparrows; if the cedars are stirred they can fly to him. "High hills are for the harts," that is, the strict commandments of God are set up for the lovers of contemplative life. "The stone," namely Christ, is the place of refuge "for hedgehogs," that is, for those who are covered with small sins; to him they run when troubles come.

(19) *Fecit lunam in tempore, sol cognovit occasum suum.* "He made the moon in time, the sun knew his setting." The moon is holy church, which passes with time to heaven; the sun is Jesus Christ, who knew his death, which he suffered for his church.

(20) *Posuisti tenebras et facta est nox; in ipsa pertransibunt omnes bestiae silvae.* "You set darkness and the night is made; in that night all the beasts of the wood shall pass by." That is, you imposed blindness on sinful men and dark encumbrance of the heart in them. In the night the devil who leads them "will pass by."

(21) *Catuli leonum rugientes ut rapiant, et quaerant a deo escam sibi.* "The cubs of lions roaring that they may seize, and seek from God food for themselves." Those whom he called beasts he calls "cubs" and "lions," for some are princes of devils, some, like cubs, are more contemptible devils, who attempt to deceive souls in darkness; they are fed from the wrongs of men, and they are not allowed to do anything except by God's permission,

(22) *Ortus est sol, et congregati sunt, et in cubilibus suis collocabuntur.* "Risen is the sun, and they are assembled, and in their dens they

shall be laid." When Christ dies in us through sin, many harms strike us, but he, rising in us through grace, puts to flight the lions, and they are terrified of making an attack on us, because of the sign of *tau*[31] which we bear. The "dens" of fiends are bad men who remain in deadly sin.

(23) *Exibit homo ad opus suum, et ad operationem suam usque ad noctem.* "Man is to go to his work and to his labor all the time till evening." A good man must "go to his work," beginning well, and "to his laboring," enduring well, "all the time" to the end of his life, and then he will be at rest, for you, God, have done all these things.

Psalm 118:1–8 (119)

(1) *Beati immaculati in via, qui ambulant in lege domini.* "Blessed the undefiled on the way, who walk in the law of the Lord." Other psalms like stars give light, but this psalm like the sun blazing at midday in full light is radiant with holy teaching and moral sweetness; in it the just man speaks, now giving thanks for what he has received from God, now hoping once more for what he has deserved. As one might say, different men seek different things to take delight in, but let those who wish to be blessed by God be undefiled by sin on the way, that is, in Christ, and these are they who "go," that is, do not live idly in God's law as he is leading them in it. Yet they cannot do this unless they know his teaching.

(2) *Beati qui scrutantur testimonia eius: in toto corde exquirunt eum.* "Blessed he who thoroughly examines his testimony, they seek him with their whole heart." First a man ought to reform his life and then scrutinize God's testimony, that is, his words, to understand them, and so they are blessed if they seek Christ with their whole heart so that no part may be given to any creature. Wicked men refuse to do this.

(3) *Non enim qui operantur iniquitatem, in viis eius ambulaverunt.* "For those who perform wickedness have not walked in his ways." The greatest wickedness is that men should love the things which God made and not himself, and all who do this are not on God's ways but on the world's ways, which led them to hell, and not for this purpose

(4) *Tu mandasti; mandata tua custodiri nimis.* "You commanded that your orders should be fully observed." That is, until death, so that men should choose to die rather than wish to anger you a single

time, except that I am not sufficient to perform your will without grace.

(5) *Utinam dirigantur viae meae, ad custodiendas iustificationes tuas.* "God grant that my ways be directed, in order to keep your justifyings." I cannot keep them any other way unless my ways, that is, my actions in this life, are directed toward heaven and not bowed down earthward.

(6) *Tunc non confundar, cum prospexero in omnibus mandatis tuis.* "Then may I not be shamed, when I have looked into all your commandments." He who looks into God's commands and has not performed them will be "shamed" before God, for whoever has broken one is guilty of them all; therefore he who performs them all shall not receive shame but honor when he looks into them.

(7) *Confitebor tibi in directione cordis, in eo quod didici iudicia iustitiae tuae.* "In directing of the heart I shall confess to you, in that which I have learned, the judgments of your justice." That is, I shall love you in that you have "directed" my heart aright, through what "I learned" of your righteous decrees, by which you judge this world now and at the end, and set your servants free.

(8) *Iustificationes tuas custodiam, non me derelinquas usquequaque.* "Your decrees I shall observe, do not entirely forsake me." That is, I shall perform good deeds and therefore, if you abandon me for a time in order to test me, so that I find out how weak I am, do not "entirely" abandon me in case I perish.

Psalm 121 (122)

(1) *Laetatus sum in hiis quae dicta sunt mihi: "in domum domini ibimus."* "I was glad about those things which are being said to me: 'Into the house of the Lord we shall go.' " No love can be idle: If it is earthly, it constantly pulls downward toward the thing which it loves. If it is of heaven, it is constantly on the upward (way) toward God, and sighing for the companionship of angels, saying, "I was glad," that is, I had hope and joy in the thing which is "being said to me" by prophets and apostles, who summon us to run to heaven, which are those things that "I was glad" about: "we shall go to God's house," and when they were said,

(2) *Stantes erant pedes nostri in atriis tuis, Jerusalem.* "Standing were our feet in your entries, O Jerusalem." This "Jerusalem" is the house of God where the feet of our will stand in thought and hope.

(3) *Jerusalem quae aedificatur ut civitas, cuius participatio eius in id ipsum.* "Jerusalem which is built as a city, the partaking of it in itself." This is Jerusalem which is formed of the company of saints, which can never be lost, "as a city" (it contains) varying degrees of renown and merit, and (is) "partaker" of God's stability "in itself"; that is (it is) everlasting in unity without transformation. We shall go:

(4) *Illuc enim ascenderunt tribus, tribus domini, testimonium Israel ad confitendum nomini domini.* "For to that place go up the families of the Lord in order to confess to the name of the Lord." Not all "go to that place," only all of those who are born spiritually of God, and who give evidence by their good works that they are Christian men, to the praise of God's name.

(5) *Quia illuc sederunt sedes in iudicio, sedes super domum David.* "For there sat thrones in judgment, thrones above the house of David." That is, just men, in whom God sits and judges, will sit there to judge Christ's retainers.

(6) *Rogate quae ad pacem sunt Jerusalem, et abundantia diligentibus te.* "Ask for whatever contributes to the peace of Jerusalem, and abundance for those loving you." You who are to judge, ask for those who performed the works of mercy, for such people will be taken up to heaven, that is, to "peace," of which there is endless abundance for those loving you. He does not say "for those giving much," for he who loves in another the good which he is not able to perform (himself) becomes such that he is as if he had himself performed that thing, out of his love and for Jerusalem.

(7) *Fiat pax in virtute tua, et abundantia in turribus tuis.* "May peace be made in your strength and abundance in your towers." The "strength" of Christian people is charity, their "towers" are perfect men who are able to be judges, in whom there is an "abundance" of merit and worth.

(8) *Propter fratres meos et proximos meos loquebar pacem de te.* "For my brothers and my neighbors I spoke peace concerning you." That is, I preached peace so that my "neighbors and brothers" could be united in charity.

(9) *Propter domum domini dei nostri quaesivi bona tibi.* "For the house of our Lord God, I sought good things for you." In other words, for pilgrims, so that they might climb up to you, I spoke of your goodness and your joy.

Psalm 131:1–10 (132)

(1) *Memento domine David et omnis mansuetudinis eius.* "Lord, be mindful of David, and of all his graciousness." In this psalm it is Christ who is speaking through his church. In this "graciousness" may Christ overcome the devil, (and the psalm urges) that he be mindful of achieving this.

(2) *Sicut juravit domino, votum vovit deo Jacob.* "As he swore to the Lord, a vow he made to the God of Jacob." Holy church vowed to be God's house in graciousness and by that vow all of us are bound. This is the vow:

(3) *Si introiero in tabernaculum domus meae, si ascendero in lectum strati mei.* "If I enter into the tabernacle of my house, and if I climb into the bed of my coverings." That is, if I seek my own advantage and not the praise of God, or if I give my body rest in pleasure, and in pleasing ways of sin—neither of these I shall do.

(4) *Si dedero somnium oculis meis et palpebris meis dormitationem.* "If I give sleep to my eyes and slumbering to my eyelids." That is, if I give bodily pleasure to my thoughts or slumbering in those things which are of less account—meaning: I shall not, for all the wealth on earth is like the dreams of the sleeper, which vanish instantly away.

(5) *Et requiem temporibus meis, donec inveniam locum domino, tabernaculum deo Jacob.* "And rest for my forehead, until I find a place for the Lord, a tabernacle for the God of Jacob." When any earthly thing begins to entice you to sin, your forehead grows heavy unless you refuse to consent to it, and then sleep [comes] to your eyes. With this thought chafe your temples, toss out sleep and the lethargy of evil pleasure and in this way you are preparing a place for Christ, that is, a "tabernacle for God" in which you are to attend on him here. This David promised and kept it, because

(6) *Ecce audivimus eum in Effrata, invenimus eum in campis silvae.* "See, we heard him in Effrata, we found him in the fields of the wood." That is, we had the sound of God in the old Law, but we found him dwelling in Christian people, who are equable in their just behavior, just as fields are smooth.

(7) *Introibimus in tabernaculum eius, adorabimus in loco ubi steterunt pedes eius.* "We shall enter his tabernacle, we shall bow down in reverence in the place where his feet rested." He who loves "enters," and he who enters is made his house, on condition that he comes from those on whom his feet rest; these are they who persevere in

sanctity until death, and they are the true adorers of God, for on them are the footsteps of his accompanying them.

(8) *Surge, domine, in requiem tuam, tu et arca sanctificationis tuae.* "Rise, Lord, to your rest, you and the ark of your sanctification." "Rise" from the dead, and rise to heaven, and may your church, which you sanctified, rise to love and life.

(9) *Sacerdotes tui induantur iustitiam et sancti tui exultent.* "May your priests be clad in righteousness and your saints rejoice." For so they may continue in hope of resurrection, and because they have the Holy Spirit among them, holy men are all saved; many priests are disloyal, and few are holy, therefore he prays for right behavior for them, which all must of necessity have to be saved.

(10) *Propter David servum tuum, non avertas faciem Christi tui.* "For David, your servant, do not turn away the face of your Christ." That is, for the promise which you made to David, to fulfil it in your elect, do not abandon those who strive to love your Son, Jesus Christ.

Psalm 150 (150)

(1) *Laudate dominum in sanctis eius, laudate eum in firmamento virtutis eius.* "Praise the Lord in his saints, love him in the establishment of his might." In this psalm the import is that God should be praised because he has assembled his saints and put an end to all their weakness. He restored them to his likeness and placed them in endless bliss, therefore he speaks here of the praising of God in his glorified saints, and praises him without end. Therefore the City of God, that is, the unity of all the elect, is exhorted to sing to God in desire and with voice. In that height of God's praise all psalmody is fashioned, which praising is sung here with sweetness in holy companionship. Therefore those to whom the prophet revealed at the beginning of this book the mode of true [conversion] are now received into the heavenly Jerusalem. He declares that God is to be praised "in" them, for he has given all good things to them. Beginning in this way, "praise the Lord in his saints," that is, for the joy and honor which he has given them. Praise him "in the establishment of his might," that is, because he overcame the devil by his death, and so in his might he established holy men so that they may never die.

(2) *Laudate eum in virtutibus eius, laudate eum secundum multitudinem magnitudinis eius.* "Praise God in his might, praise him for the magnitude of his greatness." God's "might" is what he did in those

who reign with him and in him without end, and they are "the magnitude of his greatness," for he has made them great in power and many in number. And they, the holy men, are symbolized in all these musical instruments, which he puts down as symbols of praising God, in that they symbolize the quality for which they are to praise him, and he begins with the trumpet:

(3) *Laudate eum in sono tubae, laudate eum in psalterio et cithara.* "Praise him in the sound of the trumpet, praise him on the psaltery and harp." "Praise him in the sound of the trumpet," that is, for the highest brilliance of praise which is in you. "Praise him on the psaltery," that is, for all the things of heaven. And "on the harp," that is, for all things on earth; it was he who made heaven and earth.

(4) *Laudate eum in tympano et choro, laudate eum in cordis et organo.* "Praise him on the tabor, and the crowd, praise him on strings and organs." "Praise him on the tabor," that is, on flesh changed to immortality and incapacity for suffering, for the tabor is made of dried skin. "And on the crowd," that is, in peaceful companionship and unison of voices. "Praise him on the strings," that is, on flesh freed from all corruption, for by strings he refers to all musical instruments which sound with strings. To the strings he adds "organs," which are manufactured like a tower, with different pipes, in such a way that each does not give sound by itself, but they all sound together in most harmonious diversity, as happens in organs. Therefore, holy men must attend in harmony, not discord. Harmony, as with different voices, not discordant (with each other), is a sweet song.

(5) *Laudate eum in cymbalis bene sonantibus, laudate eum in cymbalis iubilationis.* (6) *Omnis spiritus laudet dominum.* "Praise him with well-sounding cymbals, praise him in chimes of rejoicing. Let every spirit praise the Lord." "Cymbals sounding well," are our lips, which in harmony with the heart in the praising of God sound well. But praising by voice will be in heaven. Yet so that you should not think that "chimes" are to be understood here as exterior to the soul, he says, "praise him with the chimes of rejoicing," that is, revealing outwardly with the lips of joy which is conceived within, for this rejoicing is a miraculous praising of God which does not come except from the soul, and because he intends that everything should be understood allegorically, he closes his Book with an appropriate conclusion:

"Let every spirit," those of angels and of men, "praise the Lord," whom I praise, because he cannot be praised except spiritually. He does not order flesh and blood and material things of this world to praise God, but that thing which is most exalted in the nature of existence is exhorted to praise, that is, the spirit, which is redolent of heaven and receives unending glory. A brief and exquisite statement of the mode of praising God is to be learned from this psalm: that all things should love God in spirit. In these instruments[32] which he mentions is the complete representation of all music, for there are wind (instruments) in the trumpet, percussion in the harp and the cymbals, resonance in the crowd—in which musical instruments spiritual melody is symbolized, which is apprehended with pure thought more than with bodily ears. And so: let every spirit praise the Lord.

Here ends the Psalter of King David.[33]

The Ten Commandments

This rather pedestrian piece may not be by Rolle, although critics seem willing to admit it to the canon of his work (*EW* pp. xix, 155–6; *WA* pp. 276–7; Alford p. 37). It occurs in two manuscripts, the Lincoln Thornton MS, f. 194, abbreviated, and a longer version in MS Hatton 12, 209v–211v, where it follows a northern copy of Rolle's *Psalter;* in Thornton, which is printed by Horstman, the piece is ascribed to Rolle; a later hand adds this attribution in Hatton. A third copy may have existed in a manuscript from Sir Thomas Phillipps' library sold in 1897. The triple interpretation of the third commandment resembles Rolle's three degrees of love, and his emphasis on genuine prayer resembles *Ego Dormio.* Allen also suggests (*EW*, p. xix) that the references to foresters may be based on Rolle's experience of the unscrupulous John de Dalton. The piece must be fairly early among Rolle's English works, perhaps soon after the *Psalter.*

Source: Horstman, *Yorkshire Writers,* I, pp. 195–6.

The Ten Commandments

The first commandment is: You shall revere the Lord your God, and to him alone you are to be obedient. In this commandment all idolatry, all witchcraft and all magic charms are forbidden, which cannot provide any remedy for any ailment of man, woman or animal, since these are the devil's snares by which he does all he can to deceive the human race. In this commandment belief in sorcery is also forbidden, and divination by means of stars or by dreams or by any similar procedures. Astronomers observe the day and the hour and the minute that a man begins his life in, and by these symbols and others [which they observe, they] prophesy what is destined to happen to the person subsequently, but their errors are reprehended by the learned men of the church. People should do reverence to crucifixes, because they are a symbol of Christ crucified. To statues the respect is due of those whom they represent, and for that reason alone they are to be honored.

The second commandment is: You shall not take God's name in vain. Under this commandment, oaths without good reason are forbidden. Anyone who names God and is swearing falsely, may God despise him. In three respects a person may sin by swearing, namely: if he swears against what he really believes; or if he swears by Christ's wounds or blood—this is always a great sin even if what he is swearing is a true fact, because it is an expression of irreverence to Jesus Christ; third, if he contravene his oath, not carrying out what he has sworn to do. God's name is taken in vain in many ways: in heart, in speech and in action. In heart, disloyal Christians take it in vain when they receive the sacrament while their soul is not in a state of grace. In speech, it is taken in vain in every act of swearing, of promulgating new doctrines which are frivolous and irreligious, and in prayer which worships God with the lips when our hearts are far from him. In action, hypocrites take God's name in vain by making a pretense of doing good externally, but they are lacking in charity, strength and vigor of spirit to withstand all wicked impulses.

The third commandment is: Be careful to keep holy your holy day of obligation. This commandment can be understood in three aspects: First, in general, we utterly abandon all wicked behavior. Then, in particular, that we abandon all physical acts which hinder devotion to God in prayer and meditation. The third applies specifically to contemplative men who separate themselves from all worldly things so that they may give themselves entirely to God. The first aspect is essential for us to observe, the third is counsel of perfection. Accordingly, one ought, as God commands, to abandon all sin on the holy day, and not to perform any work which hinders people from giving their heart to God, so that they may sanctify the day in rest, devotion and charitable deeds.

The fourth commandment is: Honor your father and your mother. This has two aspects, in other words, a physical and a spiritual one. Physically, by support, so that they can be helped and maintained in their old age and when their powers decline. Spiritually, in respect and obedience, not speaking to them discourteously, dishonorably or disagreeably in a casual way, but attending to them politely, cheerfully and humbly, in order to gain what God promised to children who are like that, to be precise, the land of light. And when they are dead, one is bound to help their souls by giving alms and by prayers.

The fifth commandment is that you kill no one, neither by plotting, nor by committing the deed, nor by ordering it or condoning it. And under this commandment, illegal striking of any person is also forbidden. There are spiritual murderers, those who refuse to feed the destitute in their need, those who slander others, and those who mislead the innocent.

The sixth commandment is: Do not be lecherous. That means: You are not to have sexual relations with a man or a woman unless you have taken them according to the rites of holy church. Under this commandment additional prohibitions are: every kind of deliberate self-pollution brought about by any method contrary to natural behavior, or any other way.

The seventh commandment is: You shall not commit theft. In this are prohibited all types of removal of other people's property illegally against the wishes of the owner, except in a situation of direst necessity, when all property is held in common. Under this commandment it is also forbidden to use deceptive weights, counting, volume or measure, or usury or force or intimidation, as, for example, the under-officers at courts, or the foresters, and the King's ministers do, or extortion, as the nobles do.

The eighth commandment is that you shall not bear false witness against your neighbors, such as in the assize courts, or in matrimonial cases. Additionally, lies are forbidden in this commandment, and perjury. Yet not all lies are mortal sin, only if they harm someone physically or spiritually.

The ninth commandment is: You are not to covet unjustly the house, or any moveable or fixed property of your neighbor, nor are you to retain other people's property if you can restore it to them, or your penance will not be any advantage to you.

The tenth commandment is: You shall not covet your neighbor's wife, nor his servant, nor his maidservant, nor his property. Anyone who keeps these commandments through love, loves God. He is bound to love his neighbor as himself, in other words, (wishing) for him to have the same good things which he values for himself, for him not to have any harm at all, and to love his neighbor's soul more than his body or any worldly goods. Etc.[1]

The end.

Meditations on the Passion

There are two versions of these meditations on the Passion, termed the *Shorter Meditations* (*SM*) and the *Longer Meditations* (*LM*). *SM* survives in only a single manuscript (CUL MS Ll.i.8), from which Hope Allen prints three extracts; I have translated the complete work, using Horstman's edition for the passages omitted by Hope Allen. *LM* survives in four manuscripts, of which three were known to Hope Allen and to Horstman. Hope Allen printed the opening of the work from the Oxford manuscript (Bodley MS e Mus.232 [O]), corresponding to folios 1v–8v of O. Closely related to O in many readings is the version in B.L.MS Cotton Titus C xix (T), printed by Sr. Mary Madigan as an appendix to *The "Passio Domini" Theme in the Works of Richard Rolle;* less closely related, it seems, is the version in Upsala MS C 494 (U), printed by Lindqvist, and CUL MS Addit.3042 (C), from which Horstman prints the complete text of *LM*. I have attempted to collate COTU, and the translation follows my attempt to identify the original readings which lie behind the four manuscripts of *LM*. C contains many careless additions, but has one sentence not in OTU which is either scribal or shows that OTU descend from the same hyparchetype. It is difficult to determine which are the right readings in many cases: C modernizes lightly, while T, a late fifteenth-century MS, transposes words and repeats grammatical words; none of the four manuscripts of *LM* is in Rolle's dialect.

SM, however, survives in a manuscript closer to Rolle's dialect. The difficulty with this manuscript is to decide whether it is a careless version of *LM*, copied by a scribe who began by abbreviating and then copied more fully, as Lindqvist thought, or whether it is an original version, preserving Rolle's alliterative and rhyming patterns, which were lost in the expanded *LM*, as Horstman and Allen suggest. Hope Allen attributes both *SM* and *LM* to Rolle, as do all manuscripts except U. Others, notably Margery Morgan (in an article in *Medium Aevum* 22 in 1953), have doubted Rolle's authorship of *LM*. Hope Allen ceased quoting from *LM* after it becomes more similar to *SM* in the second part. In the first, there are whole paragraphs which have been added in *LM* (or heavily abbreviated in *SM*), giving *LM* a closer literal account of the passion sequence, while *SM* remains more personally meditative. *SM* continues the passion narrative further than *LM* yet closes with "etc.," perhaps indicating that both versions are abridged. There are lengthy quotations from a Latin "treatise on the passion by Hampul" in BL MS Royal 8 c.xv, which seems to be either a translation of *LM* or a Latin version, perhaps expanded, made by Rolle himself.

In order to assist the reader to identify where the two versions diverge, I have tried to use identical words in the two translations where a phrase is identical in *SM* and *LM*, even if the immediate context or construction is different.

Sources: *SM:* Allen, *EW*, pp. 19–27; Horstman, *YW* I, pp. 83–91. *LM:* Allen, *EW*, pp. 27–36; Horstman, *YW* I, pp. 92–103. Both versions discussed by Allen in *WA*, pp. 278–87.

The Shorter Meditations: MS CUL L1.i.8

Sweet Lord Jesus Christ, I thank you and am grateful to you for that sweet prayer and that holy petition which you made for us on Mount Olivet before the holy passion. I beg you, sweet Lord, to listen to my prayer. "We adore you, O Christ, and we bless you because by your holy cross you have redeemed the world. Our Father. Hail Mary."[1]

Sweet Lord Jesus Christ, I thank you and am grateful to you for that great anxiety you had for us when you became so full of distress that an angel came from heaven to comfort you, when you sweated blood in agony. I ask you Lord, and implore you, for your sweet mercy, that you may be my help in all my distress and my temptations; and send me, Lord, the angel of good counsel and comfort in all my needs, so that through that sweat I might pass out of all my sickness of soul [and body][2] into a life of health.

"We adore you.
Our Father.
Hail Mary."

Sweet Jesus, I thank you and am grateful to you for the tortures and distresses and disgraceful treatment and felonies which people did to you entirely by betrayal. People tied you up like a thief, without compassion or sympathy. Lord, I thank you for these sad, sweet steps which you took, for our love, toward your own torment and your own death. I ask you, Lord, and beg you to untie us from the bonds of all our sins, as you allowed yourself to be tied up for love of us. "We adore you. Our Father. Hail Mary."

I thank you, sweet Lord Jesus Christ, for the tortures and the humiliating experiences which you endured in the presence of the bishops and lawyers, and from your enemies, and for the buffets and the blows on the neck and for many other disgraces which you suffered; and among other things, I thank you, Lord, for that look which you directed toward your disciple, Saint Peter, who had disowned you. You looked at him with a glance of compassion, when you were in your greatest distress, and in your greatest torment. Openly you revealed there the love and the holy affection which you had for us, in that neither humiliation nor torture nor anything can drag your heart away from us as far as it depends on you. Sweet Lord, full of compassion and sympathy, there we can turn to your grace by means of your blessed gaze and repent of our sins and of our misdeeds so that we are able to reach your compassion together with Saint Peter.

"We adore you
Our Father
Hail Mary"

I thank you, sweet lord Jesus Christ, for all injuries and tortures and words of derision, malicious names and insults which people directed at and did to you on that night in the harsh prison which they held you captive in. Lord, I ask and implore you that you send me patience and strength to oppose without yielding all the assaults and temptations of my opponents and of my spiritual and physical enemies.

"We adore you
Our Father
Hail"

Lord Jesus Christ, I thank you for all the injuries and disgraces which you endured at the judgment of Pilate, and for all your steps and your footprints which you made for me in all that sorrow, now in this direction and now that, now in being judged by one, now by another. I ask and beg you, lord, for all these injuries and these disgraces and these hardships and the steps which you made at that same time then for the love of us, that you draw and direct our ways and our steps toward you and your service.

"We adore you
Our Father
Hail"

Sweet lord Jesus Christ, I thank you for the agonies which you endured for us, and for the sweet blood which you shed for us, when you were so painfully beaten and roped to the pillar so that the blood on the pillar can still be seen. I ask and beg you as my dear lord for that sweet blood, which you bled so generously for me, to be full deliverance for my soul.

"We adore you
Father
Hail"

Sweet lord Jesus Christ, I thank you for the injuries and disgraces which by your own dear wish you suffered for us when you were dressed up in purple to deride you, and in the crown with its thorns to torture your sweet head, and when they, kneeling in mockery, called you "lord, king and leader," and after saying all that spat so filthily on your sweet face, and so filthily made your lovely face slimy with the filthy stinging spitting from the filthy accursed Jews, and cuffed and struck and hammered on your sweet head with [iron].[3] Also for your tormenting wounds I thank you, for your pains and for your sweet blood which ran down and streamed from your blessed face. I ask and beg you, dear lord, to protect us from sin, and from the disgrace which we have deserved because of sin.

"We adore
Father
Hail"

Sweet lord Jesus Christ, I thank you for being so covered in blood then, so crowned with thorns in the presence of all the people, and your sweet face so spat on and so defiled with the filth and the stinging spitting from their accursed mouths. Then on each side you were denounced[4] and driven[5] and had the outcry raised against you for a violent death, and you were condemned to the shameful death of hanging, blessed and thanked may you be for it. I beg you, dear lord, that through your great compassion you give me grace and wisdom to judge and criticize myself so that my soul may be saved.

"We adore
Father
Hail"

Sweet lord Jesus Christ, I thank you for the injuries and disgraces which you endured so graciously and so gladly, now by being tugged at, now by being butted so disgracefully, now by being struck, now by being flogged so painfully and so brutally; and by carrying your own cross on your sweet, naked back, like a thief carrying his own gallows to be hanged on it himself at Mount Calvary, where people gazed at wicked men and thieves, (deciding) whether this one was a thief or a murderer: and there you allowed them to put you on the cross.

Meditation

Dear lord Jesus, have mercy, you, the fount of mercy. Why will my heart not crack and split in two? How is it ever to endure, when it surges into my mind what a terrible plight you were in when your tunic was removed, when the traitor Herod had pulled it off you: it had stuck firmly with the blood from the violent flogging to the flesh of your back, which was beaten agonizingly raw, and ripped your poor skin; the robe stuck to it and had dried on it; your flesh was so tender, so weakened and so sore, that they ripped it off your body roughly and sharply, and took no notice of how agonizingly the stripping distressed you because some pieces of the blisters and torn skin came away with it. Then your weak body, precious lord, was all pitifully raw and bleeding, the steam arose from your body and vaporized all around, and one can imagine the dewdrops which collected as a result.

O lord, I can see your red blood coursing down your cheeks, torrents after each blow, down front and back. Your crown has torn to pieces the skin on your head, every thorn in it penetrates your skull.

I cannot bear to have to live and watch my gracious lord, so ailing and so submissive, who has never done anything wrong, being so dishonorably tricked out. The remorse and the groaning, the grief and the sighing, the pathos of his expression, I wish these would bring my death. The crown of all bliss, who crowns all the blessed, and is king of all kings, and lord of lords, he is crowned by hell-hounds with thorns. Supremely honored in heaven, he is despised and desecrated here;[6] he who created the sun and all that exists at all, out of all the teeming wealth of the world, all of which he gave, he had nothing with which he could hide his head, but has become so poor, to make us rich, that he walks along completely naked, under the gaze of everyone.

O lord, your grief—why might it not bring my death? Now they march you forward, naked as a worm, torturers surrounding you, and armed soldiers. The throng of people was exceedingly oppressive; they pulled you and dragged you along with no respect at all; they kicked you with their feet as if you were a dog. I can see in my mind how pitifully you walk: your body is so bloody, so beaten raw and blistered, your crown is so sharp, pressing on your head; your hair moves in the wind, matted with the blood; your lovely face, so pallid and so swollen with punching and hitting, with spitting, with squirting, the blood gushed out as a result, which makes me shudder to look at it; so ugly and so loathsome have the Jews made you that you are more like a leper than a healthy man. Your cross is so heavy, so high, and so rigid, and they have hung it on your bare back, lashed so tightly.

O lord, the groaning you made, so painfully and so agonizingly did it press on the bone. Your body is so ailing, so enfeebled and so exhausted what with prolonged lack of food before you were captured, and being kept awake[7] all night without any sleep, so far overwhelmed by flogging and by punching that you walk stooping right over, and your face is tense. The flesh where the cross rubs it is all raw, the swellings and the blisters are black and blue; the agony of that burden afflicts you so greatly that every footstep you take stabs into your heart. And in this way, with groaning and great torment, you are walking out of Jerusalem toward your execution. The city is so noble, the throngs so great, the crowds come rushing out of every street, then everyone stretches up to see through the great cloud of vapor,[8] everyone gazing on in amazement. No thief was ever led to his execution with such a procession of the crudely curious as that. There were some among the ordinary people who sighed deeply and wept at your anguish, who realized you were so tormented and that it was out of malice, because the princes and prelates who administered the law put you to death for your honest reproofs, rebuking them for their mistaken beliefs. The ordinary people knew that what you suffered was a crime and injustice and they accompanied you weeping and sighing bitterly.[9] You then prophesied something which later came to pass: You told them to weep for themselves and for the great retribution which was destined to descend on them and their children because of your death, and on the entire city, which was subsequently destroyed, and, in retribution for their own guilt they were expelled from their homes.

O lord, the grief which surged into your heart when your eyes fell on your mother. You saw her following behind among the jostling crowd, twisting her hands in dismay like a woman beside herself, crying and moaning she flung her arms about, the tears pouring from her eyes cascaded to her feet; she collapsed more than once deeply unconscious in anguish at the pains which went shooting into her heart. The grief she expressed and the great lamenting intensified many times over your other torments. And so, when she realized that this was the case, it affected her even more badly and you too are weeping for her; so the anguish of each of you, for the other, was increasing many times over with mounting distress. The love of your two hearts, which, above all other loves was without equal, burning ardently, made you passionate for each other with grief, unlike any other misery: as the love was unique, so the grief was unequalled; it penetrated your hearts like a death-pang.

O lady,[10] have pity on yourself; why were you so brave to follow so close among so many fierce enemies? How was it that your natural timidity as a woman or your virgin modesty did not hold you back? Because it was not proper for you to move along among a rabble like that, so despicable, so disgraceful, so hideous to look at. But you paid no attention to being afraid of any man nor to anything else which might impede you, but as if beside yourself in grief and distress at your son's suffering, all your heart was set firm.[11] Your love for each other was so intense, and so burning hot, your sighs came from so deep within you, the mourning of the expression of each of you was a killing grief. The love and the sorrow which stabbed into your breast took away concern for physical terror and social disgrace and any kind of hindrance, so that your [sorrow made you][12] as if beside yourself.

O lady, because the sorrow which you endured at your son's suffering ought to have been mine (I had deserved it and many more, and far worse, I being the cause of it and he guiltless), seeing the precious wounds were my own just desert and that you are considerate, obtain just a single one of them all for me, one pang in my heart of the same pain, a drop of that lamentation to accompany him with. If all that misery is mine by right, get for me some of what is my own, don't be so unfair as to keep back all of it. Even if you are glad to have all your misery, are you not also very generous? Go shares with someone impoverished who has little or nothing;[13] give me some of your sighings, as you [sigh][14] there so bitterly, so that I can sigh with you, I who began that misery. Dear lady, I'm not asking for castles, or towers, or other worldly riches, the sun nor the moon nor the bright stars, but wounds of deep remorse[15] are all I yearn for, anguish and sympathy for my lord Jesus Christ. [Worst][16] and most unworthy in all men's estimation, I have a craving for pain, to implore my lord for a drop of his red blood to make my soul bloody with, a drop of that water[17] to wash it with.

O lady, for that mercy, you who are mother of mercy, succor for all sorrow, remedy of all misery, appointed mother of all those who are wretched and of all those who mourn: Listen to this wretch and visit your (MS: "my") child; thrust into my heart, which is as unyielding as stone, a small spark of commiseration in that precious suffering, a wound of that compassion to make it supple with.[18]

O lord, that pain that the wicked Jews, so cruel and so savage without any pity on Mount Calvary tormented you with! They threw the cross down flat on the ground and, laying you out on it, with strong ropes tied to your hands and feet, they tugged and stretched you tightly widthways and lengthways by hands and feet, and hammered in the nails, first in the one hand, and pulled hard, and after that they hammered in the other. The nails were blunt at the point so that they would break the skin and the muscle; they gouged out your hands and feet with entirely blunt nails so as to cause greater pain. *They have dug holes in my hands and in my feet* (Ps 22:16, cf. Ps 53:5).

Glorious lord, so miserably treated
So pitifully stretched prostrate on the cross[19]

In your great humility, your mercy, your power,
Cure all my evils with the remedy of your blood.

Oh lord, the pitiful state which I now behold! Your wounds as you are strained gape so wide, your limbs and your loins are so tender. You lie raw and red-stained, straining on the cross, the sharp crown on your head afflicts you so sorely, your face, once so attractive, is so swollen up, your sinews and bones stick out so far that your bones can be counted; the torrents of your red blood gush like a river, your wounds are bleeding profusely, and hideous to look at. The sorrow which your mother is uttering increases your grief.

Oh lord, king of power, willing to leave your power,[20]
And become like one quite powerless, my sinning to redress,
What is it I am saying as I beat on empty air?
I talk of how you are feeling, but my senses fail to find you.
I stumble about, like a blind man, as I move,
I muse in perplexity; my thoughts just dissipate.
It is the token of my mortality, defilement of my sin,
That has put to death my soul, and remains transfixed in it
And blocks all the sweet aroma, so that you I cannot sense
Having with such dishonor been your traitor and disloyal.

It could be a prison, lord, for your divine nature, this stench of my dishonor, this grief of my spirit, this defilement in my mouth; if I set my tongue to your name it defiles it, so I can taste nothing at all of your sweetness, which I [have lost][21] through sin, by taking pleasure in such gratification, for I stumble about merrily in desiring many different kinds of sinful pleasures.

But you, glorious lord, you bring the dead to life,
Great numbers you have converted, and brought them to heavenly
  reward;
Those born blind you have enlightened, in the scriptures I may read,
Signifying spiritual actions, there can be no doubt of this.

Bring me to life, lord Jesus Christ, and give me the grace to be able to sense some of your light (MS: "sight") so that I may have some degree of sight in my soul to assuage my thirst.[22] But I am well aware of what I have seen written: that anyone who desires and seeks in the right way, although he is not able to feel you at all, already possesses what he is not aware of; that is, the love of your divine nature.[23] It has supplied [us][24] this quotation, and another like it: that if a man cannot detect any taste, he should reckon himself an outcast,[25] and, despising and abusing himself, and confessing his weakness, surrender himself as undeserving of having any fervor of devotion or any such sign of special affection[26] from our lord God whenever he cannot experience devotion, and that will be the quickest way for him to gain the gift of his grace.

Then there went over to the cross a great crowd of Jews, who picked it up and lifted it in the air, with all the strength they had, and thrust it hard down into the shaft which had been prepared for it in the hill. Your wounds burst and ran out painfully, so that your body hung there utterly jarred; wretched indeed was your condition!

Lord, you were in a terrible plight then, when the ghastly injuries of your feet and of your hands—which more than all other men's were extremely sensitive—supported all the weight of your blessed body, so handsome and so well-proportioned. That agony and that grief your mother observed, she who was so lovely and so submissive and so humble. She fell down again and again, moaning at the same time, and grief pierced her in the breast like death; her head hung down so despairingly, she twisted her hands, the tears she wept there were most abundant.

The sighings and the griefs which she expressed there went to amplify your torment, and made it intense. The spot was so loathsome and a place of lamentation, the stench of the corpses assaulted your nose. In this way you were tortured in your five senses, to heal our transgressions which we have committed with those senses.

To counteract our transgression through our sight, you agreed to be blindfolded by the Jews.

To counteract our transgression in the sense of smell, the smell of the corpses as you hung on the cross assaulted your nose, and was deeply offensive to you.

To counteract our sins of taste, you tasted the gall; so destitute were you made by your great loss of blood.

To counteract the listening to lascivious talk which we have assaulted you with, you agreed to hear much injustice with your ears: when men wrongly accused you of sin, shouting out in derision and hatred the words "God save the king!" and spat in your face; having to listen to the odious shout when they all shouted out "put him on the cross; let the cross be his punishment!" And also when they said,

"He knew how to save other men; let him save himself now, if he knows how."[27] Listening to these and other injurious words you agreed to be tortured for our sake in that sweet sense.

To counteract sinning in the sense of touch and of walking in evil ways, your hands and your feet were pierced with hard nails, and from the head to the feet, with crowning and flogging, with punching and beating, with jostling and butting, with tying by tough ropes, and straining on the cross, you agreed glorious lord, to be severely tortured for my sake. There you hang, so destitute and so oppressed by misery, that, out of all this world's goods, and they were entirely yours, you have nothing but a rag of cloth to cover your private parts with. You who are king of kings and lord of lords—hell, heaven and all this world are your possession—at the moment of your death for my sake you determined to be so destitute that you did not even have so much earth as you could die on. No, on the rough cross hanging in midair, there your deathbed was most deplorably arranged; the cross had only a foot of earth, or very little more, on which it stood, and that was your appointed punishment.

You spoke regretfully of your situation, glorious lord, in observing that foxes have their earths and birds their nests, but you at your death did not have anything to rest your head on. Jesus, why must I live and see the grief and sorrow, when I turn over in my mind how piteously you spoke when you said: "All who pass along the road, stop to look to see if any pain which any man suffered, or any grief on this earth is like the sorrow which I am suffering for the sake of sinful man."[28] No, lord, no, there was never any so harsh;[29] it was indeed unique; of all the torments there ever were, none so grievous has ever existed. And still you said, lord, so sweetly and so humbly, "My chosen vine, I have planted you" (Jer 2:21), that is: "My dear vineyard," you said, or in other words, "My beloved chosen one, haven't I planted you myself? Why are you so bitter?"

"My people, what have I done to you?" (Micah 6:3). That is: "My sweet, what have I done to you? Have I made you resentful, that you cause me all this misery? Haven't I given you my whole self, and everything which you've ever had, and life without end, if you're willing to accept it, my body as your food, to get death on the cross in return, when I promised you all of myself as your reward in heaven? Have I injured you so badly by my good deeds, or outraged your feelings by my sweet fondling?"

Lord, you entreated your father in heaven for the wicked traitors, tyrants and tormentors, for him to forgive them for your death, and for all sins which they had committed, and said the wretches did not know what they were doing, and in addition, said to the thief hanging beside you, who had been committing theft ever since he knew how to, that he would be in bliss with you that same day. From which can be seen that you were not in any way imposing[30] long-lasting punishment, which he ought to endure for his sin, but at his first request, when he begged for mercy, acknowledged you as God, and admitted his own sin, immediately you gave him the privilege of grace and mercy, without any longer postponement of the state of bliss.

Lord, in your mercy, you who are the fount of mercy, tell me who am your thief[31] what you said to him, for I have stolen your good deeds, and abused your graces, the senses and the virtues which you have bestowed on me. You who were so gracious and so courteous and so submissive as to bestow that grace on him in your greatest anguish, now that you are in bliss, where there is nothing to afflict you, and it is only our wrongful acts which hold you back, don't be aloof and reserved about granting a request, but be many times more generous—for seldom to be met with is any man who is not more benevolent when things are going well with him than he was in his greatest affliction.[32]

O lord, your mother was dismayed and you were troubled about her too, when she was forced to be deprived of you, and you took your leave, entrusting her to Saint John, to attend her and support her as her son in your place. As a sign you said: "Lady, see here your son" and to John, "See here your mother." You entrusted a virgin to a virgin for protection; as you were divine wisdom, in your wisdom you did not want to leave your mother on her own, but wanted there to be someone assigned to her in the capacity of a supporter.

O lady, you were afflicted then when your ears took in those words! That grief could have killed you, what with that parting and your son's anguish. The tears streamed down rapidly from your eyes, your sighings and your sorrows oppressed your heart deep down, you fell down unconscious with all your limbs sprawling; your arms fell to your sides, your head lolling down, your rosy complexion[33] grew quite blanched, your face deathly pale. The sword of your son's anguish transfixed your heart.

"A sword shall pierce your own soul (also)"[34] that is: The sword shall pass through your heart.

O lady, no tongue can describe that sorrow which you endured there at that same substitution, when in place of your son, your flesh and your blood, you had to take another companion; instead of almighty God, a mortal man, a disciple instead of the master, John instead of Jesus Christ. That substitution was as grievous to you as a spasm of your death agony. Lady, why could I not have been beside you, hearing what you were hearing and seeing that same scene, and taking my share of your tremendous grief, perhaps being able to alleviate your misery? After all, people have a saying about this: that it is often consolation to have a companion in trouble.[35]

Lord, after this you cried out so mournfully on the cross, saying that you were thirsty—which was hardly surprising. Then you were served with vinegar and gall, by those for whom you were willing to shed your heart's blood.

O lord, you took it and tasted it, because you wished to be made to suffer in each sense for our sake. That thirst was of two kinds: physical and spiritual. You were thirsting with a great longing for the spiritual recovery of those who were putting you to death, and also for the souls who were in hell at that time, who throughout their [lives had kept your laws. Happy that same man, glorious, sweet Jesus, who can in his lifetime endure for your sake any degree of physical pain or worldly disgrace, or for the love of your name wholly abandon in body or in mind any urges of the flesh, or can in any respect accompany you here under the][36] shadow of your cross, in other words, harsh living.

O lord, the compassion, the mortal anguish that ought to surge into human hearts when men meditate on those words which you spoke on the cross, complaining so bitterly to your father:

Eloi, eloi, lamasabactani

that is, "My God, My dear God, why have you completely abandoned me, why do you not spare me at all?"

Glorious lord, for our sake your human nature was left totally abandoned; such a despicable and agonizing death no man has ever endured. Your divine nature intended this for the sake of sinful man, without any remission of the circumstances of your wretched plight, with no martyrdom or physical agony ever resembling yours. Your human physique was so sensitive, both in body and spirit, and the torment, in spite of this, greater than all torments. The supremely high rank—son of the heavenly Father—and yet you hung on the cross between two thieves, and in the very centerpoint of the world at that;[37] there was nothing covert about your disgrace, as if you were the commander of all brigands, you hung between them, entirely naked, your skin flayed off you, and every limb wrenched from the socket, the sharp crown on your head that you had been crowned with. Your wounds were so ghastly and tugged apart, so gaping, the blood which you lost was horrifying to see. Your mother's grief was more torture to you than all your physical anguish, and this exceeded all the other anguish: the perdition of the souls of those who tortured you so.

Lord, no heart can conceive your great mercy, nor the limitless love and lovely compassion which you settle on the good who act in accordance with your wishes, considering how great your sorrow was for those who were your enemies.

Lord, in my imagination I want to embrace the foot of the cross prostrate on the ground as you were lying with the stench of the bones of dead men lying there so revolting under your nose. Then nothing can ever disturb me or change my mind, so that it will be a great consolation[38] to me with pleasant thoughts. I will not turn my gaze upward to see that[39] splendid spectacle, the vision of your wounds, because, glorious lord, I am guilty in many ways and am the perpetrator of them, and someone unworthy to look at that sight.

I would like to prostrate myself on the ground among the dead, who lie stinking horribly, and lower still if I could, to retain the power and the grace of your blood. From there I refuse to get up or move away in any direction until I am completely reddened with your precious blood, until I am marked with it as one of your own, and my soul is softened in that sweet bath. May it come about, glorious lord, that my hard heart which is now as hard as stone, may unfold as a result, and become quite soft and spring to life in sensing you.

Lord, your sweet passion raised the dead from their graves and they walked about; it opened the gates of hell; the earth trembled at it, and the sun[40] lost its light. Yet my worthless heart, which is of the same species as the devils, harder than the stones which split apart at your death, cannot sense the least part of your passion; I neither rise with the dead at the pity of it, nor do I tear apart like the temple, nor tremble like the earth, nor open the enclosure which is so firmly bolted.[41]

My lord, is the unkindness of my feeble heart greater than the power of your precious death, which worked such miracles and many others besides, if the commemoration of it doesn't stir up my heart? Please,[42] lord, a drop of your blood to drip on to my soul in memory of your passion can heal all my disease, make pliable and soft what is so hard,[43] and make it undergo dyeing when you wish it too.[44] I know very well, glorious lord, that my heart is not worthy of your approach, for you to descend into it; it is not of the same status as your holy sepulchre which enclosed you in your human nature, but, lord, you did descend to hell, to make visitation and to give justice, and in that very way I'm requesting your coming to me. I acknowledge freely, glorious lord, that I never did deserve to be your mother's companion, to stand with her and with John at your passion. But, lord, honestly, if I am not qualified to be there because of my total lack of fitness to see that blessed sight, I do consider myself fit, because of my great wrongdoing, to hang alongside you as the thief hung.

So, lord, if I can't be present there as one who has merited it, I request some share in your death as one of those who are guilty; I request that even if I do not merit being enlightened in spirit, yet my urgent needs and my wickedness demand to be given their just dues.[45]

Come then, heavenly healer, as it is your wish, and enlighten me as you know my need; kindle in my heart a tiny spark of your passion, of love and of compassion, to bring it to life with, and so, completely aflame with love above everything else, I may forget the entire world and lave myself in your blood. Then I shall bless the time when I shall be able to feel your grace so arousing me[46] that all worldly possessions and all physical pleasure seem distasteful to me compared with the recollection of your death.

O the pity of it, lord![47] You committed your glorious spirit into your father's hands when you were at the point of death, saying: *Pater, in manus tuas*, etc., that is: "Father, into your hands I entrust my spirit." And as a true sign of the healing of our souls, showing that all had been completed by the blessing of your blood, you last spoke: *Consummatum est*, that is: "All is finished." Then your head fell down and the breath of life went out. The earth trembled then, the sun lost its light[48] so that the weather was all dark as if it had been night-time. The dead rose, as proof of their recognition of the divinity; the temple then split, the stones splitting completely apart. They struck your heart with a sharp spear; the blood and water gushed out from it.

Glorious lord, this is how my mind is aroused by it: I see your blood flowing out of hands and feet, your sides pierced with the spear, your wounds dried up and completely run out, your body all soiled with blood, your chin lolling down, and your teeth exposed; the whites of your eyes are turned upward, your skin, once so lovely, has gone quite livid, the crown pressed into your head makes me shudder to look at it, your[49] hair is matted with blood and blows this way and that. I really wish that reflecting on this scene would bring about my own death.

Lord, I can see your mother standing at your side; she is sobbing and fetching sighs and collapsing; John on your other side is so full of misery; both are twisting their fingers, are giving vent to deep grief. When they gaze[50] upward, the sight of the cross stabs at their hearts like a death-pang. They fall down weeping and moaning bitterly: and I am the reason for all that same misery.

Lady, in your mercy, since I deserved everything which happened to you, and since everything which happened to you is by rights mine, permit me, by your good favor, a glimpse[51] of your sorrow, and a fraction of your pain to busy myself with, so that in some measure I can feel something, and a share of your sorrow, all of which I caused.

O lord, they are casting lots for your clothes, as the Bible described long before in prophecy; and they left you naked between two thieves—no man ever suffered anything as horrible as your death was. Then the crowds began to flock back to the town from the hill of Calvary where you hung on the cross. The spectacle is so amazing, they move so thickly, like waves, each man off to his own home, along every road. Then in your divinity you were swiftly in hell, to gladden the souls who were waiting for your coming. The happiness and the rejoicing, the gladness and the pleasure which they enjoyed then no human tongue could ever recount. You opened up the gates of hell, lord, through your divine strength, and took out of suffering many who were there: Adam and Eve, and all who were dear to you, who had observed your laws during their lifetime. After that, lord, Joseph of Arimathea obtained permission from Pilate to take you down, as it was the time of evensong, with the help of Nicodemus, and of your mother and John, who were standing there mournfully. They took your blessed body from the cross, they straightened out your arms, which had become stiff, and stretched them down along your sides. They carried you to the place where you were buried; they washed off the cold blood and made you clean, laid you in the new sepulchre which Joseph had had built for himself; they anoint you with sweet-smelling ointment. The grief your mother was feeling for you is grief itself to hear.

Lady, the tears you cried there made your breast and cheeks all water![52] You fell down to his feet, and kissed them most sweetly and all the time you were kissing, you were crying bitterly.

Then a watch of armed knights was placed there, to guard the tomb until the third day. Etc. Amen. Jesus.

Here ends the *Meditation on the Passion of the Lord* of Richard Hermit of Hampole, who died in the year of our Lord, 1348, etc.

The Longer Meditations

Lord who made me of nothing, I implore you to give me grace to serve you with all my heart, with all my ability, with all my strength, with all my knowledge, with all my endeavor, with all my understanding, with all the powers of my soul, with all my attention, with all my speech, with all my senses, with all my acts, with all my employment, with all my activity, with all my rest.

Lord who made me like yourself, I implore you to give me the grace to love you with all my soul, with all my love, with all my intention, with all my pleasure, with all my enjoyment,[1] with all my memory, with all my wanting, with all my devotion, with all my longing, with reforming of my life, with all my desiring, with enduring in virtue, with contrition and confession to you and penance for my sins.

Lord who made me and all my limbs, I implore you, give me grace to serve you with all my limbs [so that my limbs may be your limbs] and all to be employed in your service, and constantly bending as you direct me, constantly ready to move or rest at your command, always immobilized to acts of sin, always fresh and eager for your instructions.

(The text printed by Hope Emily Allen begins here).

Lord who made me and have given me many gifts, spiritual, physical and material, I implore you, grant me grace to use all of them in your service and for that purpose for which you gave them to me, so that I may constantly worship you in your gifts, and grant me the grace constantly to be humble in possessing your gifts, to reckon myself contented with your gifts, and never to be presumptuous nor proud of your gifts, but constantly to recognize myself for what I am, a sinful and worthless creature.

Lord who came down from heaven to earth for love of the human race, from so high to so low, from such high dominion to such low poverty, from such high splendor to such low misery, from such high magnificence to such low affliction, from such high happiness to such low sorrow, from such a pleasurable life to such a painful death, now, lord, for all that love which you revealed to mankind in your incarnation and in your passion, I implore you for mercy and help.

Sweet Jesu, I thank you, lord, with all my heart, because you set out toward that place where you knew your death was prepared, and I thank you, lord, that you indicated so unmistakably there that you were willing to die for us; and so I believe, lord, that you chose the day and the time when you wished to die, and every detail of your passion was performed according to your plan; and I believe, lord, that you gave up your soul when you desired to, and when you desired to took it up again. Now here, sweet Jesu, I implore you, grant me grace to offer myself to you with my whole intent, in heartfelt sorrow for my sins and calling out for mercy to reform myself in my motivation, by admitting my sins to you and doing penance for them, by perseverance in virtuous living, by total love for you who made me; and allow me to turn to you through frequent confession in every difficulty, in every temptation of my body, of the world around me, or the devil; and bestow on me the grace that every thought, word or act which emanates from me may reveal that I am converted to you; and give me the grace gladly to turn with full inclination to [those] activities which you have appointed for me. Sweet [Jesu], lord, I implore you, hear my prayer. *Our Father . . . and lead us not . . . but deliver us from evil.*
We adore you, O Christ, and we bless you, because by your holy cross you have redeemed the world.
Let us pray.

(This prayer is given in Latin in MS C; it is abbreviated in the other manuscripts, and is intended to be prayed after each *Pater nos-*

ter throughout the meditation. I have included it only this once, as in the manuscript.)

Lord Jesus Christ, son of the living God, set your passion, cross and death between your judgment and our souls now and in the hour of our death, and deign to confer your mercy and grace on the living, and pardon and peace to the departed, to the government of the church peace and mercy, and to us sinners life, happiness and eternal glory. You who live and reign, God, world without end. Amen.

Sweet Jesu, I thank you with all my heart and mind for that sweet prayer and for that holy petition which you made on Mount Olivet before your most holy passion, and, lord, I thank you because there you taught us to pray when you said, "Father, not my own, but may your will be done," because your will, Lord Jesu, and your father's will are all one will. And so you were praying not for yourself but for us, to teach us, whose wills are often rebellious to the Father in heaven, to give up our will and to pray that the Father's will be done in us. Now here, sweet Jesu, I implore you that I may be constantly prepared for your will, and [that I eliminate my own will][2] except when my will is in agreement with yours; and bestow on me grace always to find out what is your will, [which is my happiness][3], and so turn to [it].

Our Father . . . and lead us not. We adore you. Lord.

Sweet lord Jesu, I thank you as much as I know how to for all the terror and the spiritual agony which you endured for us when an angel came from heaven to comfort you, and when you sweated blood in agony. Here, sweet Jesu, I implore you for your sweet mercy, that you may be my help and consolation in [every] temptation, agony of spirit, or disturbance, so that with your sweet consolation I may pass out of all turbulence of soul and body into the healthy state of virtue and penance. *Our Father.*

Sweet Jesu, I thank you for the distress which you experienced when Judas betrayed you, and you foretold this to him, and gave him fair warning, and for that reason it was the greatest sin that ever occurred.[4] Now, lord Jesu, I implore you, protect me from serious sins such as presumption, despair, and all kinds of sins against nature, and give me the grace to reckon each sin as a serious one which might in any sort of way grieve you, [for nothing is little that grieves you, lord] Jesus. *Our Father.*

Sweet Jesu, I thank you for all the distresses you endured when you were captured by the Jews, when some pulled you, some shoved you, some dragged you, treated you with contempt, jeered at you, mauled [you] and tore at you; and, sweet Jesu, I thank you for all the patience which you demonstrated there when you allowed them to do as they wanted. Now, sweet Jesu, I implore you to lay hold on me and make me entirely yours, and if I should run off to any sin caused by the world around me, my own body or the devil, sweet Jesu, fetch me straight home again, as a lord does his serf, and urge me on with hardship to immediate penance.[5] [Furthermore], sweet Jesu, in you resides every sovereign remedy, and I, lord, am desperately ill with sins; take hold of me therefore, sweet Jesu, and place me under your treatment, and move close to me with your grace, as the Samaritan did, and pour into my wounds the oil of forgiveness and the wine of invigoration, and lead me into the shelter of love, always keeping me under your treatment.[6] Further still, sweet lord Jesu, this life is full of temptation and enemies and there is no support except from you, sweet Jesu; for this reason, sweet Jesu, take me into your tutelage and protection and never permit your handiwork to be [destroyed]. Yet again, sweet Jesu, you are all goodness and to you belongs all the love there is, and accordingly, take complete possession of my heart so that my love may rest entirely on you who purchased everything, and then my heart will never turn from you no matter what tempts it but will always cling fast to you, since to love you, sweet Jesu,

[is] most rewarding
with most succeeding
for those most needing.

Our Father . . . and lead us.

Sweet Jesu, I bestow on you words of thanksgiving and gratitude in recompense for that betrayal and the disgraceful treatment which you experienced when they tied you up to a [post like a] thief. Now, sweet Jesu, I implore you, tie me up to yourself so that no difficulty nor temptation may ever separate us from one another; tie me up to yourself, sweet Jesu, (with the ropes of) faith, hope and love. Fasten men to you with faith, sweet Jesu, so that no [evil advice] nor error nor heresy may ever turn me away from my faith; and permit my faith, sweet Jesu, to be in moderation, not too lax, believing things which should not be believed, nor too limited, leaving out things which should be believed; in addition, sweet Jesu, make me believe in all the sacraments of holy church and in all its decrees, [and] trust entirely in God for my salvation. Sweet Jesu, tie me up to you in hope so that all my hope, [confidence, strength, consolation and happiness may lie in you; in each situation, pleasant or miserable, may my hope] and confidence be solely in you; never let my hope become too limited in case I lapse into despair, nor too lax in case I soar into presumption; and bestow on me your grace, sweet Jesu, to persevere in good works in your service with such discernment that my hope and reliance on you may be in proportion to what is reasonable. Sweet Jesu, tie me up to you in love so that all my love may be solely in you, in will, speech and action, and let me love nothing but you and for your sake;[7] and let me love friend and enemy as you commanded; and send me the grace to prevent any immoderate anger, hatred or malice from breaking my rope of Christian love; and allow me, lord, to love you better and better as time goes on, with more and more commitment, and allow me to love what you love and to hate what you hate.

Our Father.

Sweet Jesu, I bestow on you words of thanksgiving and gratitude for all the steps and paces which you made toward your own torment and your own death. I implore you, sweet Jesu, to direct all my movements and all the emotions of my heart. *Our Father.*

Sweet Jesu, I thank you for all the humiliating experiences, excruciating pains and disgraceful acts which you endured in the presence of Annas and Caiaphas, Pilate and Herod, and particularly I thank you, sweet Jesu, for that compassionate look which, turning back, you directed on your disciple Saint Peter, who (had) disowned you, but even so, in deep mental distress, you revealed openly to him that your love was such that neither humiliation nor torture was able to drag your heart away from him. Now, sweet Jesu, turn your eye of mercy toward us sinners so that through your compassion and grace we are able to repent of our disobedience and misdeeds [in order to reach your compassionate forgiveness] with Saint Peter. *Our Father.*

Sweet Jesu, I thank you for that patient and silent way you stood in Pilate's presence and amid all the false accusations of the Jews. Now here, sweet Jesu, I implore you, send me the grace to remember with full conviction in every temptation that I am standing in your presence, as my judge, and send me the grace to endure patiently my enemies' accusations, reprimands and wicked language on account of my love for you, and let me acknowledge that everyone else is better than I am, and be patient at all times and reckon myself inferior; and, sweet Jesu, when I am to be judged, be merciful with me, and let your own humility and that judgment you so unjustly underwent excuse me from that punishment which in strict justice I should receive. *Our Father . . . and lead us not.*

Sweet Jesu, I bestow on you words of thanksgiving for all that humiliation and excruciating pain which you endured when they spat in[to] your face, on that sweet mirror and glory of heaven in bodily form, which angels and saints take delight in gazing upon.[8] Now, sweet Jesu, allow me the grace to take my greatest delight in gazing inwardly and meditating on that glorious face; and, sweet Jesu, restore the image of your face in my soul, which has been faded by the filth of sin;[9] and, beloved lord, let me never be titillated by the face of sin when I am tempted, and send me the grace never to give in to the allure of sin; and [send] me the grace to honor you in every creature; and let me never be conceited about the appearance of my own face, nor feel the urge to commit sin because of the appearance of anyone else's face; and, sweet Jesu, afford me [the grace] to behold your glorious face in heaven, Amen. *Our Father . . . and lead us not.*

Sweet Jesu, I bestow on you as many words of gratitude as I know for all [the] wicked words, bad names, derisive remarks, [profanities], grimaces and insults which the Jews directed at you throughout the time of your precious passion, and for all the strongholds and prisons which they held you captive in when you were dragged and hustled to Annas and Caiaphas, and next moment to Herod and Pilate, and confined inside their palaces. Now, sweet Jesu, here I implore you to send me [endurance] and the strength to stand resolutely, patiently enduring words of contempt and reproach on account of my love for you, and never complaining because of hardship nor affliction nor illness which have been sent by you; and bestow on me [the grace] to stand firmly in all the assaults and temptations of my enemies, spiritual and physical. *Our Father . . . Hail Mary.*

Sweet Jesu, I thank you for all the steps and footprints which you made in this direction and that at the time of your passion, and, I implore you, send me the grace on all my paths and ways that they may be directed toward your honor and the salvation of my soul; and send me the grace to move to your service of my own will, and not to give up, whatever the discomfort or sacrifice; and make me feel disgust at the notion of moving toward any physical pleasure that is against your will, sweet Jesu. *Our Father . . . and lead us not.*

Sweet Jesu, I bestow on you words of thanks for that contemptuous blindfolding which the Jews did to you, and here I ask you, sweet lord Jesu, to protect me from the way in which sin blindfolds me when I get into the habit of it, and when I go for a long time without confessing it, when I am presumptuous (of forgiveness), when I despair, when I have too high an opinion of myself; and protect me from the total blackout of damnation and from being shut out from the blessed vision of your glorious face, and allow me to look clearly into the face of my own conscience, and send me the grace, sweet Jesu, to protect my eyes from all the harmful sights which entice me to sin; and allow me to view your blessed self unendingly. *Our Father.*

Sweet Jesu, I thank you for ever for that disgrace and ignominy which you endured when you were beaten up, and indeed you endured many vicious punches then because each of them was in competition with the rest to hit you first. Now, sweet Jesu, permit me to endure discomfort and severe hardship willingly for your sake, and never to complain at human diseases and injustices, but always to thank God for everything which he sends; and permit me, lord Jesu, to be tormented because of my sins before I die, and grant a constant heart, lord, to pray for it,[10] and when it comes, lord, give me composure and courage to thank you unreservedly for your [holy and gracious] gift (of suffering). *Our Father.*

Sweet Jesu, I bestow on you thanks and words of gratitude for all that painful, protracted and severe agony which you endured for us, and for all that precious blood which you shed when you were roped tight and naked to a pillar and violently flogged. That was a cruel agony and this is why: [they picked men to flog you who were strong,] robust and keen to kill you, and it was a long time before they got tired; and the whips were made very stout and stinging. As a result, your whole body was nothing but gashes and many gashes on each lacerated place at that, because the thongs struck so often in the same spot, and struck ever more deeply with each stroke, and what a generous and abundant proof of your love that was, sweet Jesu! Your body at that time was like heaven, because just as heaven is full of stars, so your body [was] full of wounds. But your wounds, lord, are better[11] than the stars, because stars only shine at night, and your wounds are powerful by night and by day; all the stars (in existence) only give a little light at night, and a single cloud can hide all of them; but a single one of your wounds, sweet Jesu, was and is sufficient to dispel the clouds of sin and to clear the conscience of every sinful person. Here, sweet Jesu, I implore you that these wounds may be my [meditation night and day, since in your wounds lies the complete remedy] for every disease of the soul. In addition, sweet Jesu, the stars are the cause of everything on the earth which is green, or growing, or fruit-bearing; now, sweet Jesu, make me (fresh and) green in my faith, growing in grace, and bearing fruit of good works. Finally: the stars are the origin of mines, of metals, and of precious stones; now, sweet Jesu, make me as tough as metal to repel temptations, and precious as a gemstone for the exalted ranks of love. *Our Father . . . and lead us not.*

And again, sweet Jesu, your body is like a net, because just as a net is full of holes, so your body is full of gashes. Here, sweet lord Jesu, I implore you to catch me in the net of your flogging so that all my feelings and love may be for you, and draw me closer and closer to you, and alongside you, as a dragnet draws fish, until I arrive at the bank of death, so that no temptation, time of hardship nor time of prosperity may ever tug me away from you; and as a net draws fish ashore, so, sweet Jesu, gather me up for your perfect joy. Catch me, lord, with the net of [mercy which is] holy church, and restrain me, lord, so that I can never break out of the fetters of charity. Catch me, sweet lord Jesu, in [the] net [of] your [commandments] so that sin can never set me free from the confining walls of virtue. *Our Father . . . and lead.*

Once more (a comparison), sweet Jesu: Your body is like a dove-house, because, just as a dovecote is full of openings, so your body is full of wounds, and just as a dove being chased by a hawk is safe enough if she can only get to an opening in her dovecote, so, sweet Jesu, your wounds are the best refuge [for us] in every temptation. Now, sweet Jesu, I implore you: In every temptation honor me with the supply of one or other hole among your wounds and the inclination to remain constant in the memory of your passion. What is more, sweet Jesu, your body is like a honeycomb, because in each direction that is packed with cells, and each cell is so stocked with honey that it cannot be touched without exuding some of its sweetness; in the same way, sweet Jesu, your body is full of cells of devotion so that it can't be touched by a pure soul without the sweetness [of] affection (appearing). Now, sweet Jesu, bestow on me the grace to touch you by calling out for mercy on my sins, by my yearning longings for spiritual contemplation, by reforming of my life and by my persevering in virtue, endeavoring to fulfill your commands, and remaining in tender recollections of your passion. *Our Father . . . and . . . not.*

Yet another (comparison), sweet Jesu: Your body is like a book entirely inscribed in red ink, (which is) compared to your body because that is entirely inscribed with red wounds.[12] Now, sweet Jesu, send me the grace to read this book again and again, and to understand something of the sweetness of that reading; and allow me the grace to grasp something of the matchless love of Jesus Christ, and to learn from that example to love God in return as I should do; and, sweet Jesu, send me grace that in this book I may ponder over my matins, [other hours of the Office] with Evensong and Compline [and that it may be my constant] meditation, conversation and discussion. *Our Father . . . and lead us not.*

Sweet Jesu, once again (a comparison): Your body is like a meadow full of scented flowers and health-giving herbs; in just this way your body is full of wounds, sweetly aromatic for a devout soul and as health-giving as herbs for each sinful man. Now, sweet Jesu, I implore you, allow me the sweet aroma of mercy and the health-giving medicinal prescription of grace.

(At this point the extract from the *Longer Meditations* in Allen's *English Writings* ends; it has covered about eight folios of Bodley MS e Mus.232. The text given by Horstman from CUL MS Addit.3052 continues:)

Sweet Jesu, I bestow on you words of gratitude for all the injuries and disgraces which you suffered by your own dear wish when you were dressed up in purple to deride you; [they] crowned your head with thorns to prove your sweet tolerance and composure and then fell on their knees and mocked you and called you "lord" and "leader" and spat in your face and cuffed you and spoke as many insults as they could to you. Here, sweet Jesu, I implore you to remit the disgrace and injury which we have deserved for our sin in committing all the disgraceful and shameful acts we have done, and send us the grace to worship you in as many ways and as amply as the Jews found to disgrace you in your passion; and, sweet Jesu, send us the grace of such clothing and outfits as are most agreeable to you, and never to crave for modish fashions nor newfangled attire; and, sweet Jesu, send me the grace to carry my head low and never to exhibit ostentatious mannerisms in appearance nor in expression; and, sweet Jesu, send me the grace to employ my five senses in your worship and send me the grace never to covet honors nor position beyond what you have appointed for me. *Our Father . . . and lead us not.*

Sweet Jesu, I thank you with all my heart for all the blood which you so copiously shed in your crowning in front of all those people, when your sweet face was covered in blood and on every side you were vehemently shouted at and scoffed at and pushed along to that violent and repulsive death, and judged so unjustly to it: may you be blessed and thanked, sweet Jesu, as one deserving of being loved by all creatures. Here, sweet Jesu, I implore you, wash my soul with that blood and anoint and decorate my soul and my consciousness with that precious blood, and send me the grace, through your great compassion, to judge and criticize myself with full comprehension, so that my soul may be saved. *Our Father.*

Sweet Jesu, I bestow on you words of gratitude for all the injuries and disgraceful acts which you endured while carrying your own cross and punishment on your bare back; they dragged you and tugged you so roughly that it was a most pitiable sight, and in addition, sweet Jesu, they pushed you, struck you so ignominiously like a thief carrying his own gallows. Oh my dear lord, my sweet Jesu, what a terrible plight you were in when, on Herod's orders, your tunic was stripped from you; it had stuck very firmly to your body with the blood from your flogging when you were slashed and lacerated and beaten so severely and for such a long time until all your skin was bloodless[13] and scarcely hung on you; and so the material was stuck to your skin with dried blood, and yours was tender skin because you were young and in the bloom of health. Then, as they ripped off the cloth, they took no notice of how agonizingly that contemptuous stripping was paining you, with many fragments of your tender skin coming off attached to it. Then it was pitiful to see your body all streaming with blood. O lord, sweet Jesu, in my imagination I can see your red blood coursing down your cheeks, gushing out after each blow as you are crowned, in front, behind, and on both sides. The thorns tear your scalp to pieces; each thorn penetrates your skull. I cannot bear it, sweet Jesu; how can a Christian soul watch his lord who has never done anything wrong suffering so much torment? Your grunting and groaning, your grieving and heaving sighs, the pathos of your expression—all these pierce my heart. The crown of all bliss, who crowns all the blessed, the king of all kings, the lord of all lords, the emperor of [all emperors is now by hell-hounds][14] crowned with thorns, supremely honored in heaven, he is despised and desecrated, he who created the sun and all creatures, all of which he gave, has nothing with which he can hide his head, and he is so poor that he walks along completely naked under the gaze of everyone. Here, sweet Jesu, I implore you, give me the grace to carry with you the cross of penance, for the sake of your love and [because of my sins, just as you did for my sake and because of] my sins, and allow me to carry it just as you did until the time of my death, and don't let me get [tired or] start grumbling because I'm suffering for love of you; and give me the grace to perform penitential acts for my sins during this life, and allow me to have my purgatory here, and give me the grace to endure calmly contemptuous remarks occasioned by my love for you. *Our Father . . . and lead us not.*

Sweet Jesu, I bestow on you words of gratitude for all that suffering and grief which you endured as you carried your cross to your execution, and in my mind's eye I am watching as they march you forward, naked as a worm, torturers surrounding you, and armed soldiers, the throng of people exceedingly thick, and they are dragging you along with no respect, they are kicking you with their feet as if you were a dog. Oh, this is a pitiful picture! Your head is full of thorns, your hair is full of blood, your face is totally pallid, your expression is of deep grief, your cheeks and head are all swollen from being punched, your face is all besmeared with spit; after the attentions the Jews have paid you, you are more like a leper than a healthy man.[15] The cross, massive and heavy, is so tightly lashed to your [bare] back that you are crushed to a stooping position and are crouching underneath it. O sweet Jesu, you groaned most bitterly when it pressed so painfully on your naked body, which is so ailing, so crammed full of agonies, so enfeebled and exhausted, what with prolonged and complete lack of food beforehand, what with being kept awake all the preceding night without any sleep, what with flogging and punching and disgraceful things said and done (to you) beforehand. Your flesh where the cross is rubbing has lost all its skin and is pouring with blood from raw weals. The agony of that burden makes you so distraught with pain that every footstep you take stabs into your heart. And in this way, sweet Jesu, you are walking [out of] Jerusalem toward your execution; all the onlookers come and walk alongside and yell at you and are inquisitive. No thief was ever led to his execution with a procession like that! Here, sweet Jesu, I entreat you, send me the grace to accompany you by commemorating your passion, by suffering in some measure for love of you, and by feeling sympathy with you. *Our Father.*

Sweet Jesu, what grief surged into your heart when your eye fell on your beloved mother! You saw her moving along with the jostling crowd like a woman driven completely [insane because of unspoken misery which exceeded all human miseries]. At one moment she was twisting her fingers in dismay, crying and moaning, at the next she was flinging her arms wide, tears pouring from her eyes and cascading to her feet, then she would collapse deeply unconscious over and over again because of her anguish and distress. Her distress, my sweet Jesu, and her mourning the whole time greatly intensified all your other torments many times over; and when she realized that her unhappiness was causing you such severe distress, it affected her even more badly, and so the anguish that each of you felt for the other increased many times over. The deep affection of your relationship with each other, an unparalleled ardor, made your grief for one another quite unlike any other grief or misery in the world, because since your love was unique so your grief was unequalled; it penetrates your hearts like a deathblow. O lady, have pity on yourself, how could you be so brave as to accompany him so closely among so many fierce enemies? How was it that your natural timidity as a woman or your virgin modesty did not hold you back? It wasn't proper for you to move along among a rabble like that one! But you paid no attention to being afraid of any man, nor to anything else that might impede you, because you were beside yourself with distress about your son. [And so your whole awareness was focused on him; your love was so keen within your breast, directed toward your son], your sighing came from so deep within you, your emotions so choked with mourning and distress, your expression so downcast with killing grief, that it deprived you of all concern for physical disturbance or fear, of social disgrace and of any kind of hindrance. See now, lady, that anguish and that suffering ought to have been mine; I had deserved it and I [was] the cause of it; so, dear lady, seeing those torments and wounds were justly my own, and because you are considerate, obtain just one of them all for me, and then it can stay like a goad at my heart;[16] obtain for me, dear lady, a drop of that lamentation you made, to accompany him with, as you did. All that misery is mine by right: [get] for me [some of what is] my own, don't be so inconsiderate as to keep back all of it. Even if you are glad to have all your misery, you have a reputation for generosity; go shares then with someone impoverished who has little, and give me some of your sighings as you sigh there so bitterly, and allow me to sigh with you, since I started all that misery. I'm not asking for castles nor towns, dear lady, nor for any other worldly wealth, nor for the sun, nor the moon, nor any of the cosmic bodies, nor for any object; but it's wounds I yearn for, wounds of deep remorse, of anguish and sympathy for my sweet lord Jesu's suffering. I have a craving for pain, and I'm imploring my lord for a drop of his red blood to make my soul bloody with, or else a drop of his water to wash my soul with. O mother [of mercy and of compassion, help for all sorrow and eliminator of all evil, mother of all] those who are wretched and of all those who [mourn], visit my ailing soul and insert your son with his wounds within my heart; send a little spark of sympathy into my heart, which is as unyielding as stone, a single drop of that suffering to make it supple with. *Our Father*.

Sweet Jesu, I thank you with all my heart for all that torment you endured when the cross was thrown down on the ground and they spread you out flat on it, and tugged your hands and feet with ropes to the holes, and nailed the one hand securely while they were stretching the other toward the other hole; and then, sweet Jesu, they dragged your whole body downward until your feet reached the holes,[17] and those nails, lord, were blunt in order to tear your skin and bruise your muscles. Now, sweet Jesu, in my mind I can see your body on the cross, dehydrated from loss of blood, strained so that the joints pull apart; now your wounds open, the taut skin is completely ripped asunder and gapes so wide that it's a marvel it holds together; your head is crowned with thorns, your body one mass of injuries, nails in your soft hands and feet, and in your nerves, what's more, where the most painful sensation is; there is no support for your head, your body is taut like a skin prepared for parchment on the stretching-frame;[18] your face, once so attractive, is completely swollen up; your joints are separating; you are hanging and standing on nails; torrents of blood gush down the cross; the sight of your mother increases your agony. O my sweet Jesu, my lord, willing to become powerless in order to make me powerful [by cancelling out] my sin, I am talking, lord, of your suffering and talking out of deep reverence, yet I cannot devise any harmonious syllables for it, but gabble like a parrot with no idea what I am talking about; I am observing your passion intently and can detect no sensation of it; my sins are so numerous and so [black] that they have obliterated reverent love and blocked off all detection of sweetness from my soul, and so I am talking and blundering about like a blind creature, and talking without understanding or knowledge of such a revered topic. *Our Father.*

But you, sweet Jesu, you who bring the dead to life and convert them to a good life from the death of sin, enliven me, lord Jesu, and give me the grace to detect some of that sweet taste and spiritual reverence. Send me, lord, the radiance of grace so that I may have some insight within my soul. But, lord, I am well aware that anyone who honestly desires you, even if he can't feel anything, already possesses what he is not aware of, that is: the love of your divine nature; and if anyone can't detect any fervor,[19] he should reckon himself a weakling and an outcast [and reproach himself] and consider himself undeserving of having any fervor of devotion or any such sign of special affection from God, our Lord—and that will be the quickest way for him to gain the gift of his grace! *Our Father.*

Sweet Jesu, next the Jews heaved the cross up and made it jolt painfully into the shaft which had been prepared for it, and (it) burst your wounds and completely jarred your body to pieces as it so agonizingly hung there. Sweet lord Jesu, you were in a terrible plight then, with the ghastly injuries in your hands and feet supporting all the weight of your body! Sweet Jesu, then your mother really was distressed, seeing all this, and moaned and twisted her hands and wept with copious tears; all this, lord, went to amplify your torment. And that spot was so loathsome, with the stench of various corpses, that anyone would feel repugnance to come close to it. In this way all your five senses were seized by torments, in order to remedy the transgressions of our five senses. In your sight: you were blindfolded, then you (suffered in) seeing your mother so anguished, and then in seeing as enemies people who were most reckoned to be your friends, like the Jews. In your sense of smell: through the stench of innumerable corpses, because you were executed in the most contagious place in Jerusalem, where all the dead bodies from the town were thrown out, and that smell in your nose, sweet Jesu, was deeply offensive. In your taste, lord: the gall caused you great distress when you were thirsty—because, sweet Jesu, overwhelming pain produces thirst and dehydration—that (substance) being bitter to the taste; and the Jews gave you vinegar mixed with it, to exacerbate the sense of bitterness for you. In hearing, sweet Jesu, you were assaulted by false accusations, and insults; by hearing them cry "hail king" as they spat in your face; by hearing ugly shouting, when they shouted out "he knew how to save other men, now let him save himself, if he knows how." In the sense of touch, sweet Jesu, you were tormented when you were tied up and tugged along, punched, blindfolded, flogged, crowned, while you were carrying the cross, during the heaving on the ropes on the cross, as your feet and hands were nailed on the cross. And there you hung, so destitute, sweet Jesu, and so oppressed by misery, that of all the wealth on earth you had nothing but a scrap of material to hide your private parts with: and yet you are king of kings, and lord of lords, and heaven and earth belong to you. Nevertheless, lord, you determined to be so destitute at that time that you did not even have any earth to die on, but (died) on the cross in midair. And that was why you said, sweet Jesu: "Foxes have earths and birds have nests"—but at the moment of your death you yourself have nothing to rest your head on. O sweet Jesu, you said something piteous when you cried out, "All you who pass along the road, stop and look to see if there is any grief like my grief, which I am enduring for the human race."[20] Even so, sweet Jesu, you prayed to your father to forgive them the guilt of your death, so abundant, lord, is your mercy. And, sweet Jesu, in spite of all your terrible pain, you attended to the needs of the thief on your right side, when he begged for mercy, and, [sweet Jesu, in spite of all your terrible pain you] gave him a better gift than he asked for. After all, sweet Jesu, seeing the case is that you are now in bliss and no longer in torment, don't be too aloof or reserved in your mercy; it's a rare thing for a man to be more benevolent in misery than in a state of content. O lord, you were gravely troubled about your mother, when you said goodbye to her and were on the point of death, handing her into Saint John's care to look after her and give her support. Here, sweet Jesu, I implore you, abounding in sins as I am: in your bliss, lord, have mercy on me now, send me the favor when you choose to for me to be with you in paradise. *Our Father. Hail Mary . . . and lead us.*

Sweet lady, virgin and mother, you really were dismayed when Christ had said goodbye to you and handed you into Saint John's care; that grief could have killed you at that parting. The tears streamed down rapidly from your eyes, sighings and sorrowings oppressed your heart deep down; you fell down unconscious, your head lolling down, your arms fell to your sides, your color grew livid, your face totally blanched; the sword of sorrow for your son's death transfixed your heart. That substitution, lady, when you received John in place of Christ, was deeply grievous and [like] a spasm of death at your heart. O sweet lady, why could I not have been beside you, hearing what you were hearing, seeing that scene right beside you, taking my share of that tremendous grief, perhaps being able to alleviate your misery? After all, people say it is a consolation to have a companion in trouble.[21] Now, sweet Jesu, since I wasn't able to be there at your death, allow me the favor correspondingly to have that death constantly in my consciousness, in prayer, and in conversation, and allow me frequently to be aware of [my] own death, to reform my life and have sincere sorrow for my transgressions. *Our Father.*

Sweet Jesu, then you called out mournfully on the cross, [gently] saying that you were thirsty—and that wasn't surprising, because pain is very parching—and they gave you, lord, vinegar and gall. Sweet Jesu, that was no refreshment for thirst but an adding to it. O sweet Jesu, they gave you poison to quench your thirst with, and you gave them your heart's blood to assuage their sins and to heal[22] their souls. But, sweet Jesu, your thirst was of several kinds: in your body because of the pain, and in your soul where you were thirsting for the spiritual recovery from sin of those who were putting you to death, and you were thirsting for the release of the souls in hell who throughout their lives in this world had kept your laws.

Here, sweet Jesu, I implore you, give me grace to endure hunger and thirst for love of you, and to resist the urging and the promptings of every temptation of my physical nature, of worldly attractions or of diabolical seduction, and give me composure in my endurance as I accompany you in the shadow of the cross, thirsting for your service, your love and your presence in my heart, while desiring and wishing for your holy love. *Our Father . . . Hail Mary full of grace. And lead us not.*

Sweet Jesu, I thank you with my whole soul for those mournful words which you spoke aloud to your father before you expired: "Dear God, why have you abandoned me, why do you not spare me at all?"[23] Sweet Jesu, for our sake your human nature was left totally abandoned; such a horrible and such an agonizing death no man has ever endured. There is no physical agony which resembles yours; your human physique was sensitive, your rank supreme; the son of the heavenly Father is hanging between two thieves, and at the very centerpoint of the world, so that everyone should know about it; and on the greatest festival day, when everyone thronged to that city, so there was nothing covert about your disgrace at all. You are hanging entirely naked, your skin all torn to shreds, every limb wrenched from the others by cords, crowned with thorns, wounds gaping, countless and ghastly. Your mother's grief was more agonizing to you than all your [physical] anguish. See now,[24] [this exceeded all your other anguish]: the perdition of the souls of the men who were tormenting you so cruelly. Sweet Jesu, your great mercy, your boundless love and compassion, these no one can possibly reckon or even imagine, seeing you suffered so terribly for those who were your enemies. *Our Father . . . Hail Mary . . . And lead us.*

Sweet Jesu, in my imagination I will prostrate myself on the soil, and lower still if I can manage, because I am the perpetrator and the criminal in [all your] painful death. I want to embrace the foot of the cross, prostrate on the ground as you were lying, sweet Jesu, among those stinking dead bones lying there repulsive to look at: it won't disturb me at all, rather it will be (an act of) praise and pleasure for me, so much so that I will not direct my eyes upward to that splendid spectacle of your wounds, because, being the perpetrator of them, I am not worthy to gaze on them. Like this I will lie here to catch some of your blood, sweet Jesu; I will not stir from here until I am completely reddened with your precious blood, until I am marked with your precious blood as one of your own (flock), and my soul is softened in that pleasant bath; and in this way it may come about, sweet Jesu, that it may open my hard heart, which now is as hard as stone, to make it soft, to make what was dead in sin spring to life for your sake through the special influence (of your blood). Sweet Jesu, your precious passion raised up dead men out of their graves, it opened heaven, shattered the gates of hell, the earth trembled at it, and the sun lost its light; yet my worthless heart, related to the devil's species, is harder than stones, since they split apart at your passion, while my heart cannot sense the least part of your passion, nor rise with the dead at the pity of it. Now the unkindness of my wicked heart is greater than [your passion, which is] your precious death that worked such miracles and others many times greater, if the commemoration of these things does not arouse my [heart]. But, sweet lord, a single drop of your blood [dripping] on my soul in memory of your passion may make my soul pliable and soft, which is now so hard, that it melts under influence of your grace. I know very well, sweet Jesu, that my heart is not worthy of your coming to it and descending into it; I am not requesting even the status of a sepulchre for my heart, but, sweet Jesu, you did descend into hell to make a visitation there and to give their just dues to the holy souls of our devout forefathers, and in that very way I'm requesting your coming to my soul. Sweet Jesu, I acknowledge freely as well that I never did deserve to be your mother's companion, to stand with her and with John at your passion. But sweet Jesu, if I'm not qualified to be present there in that way because of my total lack of fitness, then I do consider myself fit, because of my great wrongdoing, to hang alongside you, like one of the thieves. And so, sweet Jesu, if I can't be present there as one who has merited it, I request some share in your death as one of those guilty of it. And so, even if I do not merit being enlightened in spirit, my urgent needs and my wickedness demand to be given their just treatment. Come then, sweet Jesu, as it's your wish, and set alight a tiny spark of love within my soul, as you best know how, a touch of compassion for your suffering, from which my heart can be set ablaze and I can be brought to life through it, until I would be aflame with your love above everything else; and lave me in your blood so that I may forget all the prosperity of the world, and all physical attractions. Then I can bless the time when I shall be able to feel your grace so arousing me toward you that no other possession has any pleasure for me, except your death alone. *Our Father.*

Sweet Jesu, then you spoke: "Father, into your hands I entrust my spirit." Here sweet Jesu, I implore you, have and hold my soul firmly in your hands all the time so that neither prosperity nor adversity can wrench my soul away from your control; and at my final ending, sweet Jesu, accept my soul into your custody so that no devil can obstruct my way to your glory. *Our Father. Hail Mary.*

Sweet Jesu, then you spoke for the last time: "All is finished." Then your head fell down, your breath of life went out of you, the earth trembled, the sun lost its light, dead men rose from their graves, the temple split in half,[25] stones shattered completely in pieces: (all) these were evidence of your divinity. Sweet Jesu, then the sharp spear penetrated your side, and blood and water gushed out. O sweet Jesu, then there were five great rivers of blood: from hands and feet and side. Your chin lolls on your breast, the whites of your eyes are turned upward, your lips shrivel, your white teeth are revealed, your lovely face has gone quite livid, your hair [matted] with blood. I really wish that reflecting on this scene would bring about my own death. O sweet Jesu, then your mother was completely wretched; she stared now at your head and at the crown, now at your face, now at your hands with the nails, now at the wide gash in your side, now at your feet nailed to the cross, now at your flogged trunk, and at every place she found a fresh (cause for) lamenting; she cried, she twisted her fingers, she sighed, she sobbed—now she collapses. John on your other side is full of misery. [Both are twisting their fingers and giving vent to deep grief. When they gazed upward], the sight of the crucified one[26] stabs into their hearts like their deathpang. Now, sweet lady, in your mercy, since I am the perpetrator of all that misery and pain, permit me through your [great] favor a fraction of your pain, a glimpse of your sorrow, to sigh and grieve with you, so that in some measure I can feel [a share of your sorrow], I who caused it all; allow me, sweet lady, to have and to hold this passion in my awareness as sincerely and attentively all my life as you, lady, and John, were aware of it when all the spectators had gone away and you were still lingering there at the foot of the cross. *Amen. Our Father. And lead us not. We adore you, O Christ, because by your holy cross. Lord Jesus Christ.*

Ghostly Gladness

This "prose lyric" is found in MS Dd.v.64, where it is included among the *cantica divini amoris* in the colophon which immediately follows it, and in Longleat MS 29, where it is somewhat southernized in dialect. There seems to be no authority beyond conjecture for Hope Allen's connection of this lyric with an incident described in two extant manuscripts, and in two now lost but recorded by commentators (one of them Bale), in which Rolle had a vision on the night of February 1, 1343, informing him that he would live another twelve years. The longing for death in this piece is typical of Rolle's writing and can be seen in the *Meditations on the Passion*, in the lyrics in *Ego Dormio* and Chapter 8 of *The Form;* and in his Latin *Incendium* and *Melos*. This piece may well have been composed about the same time as the lyrics, probably in the early 1340s.

Sources: Hope Allen, *EW*, pp 51–2; Horstman, *YW* I, p. 81. Discussed in Allen, *WA*, pp. 272–4.

Ghostly Gladness[1]

Holy happiness in Jesus, and joy in heart, with spiritual sweetness in expectation of the sweet taste of heaven, is health for salvation; and my life continues in love, and lightheartedness envelops my thoughts. I dread nothing which can inflict anguish on me, so much am I aware of well-being.

No wonder that death would be dear, since I would be able to see him whom I seek. But now it lurks far from me and I must live here till he will release me. Listen and learn from this lesson, and you shall not dislike it. Love makes me murmur and joy brings me to joking. See you lead your life in lightheartedness; keep hopelessness far away; do not let gloom remain with you; but in God's cheerfulness forever sing out merrily. Amen.[2]

The Bee and the Stork

Only two manuscripts contain this piece of moralized natural history: the Lincoln Thornton manuscript, and the Durham, Cosin Library MS, V.i.12. A long tradition of allegorical interpretation of nature in the form of bestiaries lies behind *The Bee and the Stork*, and fragments of Old and early Middle English bestiaries survive. When the bestiary that had ultimately derived from Greek and Oriental sources in the fourth century A.D. was translated in the eleventh century by "Thetbaldus," possibly a monk from Monte Cassino, this gave rise to much further allegorizing of the animal world in medieval literature. Originally the animals treated were those mentioned in the Bible, as Augustine had treated the animals in Psalm 102 (see Rolle's translation and commentary on this psalm on p. 76, above). Rolle's comment on Psalm 90 contains moralizing on the basilisk and weasel, mostly original. His source for the material on the bee and the stork is ultimately Aristotle, *History of the Animals*, ix.40 (or Pliny, *Natural History*, xi,10) for the bee, and *History of the Animals*, ix.8 for the stork, with moral supplied from Gregory, *Moralia* xxxi, cap.39. There is a version of Gregory's moral in *Ancrene Riwle*, some manuscripts of which read "stork" (for "ostrich") which error appears in Rolle, whose source may therefore have been *Ancrene Riwle*, at least as a supplement to other sources. A Latin abbreviated comment on the bee in BL MS Harley 268 from the second half of the fourteenth century may be a copy of Rolle's immediate source for the bee, or could be derived from him; the work contains other "fables and similitudes." Rolle may also have drawn on one of the great thirteenth-century encyclopedias, such as Vincent of Beauvais, for his material.

Sources: Allen, *EW*, pp. 54–6; Horstman, *YW* I, pp. 193–4. See also Allen, *WA*, pp. 268–71.

The Bee and the Stork

An Allegory of Richard Hermit on the Nature of the Bee.

The bee has three qualities. The first is that she is never idle, and she never associates with those who refuse to work, but throws them out and drives them away. A second is that when she flies she picks up earth in her feet so that she cannot easily be blown too high in the air by the wind. The third is that she keeps her wings clean and bright. In the same way, good people who love God are never unoccupied;[1] either they are at work, praying or meditating or reading or doing other good works, or they are rebuking lazy people, indicating that they deserve to be driven away from the repose of heaven because they refuse to work. Here good people "pick up earth," so to speak, by reckoning themselves despicable and made of earth, so that they may not be blown by the wind of frivolity and pride. They keep their wings clean; in other words, they fulfill the two commandments of love with a clear conscience and they retain other virtues uncontaminated by the filth of sin and impure desires.

Aristotle states that bees are in the habit of attacking the man who wants to extract their honey from them.[2] That is what we should do to counteract the devils who do their best to plunder from us the honey of a simple life and of God's grace. For there are many who are never able to maintain proportion in love where their friends are concerned, both related and unrelated; either they love them too much, focusing their thoughts immoderately on them, or they love them too little if those friends do not treat them in exactly the way they would like. People like that do not know how to fight for their honey with the result that the devil converts it into wormwood[3] and frequently makes their thoughts most bitter, in distress, and misery, and the whirling of futile thoughts and other worthless things, because they are so heavy with earthly friendship that they cannot fly up into the love of Jesus Christ, with which they could so easily relinquish the love of all creatures living on this earth.

In which connection, correspondingly, Aristotle says that some birds excel in flight, and these migrate from one land to another; some are inadequate fliers because of the heaviness of their bodies, and accordingly their nests are not far above the earth.[4] So it is with those who are converted to the service of God: some excel in flight, for they soar from earth to heaven and rest themselves there in contemplation and are made replete with God's love, having no thought for worldly affection; but there are some who do not know how to fly from this land, but allow their heart to relax on the journey and take great pleasure in many affections for men and women as they come and go, now this one and now that, and in Jesus Christ they do not know how to detect any sweetness, or, if on any occasion they do feel something, it is so little and so brief because of the other thoughts that they harbor that it does not have a stabilizing effect; they are like a bird which is called *strucyo* or the stork,[5] which has wings but cannot fly because of the weight of its body. And so they do have intellect, and they fast and keep vigils and appear holy in people's eyes, but they are not able to fly up to love and contemplation of God, so weighed down are they with other affections and other trivialities.

The End.

Desire and Delight

With some differences, even of the opening phrase, this is found in two manuscripts, MS T, the Lincoln Thornton MS, and Longleat 29 (Lt). The former is a northern copy, and substitutes the non-alliterating "yearning" for "desire" in the first line; Lt is southernized in dialect but slightly more accurate, at least at the opening. I have attempted to assess the original readings from these two copies. T terms this a song, "carmen," a term applied by the Cambridge scribe to *Ghostly Gladness* and concludes "etc." implying that the scribe had access to a longer form; however, Thornton ends many of his pieces in this way and it may have no significance.

Sources: Allen, *EW*, pp. 57–58; Horstman, *YW* I, 197. Discussed in Allen, *WA*, pp. 272–4.

Desire and Delight

Another by the same [Richard] concerning the love of God: Delight and the Longing for God.

Jesu, son of Mary, be merciful to me and gracious. Amen.

Desire[1] and delight in Jesu Christ, which has no part in worldly ideas, is wonderful, pure, holy[2] and firm, and one feels oneself in that degree at the stage of having been spiritually circumcised, when all other exertions and pressing[3] preoccupations are cut right away from the soul so that one can take repose in God's love without any encumbrance of other matters. Such delight is wonderful when it is so elevated that no thought can reach up to it to bring it down. It is pure when it is mixed with[4] nothing which is inconsistent with it, and it is firm when it is clean, secure and delightful by its very essence.

Three factors elevate one's delight in God. The first is to curb physical desire in one's bodily constitution; a second is eliminating or restraining our inclinations to commit wrong and temptations to consent to it; the third is controlling or uplifting of the emotions by the irradiation of the Holy Spirit, who raises one's heart up from all earthly thoughts so that one is unable to interpose any obstacle to the entry of Christ into one's own self. Everyone who desires unending happiness must endeavor night and day to fulfill this directive, otherwise they will not be able to reach Christ's love, since it is high and it lifts all who live in it up above the mire of earthly longings and base materialism, and above all thoughts of tenderness for any material object.

Two factors make our delight pure. The first occurs by redirecting our sensuality through reason; when anyone is diverted to take pleasure in his five senses at once impurity makes its way into his soul. The second is that the reason should be submissively employed in spiritual exercises, for example in meditating, praying and reading books dealing with religious topics. Accordingly, the delight which has no trace of uncontrolled arousal but is gently aroused[5] by Christ's loving, and in which sensuality[6] is redirected toward the reason, totally orientated and deployed toward God, sets a person's soul in repose and in security and causes it to remain constantly in good hope and to be pleased with all that God sends, without any resentment or depressive thoughts. Etc.[7] *The poem ends here; may the scribe have a blessing. Amen.*

Ego Dormio

Like Rolle's other two letters in English, *The Commandment* and *The Form of Living*, *Ego Dormio* was written for a female recipient. The colophon in MS Dd.v.64 claims that *ED* was written for a nun at Yedingham. Yedingham was only a mile from the Dalton's manor of Foulbridge on the borders of the north and east ridings, and the convent there must have been well-known to Rolle, but the tone of the work does not seem particularly appropriate to someone already in religious orders; the observation that in the second degree of love one abandons the world and leaves father and mother would seem to fit a girl about to embark on the religious life. In this, the earliest of Rolle's epistles, the grades of love are not given names, as they are in the two other English letters and in the Latin *Emendatio Vitae.* (This translation is based on a collation of MS C [CUL Dd.v.64] with Longleat 29.) There are twelve manuscripts of *Ego Dormio*, one of which gives it twice; all save four attribute the work to Rolle. The text in MS C has been partially adapted for a general public, but as Dr. Ogilvie-Thomson notes in her edition of the Longleat MS, this attempt has not been carried through consistently. The translation follows Lt more closely than C for this reason, and incorporates a substantial paragraph from Lt which does not occur in any other extant manuscript, but which carries the stamp of Rolle's other writing and may well be authentic. There is also a Latin version of *Ego Dormio.*

Sources: Allen, *EW*, pp. 60–72; Horstman, *YW* I, pp. 49–61. Also Allen, *WA*, pp. 247–51. A modernized version of *Ego Dormio* is given in Eric Colledge, *The Medieval Mystics of England* (1962), pp. 143–54. His version of the lyrical passages is beautiful—but very free.

Ego Dormio

Ego dormio et cor meum vigilat.[1] [You] who desire love, [open your ears] and hear of love. In the Song of Love I find the expression [which I have quoted at the beginning of this piece of writing]: "I sleep but my heart is awake." Great love is demonstrated by someone who is never halfhearted in loving, but unremittingly, whether standing, sitting, walking or [performing any other activity], is constantly meditating on his love, and frequently even dreaming of it. Because I love [you] I am courting you in order to have you exactly as I would wish—not for myself, but for my lord! I want to become [a] go-between to lead you to the bed of the one who has set you up and paid for you, Christ, son of the king of heaven, because he is eager to [marry] you if you are willing to give him your love. He is not asking anything more of you than your love; and you are doing what I want if you love him. Christ desires [the beauty of your soul, wanting you to give him your whole heart, and I'm not persuading] you to do anything except what he wants, just that you try very hard night and day to abandon all human affection and attraction which hinder you from praising Jesus Christ properly; because while your heart clings to the love of any physical thing, you cannot be perfectly united to God.

In heaven there are nine orders of angels, which are organized into three hierarchies. The lowest hierarchy comprises angels, archangels and virtues; the middle hierarchy comprises principalities, powers and dominations; the highest hierarchy, which is closest to God, comprises thrones, cherubim and seraphim. The angels are lowest, the seraphim highest; yet that order which is least bright is seven times as bright as the sun, [and just as you can see that the sun] is brighter than the candle, the candle brighter than the moon, and the moon brighter than the stars, so the orders of angels in heaven are each one brighter than the next, from angels to seraphim. I'm pointing this out so as to set your heart alight to crave the companionship of angels, since when all those who are good and holy depart from this world they are destined to be adopted into these orders, some into the lowest, who have loved [God] greatly; some into the middle rank who have loved [God] more; others into the highest, who love God most and are most burning in his love. The word *seraphim* means "burning"[2] and to this order are admitted those who want least from this world and, feeling most sweetness in God, have hearts which are most burning in his love.

I am writing [this] especially to you because I detect [in you] more integrity than in others, in that you will give your attention to carrying out in action what you can see is beneficial for your soul, and will devote yourself to that life in which you can offer your heart to Jesus Christ with most dedication, and be least among the preoccupations of this world. It is the case that if you are resolute in burning love for God while you live here, there can be no doubt that your seat can be allotted for you very high up and most happily, close to God's presence among his holy angels. You see, in the same rank where the proud devils were when they fell down below there are seated simple men and women who, in return for a little brief penance and hardship (here) which they have endured for the sake of their love for God, receive unending tranquility and happiness in heaven. Just now it seems hard to you, perhaps, to transfer your heart from all earthly things, from useless chitchat and from all human affection, and to go off on your own to keep vigil and pray and contemplate the joy of heaven and commiserate with Christ in his passion, to envisage the torment of hell which is appointed for the sinful. But certainly, as soon as you are accustomed to it, it will seem easier and sweeter to you than any earthly comfort ever did. As soon as your heart is touched by the sweetness of heaven you will take little pleasure in the jollity of this world; and when you feel joy in the love of Christ you will feel disgusted by the enjoyment and gratification of earthly entertainments: all the music and all the luxuries and comforts which all the people of this world are able to devise or invent [seem and indeed are] merely disgusting and irritating to the heart of someone who is really burning in the love of God, for he or she finds merriment, joy and music in the song of angels, as you will easily be able to appreciate if you abandon everything which you derive human pleasure from and cease to be preoccupied by your friends and relations but give them all up for the love of God, devoting your heart entirely to desiring his love and to pleasing him. You are bound to find more joy in him than I can conceive. [How could I write about it, then?] I have no idea whether [many] people are in such a state of love, because it is a rule that the higher the life is, the fewer followers it has here, since many things lure people away from loving God. So you may hear and observe this: God comforts his lovers more than those who do not love him can guess, since although we appear to be living abstemiously outwardly, we are bound to have very great inward joy if we dispose ourselves sensibly to the service of God, and direct all our thoughts to him, and abandon trivialities.

Devote your entire attention to understanding this letter, and if you have directed your whole desire to loving God, then listen to (this account of) three degrees of love, so that you may rise from one to the other until you are in the highest, because I don't want to conceal from you something which I think will be able to convert you into holiness.[3] The first degree of love occurs when a man keeps the Ten Commandments and keeps himself from the seven deadly sins and is firm in his faith in holy church, and refuses, for the sake of any earthly matter, to anger God, but will rather stand loyally in his service and persevere in it to his life's end. It is essential for everyone who wants to be saved to have this degree of love since no one can enter heaven unless he or she love God and neighbor without superiority, bad temper and malice, and without defaming his character, and without all other poisonous sins such as laziness, greediness, permissive behavior and materialism. This is because these vices kill the soul and force it to separate from God, [who is the life of the soul; and when a man or woman is pathetically separated from God we declare that he or she is dead, because he or she is dead to God] without whom no creature has the power to live. Just as a person poisoned by a sweet-tasting morsel absorbs venom which destroys his body, so a wretch who lives sinfully destroys his or her soul by pleasure-seeking and sensuality and brings it to unending death. People think that sin is something really candy-sweet, but the aftertaste reserved as payment for them is more bitter than aloes, sourer than vinegar and worse than all the misery [one can imagine in the world].

[All perishes and passes away that we behold with eyes;]
It withers into wretchedness, the wealth of this world.
Robes and riches rot in the ditch,
Couture and cosmetics slither into sorrow,
Luxuries and love-tokens very soon will stink,
Their wealth and their possessions will pull them down to death.
All the self-willed in this world are destined for one dale
Where they may see their sorrowing; where in distress lies all the rabble.
But he who has loved Jesus Christ may sing in consolation,
When all the wretched from their wealth tumble into hell.

But when you have lived fully by the commandments of God and have [strictly kept yourself] from all mortal sins and have pleased God in that degree, make the decision that you will [love God] (yet) more and do better for your soul, and become perfect. And then you will enter the second degree of love, that is, to give up the whole world, your father and your mother and all your relations, and follow Christ in poverty. In this degree you are to make every effort to be pure in heart and chaste in body and devote yourself to simplicity, endurance and obedience, and see how beautiful you can make your soul with virtue, and detest all moral weakness so that your life will become spiritual instead of physical, never again speaking harm about those around you nor returning any unkind word for another one, but tolerating everything patiently in your heart without any upsurge of anger. In this way you will experience peace, interior and exterior, and come to spiritual life, which you will find sweeter than anything on earth.

Perfect spiritual life means to despise the world and desire the joy of heaven, to destroy through God's grace all wicked yearnings in the body and forget the consolation and the affection of your relations, loving them only in God, irrespective of whether they are alive or dead, poor or rich, [in health or sickness, in misery or well-off,] you must continually give thanks to God and bless him for all [his] works. The fact is that God's decrees are so secret that no creature is able to understand them, and frequently some people have their pleasures and wishes in this world and hell in the next, while some people are in torment and persecution and agony in this life and have heaven as their reward. Therefore, if your friends are always in comfort and good health and well-off in worldly goods, both you and they might well be all the more anxious in case they lose the joy which is endless. If they are in a state of privation, poor health, or living honestly, they can be confident in God of coming to his glory. The fact is that in this degree of love you shall be so filled with the grace of the Holy Spirit that you will not experience either unhappiness or tears except for spiritual things such as for your own sins and those of other people, and for your love for Jesus Christ as you contemplate his passion; and this I would like you to [pay very great attention to] because it will set your heart alight to despise the goods of this world and all its gaiety and to desire burningly the radiance of heaven along with the angels and saints. And when your heart is entirely disposed to God's service and all thoughts of the world are driven out, then you will feel inclined to steal away on your own to think about Jesus and to be in deep prayer, for through good thoughts and holy prayers your heart is to be made burning in the love of Jesus Christ, and then you are bound to feel sweetness and spiritual joy, both in praying and meditating. And when you are alone by yourself, spend a lot of time saying the psalms of the Psalter and Our Fathers and Hail Marys, and take no notice of how many you are saying but note only that you are saying them well with all the devotion you can, raising your mind to heaven. It is better to say seven psalms, yearning as you do so for the love of Christ, and with your whole heart in your prayer, than (to say) seven hundred[4] while allowing your thoughts to drift into trivialities of physical matters. What good do you think can come of it if you let your tongue babble the words of the book and your heart rove around in different parts of the world? And so fix your heart on Christ and he will seize it to himself and protect it from the infection of worldly enterprises.

And seeing that you yearn to be God's lover, I appeal to you to love this name *Jesus*, and meditate on it in your heart so that you never forget it wherever you are. And, assuredly, I promise you that you will find great joy and strength in it; and because of the love with which you love Jesus so tenderly and as such an intimate friend, you will be filled with grace on this earth and be Christ's beloved maiden and wife in heaven. This is because nothing pleases God so much as true devotion to [his] name of *Jesus*. If you love it properly and enduringly and never stop, in spite of anything that people may say or do, you will be carried away in ecstasy into a higher life than you know how to wish for. His goodness is so great that when with heartfelt conviction we request of him one of something he will give [us three],[5] so very pleased is he when we decide to direct our whole heart to love him.

In this degree of love you shall overcome [three] enemies: the world, the devil and your body, but all the same you will have constant warfare all your life until you die, and [all the time] it is essential for you to be concerned about keeping on your feet, so that you do not sink in [wrongful] pleasures, nor in wrongful thoughts, nor in wrongful words, nor in wrongful acts; therefore your longing ought to be intense that you may really love Christ. Your body you are to conquer by maintaining your virginity for God's love alone. Alternatively, if you are not a virgin, by living in strict self-control in thought and action, and by prudent abstemiousness [and sensible attention to duty]. The world you are to conquer by yearning to have the love of Christ and by meditating on [his] sweet name, "Jesus," and on desire for heaven. For from the moment you relish the taste of Jesus, the whole world will seem to you nothing but insanity and harm to men's souls. You will not crave then to be rich, to have lots of elegant coats,[6] lots of dresses[7] and lovers' gifts, but you will value the whole lot as worthless and despise it all, and accept no more than is essential for you to have. Two sets of clothing or one will seem sufficient for you [who at present have five or six]; give some to Christ, who walks bare [and poor] and reckon all of it as nothing as far as you are concerned, since you can't be certain you'll still be alive when they are only half worn-out. The devil is conquered when you stand firmly against all his temptations in honest love and humility.

[And remember me, don't let me be forgotten in your prayers: (I am the one) who is contriving for you to be dead with Christ, whose mercy I stand in need of.] I don't want you ever to be idle, so be constantly either talking of God, or doing something significant, or thinking especially about him, [and] so that your mind may be constantly remembering him, meditate frequently in this way on his passion:

Meditation on Christ's Passion[8]

My king much water wept and much blood he let;
And was most sorely beat till his own blood ran wet,
When their scourges met. Most hard they did them fling
And at the pillar swing; his dear face smeared with spitting.

The thorn crowns the king; most deep is that pricking.
Alas my joy, that sweet being is judged to the hanging.
Nailed were his hands [and] nailed were his feet,
And pierced was his side, so lovely and so sweet.

Naked his white breast and red his bloody side;
Wan was his color, his wounds deep and wide.
In five places on his flesh the blood down did slide
As streams do on the shore—such torture he can't hide.

Now contemplate great misery: how he is judged and dead
And nailed on to tree, the bright angels' bread.
Driven by men most cruel, he who is our soul's good,
And defiled just like a fool, in heaven the holiest food.

A marvel then to see, if we all but understood,
How God in majesty was dying on the rood.
In truth it can be said, love dances first in ring;[9]
What him so low has laid, if not love, was no thing.

Jesu, receive my heart, and to your love me bring;
My desire to you will dart: I long for your coming.
Make me now clean from sin, let love us ever join.
Kindle me fire within, that I your love may win
And see your face, Jesu: now let that bliss begin.

Jesu, my soul now mend: your love into me send,
That I with you life spend in joy that has no end.
In love wound now my thought, my heart lift up in glee;
My soul you dearly bought: make it your lover be.

[Save you, I yearn for nought; this world therefore] I flee;
You are what I have sought; your face I long to see.
You make my soul most bright, as love can alter sight.
How long must I be here? [When may I come you near][10]
Your melody to hear, of love to hear the song
Which is enduring long? [will] you be my loving
That I your love may sing?

If you meditate on this every day, you will be bound to find great sweetness, which will draw your heart upward and make you sink down weeping and in deep yearning for Jesus; and your heart will be snatched away above all earthly things, above the sky and the stars, so that the eye of your heart may gaze into heaven.[11]

And so you enter the third degree of love, in which you are to [be in] great delight and comfort, should you but obtain the grace to reach it. In fact, I'm not saying that you or anyone else who reads this is bound to accomplish everything; you see, it is the decision of God, [who] selects whom he wants to accomplish either what is described here, or something different in some other way, just as he gives people grace for their salvation, because individual people receive distinct gifts from our Lord, Jesus Christ, and all of those who end their lives in love are destined to be placed in the joy of heaven. Whoever is in this degree has wisdom, and discernment to [live] according to God's will.

This degree of love is called contemplative life, which loves to be solitary, without ringing bells or noise or singing or shouting.[12]

When you first reach it, your spiritual eye is carried up into the glory of heaven and there is enlightened by grace and set ablaze by the fire of Christ's love so that you truly feel the burning of love in your heart, constantly lifting your mind toward God, [filling you full of] love, joy and sweetness, to such an extent that no illness, nor mental agony nor humiliation nor harsh living conditions are able to distress you, but your whole life will change into joy. And then, because of the elevation of your heart [your] prayers turn into joyful song and your thoughts into sweet sounds. Then Jesus is all your desire, all your delight, all your joy, all your consolation, all your strength, [so that] your song will always be about him, and in him all your rest. Then you may indeed say:

"I sleep and my heart wakes.
Who shall to my lover say
That for his love I long always?"

All those who love the frivolities and intimate friends of this world, and set their heart on anything other than on God, are not able to reach this degree, nor [the] second degree of love previously mentioned. And for this reason you must abandon all comforts of this world so that your heart may not stoop to the love of any creature nor to any flurry of activity in the world, but so that you may, in silence, be constantly valiant, and resolute in thought and speech in [loving God. You must quite absolutely give your heart to Jesus if you want to reach this degree of love. As soon as you are in it you will have no subsequent need of any affection, nor any accommodation, not even a bed, nor of the comforts the world gives, but all the time you will want to be sitting so that all the time you can be loving your lord. In this degree of love you will long for death, and be happy when you hear people mention death, because that love makes you as certain of heaven when you die as you are at the moment certain of suffering, because the fire of love will have burnt away all the corrosion of sin. And I am sure that as soon as you or I or anyone else is brought into this joy of love, we shall not be able to live as long afterward as other people do, but just as we live in love, so we shall die in joy, and move on to the one whom we have loved. In this degree of love all apprehensiveness, all sorrow, all misery, all empty joy and all sinful appetites are driven from us and we live in the sweetness of heaven. Apply yourself always to persevere and to become better and better]. Our lord does not give people beauty, wealth and pleasures for them to set their hearts on and so make sinful use of them, but so that they should know him and love him and thank him for all his gifts. The greater is their disgrace if they anger him on account of the many gifts in body and soul which he has given them. For this reason, if we wish to escape the pain [of hell and the pain] of purgatory we must hold ourselves back completely from the passions and the attractions and from the evil pleasures and the harmful anxieties of this world and see that the regrets of the world are not in us, but that we fix our heart firmly on Jesus Christ and stand bravely against temptations.

Now I am going to record a song of love which you may take some enjoyment in when you are loving Jesus Christ.

Cantus Amoris: A Song of Love

My song is in sighing, my life is in longing,[13]
Till I see you, my king, so fair in your shining,
So fair in your Godhead.
Into your light me lead, and in your love me feed,
In love make me succeed, and be you ever my meed.

When will you come, Jesu my joy,
To reprieve me from care,
Yourself give to me, for me to see, living evermore?
All my desiring had come if I were with you there.
I want no thing save only you; my one wish I declare.[14]

Jesu, my savior, Jesu my comforter, or all fairness the flower,
My help and my succor—when shall I see your tower?
When will you me call? I long still for your hall,
To see you [and your] all. Such love—let it not fall.
My heart designs the frontal for seating most royal.[15]

Now I grow pale and wan for love of my dear man.
Jesu, God yet human, your love-lesson began
When I to you fast ran, the book of love to scan.

I sit and sing of love-longing which in my breast has bred.
Jesu, Jesu, Jesu, why aren't I to you led?
You contemplate my present state; in love my mind established.
When I you see, and you're with me, then I am quite full-fed.

Jesu, your love's fixed fast: love seems to me the best.
My heart, when could it burst, to come to you, my rest?
Jesu, Jesu, Jesu, for you it is I yearn
And so, my life and loving, when may I to you turn?

Jesu, my dear and my bounty, delight are you to sing.
Jesu, my mirth and melody, when will you come, my king?
Jesu, my help and my honey, my health, my comforting,
Jesu, I desire to die when it's to you pleasing.

Longing in its descent to me my love has sent.
All sorrow from me went since my heart has been burnt;
In Christ's sweet love to believe, that will I never leave
But ever to my Love I cleave: may love my grief relieve,
And to [my] bliss me bring and grant all my yearning,
Jesu, my love, my sweeting.

Longing in me alights and binds me day and night,
Until have in my sight his face so fair and bright.
Jesu, my hope most bold, my joy which is untold,
Let your love not grow cold; may I your love enfold
And dwell in your stronghold.

Jesu, with you I stop and stay, and sooner would I die
Than have this world in its array to my own mastery.
When will you pity me, Jesu, that I might with you be,
To look on you only? My seat appoint for me
And let me upon it sit: thus we together are knit,
And I your love shall sing through sight of your shining
In heaven without ending.

Amen.[16]

The Commandment

The Commandment is a letter which certainly was written for a nun: MS CUL Dd v.64 has a colophon claiming that she was from Hampole, and this might give point to the remarks in the letter about clothing, since Hampole had lax discipline, and its prioress was warned by Archbishop Melton in 1320 about her nuns' fashionable clothing, and the situation seems to have recurred again during the fourteenth century. Here the three degrees of love mentioned in *Ego Dormio* are given the names which they also carry in *The Form of Living* and *Emendatio Vitae*. Margaret Kirkby, the addressee of *The Form*, was in the community at Hampole before she was enclosed as an anchoress, and despite the repetition of the material in *The Form* from the earlier *Commandment*, it seems possible that this letter was also written to Margaret. Because of the repetition, Hope Allen thinks this unlikely (*WA*, p.256), but one might surmise that Margaret would be obliged to leave her letter about *The Commandment* behind when she went north into her enclosure, for the benefit of her former community, and have been sent another version of the three grades of love in compensation. *The Commandment* seems to have been very faithfully copied, perhaps because it has fairly limited reference, specifically to female religious, who were perhaps responsible for its reproduction and circulation; it has been little altered or debased by scribes, as Dr. Ogilvie-Thomson demonstrates in her edition of the Longleat manuscript, and the text printed by Hope Allen needs little correction.

Sources: Allen, *EW*, pp. 73–81; Horstman, *YW* I, pp. 61–71. Discussed by Allen in *WA*, pp. 251–56.

The Commandment

God's Commandment is that we should love Our Lord with all our heart, with all our soul and with all our thought. With all our heart: that means with all our understanding, without making any mistakes. With all our soul: that means with all our free will, without any refusal. With all our thought: that means we must think of him without forgetting.[1] Loyal and true love operates in this way; in other words, as an act of human will. The reason is that love is a voluntary stirring[2] of our thought toward God to such an extent that it is unable to take in anything which is against the love of Jesus Christ, and at the same time is enabled to persevere in sweetness of devotion.

Now this is the ultimate state of perfection in this life; to it all grave sin is opposed and inimical, but not, however, venial sin, because venial sin does not destroy love, but merely inhibits its application and radiant burning. Accordingly, it is essential for all who wish to love God perfectly not only to avoid all grave sins but also, as much as they are able, to avoid all venial sin, in thought, word and deed, and particularly to talk very little, and the consequent silence to be taken up with good thoughts: this greatly aids one in loving God. Now gossipers and slanderers who injure other people's lives by malevolent talk, and all those who esteem their own condition above all others, or who despise any condition which a man would find salvation in, have no more vision of the love of God in their soul than the eye of a bat has of the sun, because flippant talk and nasty remarks are the sign of an idle and malevolent nature which is emptied of God's grace, while someone whose words are always kind, and who considers every person better than himself, reveals clearly that he is constant in virtue in his principles, and full of charitable feelings toward God and his neighbor.

And so that you may attain the sweetness of God's love, I am recording here the three degrees of love; be continually developing up these (ascending degrees). The first degree is termed *insuperable*, the second *inseparable*, the third *singular*.[3] Your love is insuperable when nothing is able to conquer it, that is to say, neither prosperity nor adversity, tranquility nor severe disturbance, physical attraction nor the delights of this world, but it proceeds uninterruptedly in virtuous thoughts, however severely tested it might be; and it detests all sin, with the result that nothing is able to quench that love. Your love is inseparable when all your thoughts and inclinations are gathered together and fastened entirely on to Jesus Christ, in such a way that you are unable to forget him at any time. And that is why it is called inseparable, because it cannot be separated from concentrating on Jesus Christ. Your love is singular when all your delight is in Jesus Christ and finds no joy or comfort in any other thing. In this degree love is as constant as death, and as hard as hell, because just as death kills every living thing in this world, so perfect love kills all physical cravings and worldly materialism in an individual's soul; and just as hell leaves none of the dead unharmed, but tortures all who end up there, so a person who is in this degree of love not only abandons the ineffectual consolations of this existence but also yearns to [experience suffering] for the love of God.

Accordingly, if you feel inclined to love anyone, love Jesus Christ, who is the most handsome, rich and intelligent man of all, whose love remains constant in unending joy,[4] because all earthly love is temporary and quickly vanishes away; [nothing which pertains to it is permanent except the suffering which it has earned]. If you crave the good things of life,[5] love him and you will possess all that is good. Desire him loyally and nothing will be lacking to you. If pleasures please you, love him, because he gives pleasure to his lovers which can never ebb away. But all the pleasures of this world are faint and misleading and let us down in extreme necessity; they begin in sweetness yet their conclusion is more bitter than gall. If you cannot exist without close companionship, raise your affection to heaven so that you may find comfort among the angels and saints who will assist you on your way to God and not hold you back as your bodily friends do. Control your will for a while from all physical desire and attraction to sin, and afterward your will shall be entirely at your own disposal because it will be purified and made so free that you will not want to do anything except what God approves of. If you feel inclined to speak, desist from it from the beginning for the sake of God's love, because when your heart feels delight in Christ you will not feel inclined to speak or chatter at all, except about Christ. If you cannot bear to sit on your own, accustom yourself resolutely to his love and he will allocate you such a secure seat that all the consolation of this world will not shift you, because you will not be attracted to it.[6] When you are by yourself, until sleep comes be the whole time either at prayer or in beneficial meditation, and regulate your praying and your vigil-keeping and your fasting so that these are moderated, neither too great nor too little. But be aware all the time that above all else God desires the love of one's heart, and therefore try harder to love him than to perform any act of self-denial, because unreasonable self-denial is not worth very much, and even nothing at all, yet love is always best, whether the acts of self-sacrifice you are performing are great or small. Be striving with all your strength to make sure of being so disposed within you to the love of Jesus Christ that nothing anyone can do or say can make you unhappy because of the spiritual joy in your soul, and that your mind is inwardly fed only by the sweetness of Christ's love and not by the delightfulness of earthly recreations, nor by the admiration of people should they begin to speak well of you, [nor] by frivolous merriment. Trust in God and he will give you whatever you are [praying] to him for in a responsible way.[7]

Responsible prayer for the soul of a Christian consists in looking and asking day and night for the love of Jesus Christ, so that the soul may really love him, feeling comfort and delight in him, rejecting the ideas of the world and dishonest enterprises. And you may be certain that if you long for his love faithfully and enduringly, so that no promptings of your own body, nor vexations of the world, nor conversations, nor antipathy of other people can pull you back and embroil you in a frenzy of activity about material things, then you are bound to receive his love and find and feel that one hour of it is more delightful than all the wealth which we can behold here could supply from now to doomsday. And should you fail, and succumb to temptations or vexations or to too much affection for your friends, it isn't surprising if he should keep back from you something which you don't want wholeheartedly. He declares that he "loves those who love him, and those who rise early to meet him will find him."[8] You are frequently awake early, so why don't you find him, (you say)? Well surely, if you look for him in the right place, you are bound to find him; but all the time that you are looking out for earthly contentment, you can't find Christ, however early you wake, because he is not to be discovered in the country of those who live on physical stimulation. His mother, on the occasion when he strayed from her, looked for him in tears, both early and late, among his relatives and hers, but she couldn't find him, despite all her searching, until in the end she went into the temple, and there she discovered him sitting among the scholars, listening and answering. This is just what you must do if you want to find him: look for him inwardly, in the faith, hope and love of holy church, tossing out all sin and abhorring it with all your heart, since that is what is keeping him away from you and hindering you from finding him. The shepherds who were looking for him found him lying in a manger between two animals, as you know. If you are sincerely looking for him you have got to walk on the road of poverty not of wealth. The star led the three kings to Bethlehem, where they found Christ inadequately wrapped in swaddling-bands like a pauper's child.[9] From this you are to interpret that you will not find him while you are living in self-esteem and frivolity. How disgraceful! How could you, a mere servant follow in attendance on your lord and your husband with many changes of sumptuous clothing, when he walked around in a short tunic and you are trailing as much behind you in your train as his entire covering? And so I'm advising you to go shares with him before you and he should meet up, so that he can't reproach you with extravagance, since he wishes you to own what you have real need of and no more. He instructed his disciples not to have [two tunics, in other words, one person would not possess] as many clothes as two could be supplied with. Taking immense pains over clothing is preoccupation with extravagance, which he forbids.

The love of Jesus Christ is a most precious treasure, a most delectable pleasure, and most reliable for anyone to put their confidence in. For this reason, he refuses to give it to silly people who don't know how to guard it and preserve it tenderly, but gives it to those who will never allow it to escape from them, either through good luck or bad, but would sooner die before they would make Jesus Christ angry. As an instance of this: on no account would anyone pour precious liquid into a putrid container, but rather into a purified one; in the same way, Christ does not pour his love into a heart contaminated by sin and constricted by loathsome sensuality in physical habits, but into a heart which is beautiful and purified by virtues. Notwithstanding this, a dirty container can be made pure so that an extremely precious object can be safely put into it; and similarly Jesus Christ frequently purifies many a sinful person's soul, making it by his grace capable of receiving the delectable sweetness of his love, and of being his living-place in sanctity, and all the time, the purer it becomes, the more joy and heavenly consolation does Christ place in it; for this reason, in the early stages when someone is converted to God he or she is not able to detect that sweet liquor until they have grown thoroughly accustomed to the service of God, and their heart has been purified with prayer and self-denial and devout thoughts of God. This is because one who is indolent in the service of God cannot be burning in love unless he or she exerts all labor and strength day and night to fulfil God's will. And when that glorious love is in anyone's heart it will not permit them to remain inactive; instead it stirs him or her to do something good that is sure to be pleasing to God, like praying, or making useful things, or talking about Jesus Christ, and above all meditating, so that an awareness of Jesus Christ is never absent from that person's thoughts. This is because if you really love him faithfully he will make you glad as nothing else will, if you are willing to concentrate on him, rejecting all other thoughts. But if you are disloyal, and take someone other than him, and gratify yourself with earthly things contrary to his wish, know this for a fact, he will abandon you as you will have done him already, and will condemn you for your sin.

For the purpose of loving him loyally, you must realize that love for him can be proved by three things: by thinking, by speaking, and by acting. Turn away your thought from the world and fix it entirely on him and he will sustain you. Turn away your mouth from trivial and mundane conversation and speak of him and he will comfort you. Turn away from actions which are futile and raise them up in his name and work solely for his love, and he will receive you. Act in this way and you are loving him faithfully and [you] are walking on the path of perfection. Take such delight in him that your heart is impervious to the joy or the grief of the world. Have no anxiety about anguish, nor about affliction which may descend on your body or that of any of your friends, but commit everything to God's will and continually give thanks to him for all that he sends so that you can sense peace and relish the flavor of his love. Now if your heart happens to be swayed either by the anxiety or by the consolation of the world then you are very far from the sweetness of Christ's love. And be very careful that you don't appear to be one person outside and another inside, as hypocrites do, who are like a tomb which is magnificently decorated[10] outside and inside stinking bones lie decaying. If you take delight in the name of religion, be careful that you take more delight in the actions which are appropriate to religion. Your habit declares you to have abandoned the world, to be dedicated to God's service, to take no delight in anything worldly. Take care, then, that the condition of your heart is exactly as it appears to be in the view of other people, because nothing can make you religious except virtues and purity of soul in spiritual love. If your body is dressed outwardly as your order appoints, take care that your soul is not naked inwardly: this your order forbids. Yet naked your soul must be from all vices, and warmly wrapped up in love and humility. Be in awe of the decrees of God, so that you do not anger him in any way. Make your soul constant in his love and pour out of yourself all sins. Throw away lethargy. Exercise yourself vigorously in goodness. Be courteous and humble to everyone. Don't allow anything to rouse you to fury or malice. Decorate your soul prettily; construct inside it a stronghold of love for the Son of God and make your will eager to receive him as you would be at the arrival of something or someone you loved most of anything. Wash your thoughts clean with tears of love and burning longing so that he doesn't find anything dirty about you, because he is happy when he sees you beautiful and lovely. Your beauty of soul, which is what he desires, is this: You are to be chaste and humble, polite and submissive, never grumbling about doing his will, always finding all wickedness repulsive. In everything you do, concentrate all the time on arriving at the vision of his beauty, and place all your resolve on this, so that you can attain this on your death. Indeed, this ought to be the purpose of all our endeavor: while we are living here we should constantly be yearning for that vision with our whole heart, always finding it a long delay until it comes.

In addition, fix firmly in your heart the consciousness of his passion and of his wounds; great will be the delight and sweetness you will feel if you focus your thoughts on the commemoration of the torment which Christ suffered for you. If you exert yourself in the right way to gain his love and desire him ardently, you will conquer all temptations and anxiety about evil, and trample them under your feet through his grace. In fact, all whom he sees wishing earnestly to love him he helps against their enemies, and raises their thought above every earthly thing so that they can experience the flavor and consolation of the sweetness of heaven. Obtain for yourself the fountain of weeping, and do not give up until you have got him, because in the heart where tears well up there will be kindled the fire of the Holy Spirit;[11] and afterward the fire of love, which will blaze in your heart, will burn away to nothing all the rust of sin, and purify your soul of all filth, as refined gold is tried in the furnace. I know of nothing which is so bound to stir up your heart deep within to yearn for God's love and to desire the joy of heaven and despise the frivolities of this world as much as resolute concentration on the dire and grave wounds of Jesus Christ's death. It will raise your thoughts above earthly pleasures and make your heart blazing in Christ's love, and will achieve in your soul the delectable experience and the flavor of heaven.

But it's possible you will say: "I just can't despise the world. I can't find it in my heart to torment my body; and I've simply got to love my friends whom I know in this life, and take rest when the opportunity comes." If you should be tempted by such thoughts, I beg you to consider where, from the beginnings of this planet, the lovers of the world are now, and where the lovers of God are. There's no doubt, they were men and women just like us, and ate, drank and laughed; and the wretched creatures who loved this world let their bodies relax and lived just as they fancied in the pleasurable sensations of their corrupt desire, and spent their lives in physical gratification and sensual pleasures; and in a flash they fell into hell.[12] So now you can see that they were [great] fools and disgustingly self-indulgent, wasting in a few years the unending joy which would have been appointed for them, if only they had wanted to do penance for the sake of their sins. You can observe how all the luxuries and pleasures of this world disappear and cease to exist. Certainly all those who love them do too, because nothing can remain firmly positioned on an insecure foundation. Their bodies have been handed over to the worms in the soil, and their souls to the devils in hell. But all those who [gave] up the ostentation and the frivolity of this life and stood resolute against all temptations, and ended their lives in the love of God, those people are now in bliss, and possess their inheritance in heaven where they remain forever, at repose amid the delights of the vision of God; and this is because they didn't try to get any more relaxation and comfort for their body than they needed.

I'll give you one piece of advice: don't neglect his name, "Jesus." Meditate on it in your heart night and day as your personal and precious treasure. Love it more than your life. Root it in your mind. Love Jesus, because he made you and bought you at a very high price. Give your heart to him, because it is the debt you owe him. Therefore devote your love to this name "Jesus," which means "salvation."[13] No evil thing can have any living-space in that heart where "Jesus" is faithfully kept in mind, because it chases out devils and destroys temptations and turns out all wrongful anxieties and defects, and purifies the mind.[14] Whoever really loves it is full of God's grace and full of virtues, receives spiritual strength in this life; and when such people die, they are adopted into the orders of angels above, to behold in unending joy him whom they have loved. Amen. *Here ends the treatise of Richard Hampole written to a certain sister of Hampole.*

The Form of Living

Horstman called this "The Form of Perfect Living," but Rolle gives his own title within the work (Chap. 3, Chap. 12); only the Vernon manuscript actually entitles the work. The title means "Pattern, Model of Life," and in what were originally eleven chapters Rolle outlines a pattern of behavior covering attitudes to fellow men and relationship with God. There is a division at the end of Chapter 6 in several manuscripts, which reflects a natural dividing-point in the work; Chapter 7 begins a more "interior" and mystical account of contemplative life, and the two-part structure seems to have been intended by Rolle. *The Form* is not as carefully structured as the *Ancrene Riwle* of 150 years earlier, with its Inner and Outer Rules governing motivation, self-knowledge and worship on the one hand, and general behavior and living circumstances on the other, but like *AR* is explicitly intended for an enclosed anchoress, as both manuscript colophons (e.g. CUL Dd v.64) and the text itself (Chap. 2) indicate. The tradition seems well-founded that the "Margarete" of the concluding paragraph in many manuscripts of *The Form* was the Margaret Kirkby whom records show was enclosed on December 12, 1348, ten months before Rolle's death, and who was particularly helped by Rolle out of some kind of psychosomatic disorder (see Introduction). Rolle may have written the work a short time before Margaret's enclosure, but *The Form* must date from around 1348–September 1349. The other two English letters and *Emendatio Vitae* must antedate it by up to five or six years.

Margaret herself may have come from the La Boteler family at Skelbroke, about a mile from Hampole and in the parish of Kirkby. Her enclosure was first at Layton, in Richmondshire, near the Durham border; subsequently she moved south to Ainderby, near Ripon, and ended her days at her old convent of Hampole; the manuscript of *The Form* at Hereford (Hereford Cathedral MS. P.i.9) refers to the recipient as a "*recluse* of Hampole"; as Margaret was not at Hampole when she first entered her enclosure, it is possible that she returned to a final enclosure in the grounds of her former convent, and it has been suggested that she took Rolle's own cell, ten years or so after his death. The opening of Chapters 2 and 3, and the observation on how much to eat in Chapter 6, together with details given under the heading of the first degree of love in Chapter 8 of prayers to say, all indicate that Margaret was young and had only just embarked on (or was about to begin) her religious enclosure. There is little or no indication in *The Form* that she was a nun before her enclosure, but the records call her a "nun of Hampole"; perhaps her conventual life was brief before she became an anchoress.

Presumably we owe to Margaret herself the wide circulation of *The Form;* she must have brought back to Hampole her letter, for it to be copied and disseminated, and the original to be preserved, although it no longer survives. Hope Allen suggests that the Scropes of Masham may have helped in the dissemination of Rolle's works; they were close relatives of the Fitzhughs at Ravensworth, near to whom Margaret had her second cell at Ainderby, from 1356–57. Chapter 11 is really a separate work, probably earlier, inserted here by the scribe of MS C to give twelve chapters, matching *Emendatio Vitae;* it occurs elsewhere in two manuscripts, in one of which it is associated with an abbreviated version of Chapter 12 (BL Arundel 507). The two lyrics, in Chapters 7 and 8, may also be earlier pieces; one of them seems to echo a lyric in *Ego Dormio.*

The Form was popular and circulated widely in all parts of the country. There are thirty-eight manuscripts of the whole or part of the text extant, and also a version of Chapters 1–6 in verse, and one whole and two fragments of three distinct Latin translations. *The Form* provides a fitting and representative conclusion to Rolle's works. This translation is based on MS C, which I have attempted to emend by Lt wherever the latter is clearly superior.

Sources: Allen, *EW*, pp. 85–119; Horstman, *YW* I, pp. 1–49. Discussed in Allen, *WA*, pp. 256–68.

The Form of Living

There are, in every sinful man or woman tied down by mortal sin, three kinds of weakness which bring them to the everlasting death of hell. The first is lack of spiritual vigor: they are so weak in their inclinations that they can neither withstand the temptations of the devil nor raise up their attention to long for God's love and guide their course in that direction. The second weakness consists in putting bodily desires into practice. Because they have no willpower nor strength for resistance, they are replete with the pleasures and inclinations of this world, and because these seem sweet to them, they remain in them all the time, many to the end of their lives. And so they come to the third state of weakness. The third weakness is to exchange a permanent good for a transitory pleasure; in other words, they exchange unending happiness for a little fun in this present life. If they would only be converted, and get up and do penance, God will arrange a home for them with angels and the saints. But because they choose the vile sinfulness of this world, and take more delight in the mire of their own flesh than in the beauty of heaven, they lose both the world and heaven. This is because a man who does not possess Jesus Christ loses everything he owns, and everything he is, and everything he might acquire; he does not deserve to live, not even to be fed with the food pigs eat. All created things shall be moved to punish him at the day of judgment. Those defects which I have mentioned are not only to be found in men or women of the world, who overeat, or behave promiscuously, or do other noticeable acts which are sinful, but they exist also in others who seem to be self-controlled and living a good life. For when the devil, who is the enemy of the whole human race, sees one man or woman amongst a thousand turn completely to God and abandon all the frivolities and luxury which people who love this world crave, and search for lasting happiness, there are a thousand tricks which he uses to discover in what way he can deceive them.[1] And when he can't lead them into sins of the sort which might make all people who knew them astounded at their behavior, then he will trick lots of them so stealthily that many a time they are not aware of the cage he's trapped them in.

Some he catches with mistaken notions which he puts into their heads. Some with the idea of their unique intellectual powers, by making them think that whatever they say or do is best, so therefore they refuse to accept advice from someone else who is better and more experienced than they; and this is a filthy, putrid arrogance, seeing that person wants to rank his own intellect ahead of everyone else's. Some the devil deceives through vainglory, in other words, empty joy: When any people take pride and delight in themselves at the acts of self-denial which they endure, at the good deeds which they perform, at any special quality which they have, when any are glad when they are popular with people, resentful when people criticize [or rebuke] them, feel malice toward those who are more highly spoken of than themselves, then those people consider themselves so splendid, and so far superior to the way of life which other men are leading, that they think that no one should reproach them for anything they do or say, and they despise sinful men, and other people who refuse to act as they order them. How could you find a more sinful wretch than a person like that? And he is that much worse again because he does not know that he is bad, and is respected and honored by people as someone wise and holy.

Some are deceived with excessive desire and pleasure for food and drink, when they pass the bounds of moderation and come to excess, and derive satisfaction from it, thinking that they are not doing anything wrong. And for that reason they do not improve their behavior, and so destroy the full powers of their soul.

Some are tricked by overdoing abstinence from food, drink and sleep; this comes from the devil's tempting, in order to make them collapse in the middle of their activities, so that they do not bring them to any conclusion, as they would have done if they had been practical and observed discretion. And so they lose their reward for being too ambitious. This is the snare our enemy sets to catch us with, when we begin to hate wickedness and to be converted to God. Then many begin what they are in no way whatever empowered to accomplish: they think then that they can do whatever their heart is set on. But frequently they fall before they get inside the gate; that very thing which they thought was in their favor is a hindrance to them. Well, we have a long road to heaven,[2] and as many good deeds as we do, as many prayers as we say, as many good thoughts as we think in honesty, hope and love, so many steps do we move toward heaven. If, then, we make ourselves so weak and so feeble that we can neither work nor pray as we should use our minds and bodies, are we not greatly to blame in giving way when we most needed to be strong? And I know very well, it is not God's wish that we should do this, because the prophet says, "Lord, I shall reserve my strength for you,"[3] so that he would be able to sustain his service of God to his dying day, and not fritter it away in a short little space of time, and then languish wasting away and groaning beside the wall. And there is much more danger than people think, because Saint Jerome says that a man who torments his body violently with too little food or sleep is making an offering of something which has been pillaged.[4]

And Saint Bernard says: "Fasting and doing without sleep do not hinder spiritual actions but assist them, so long as they are done with discretion; without that, they are vices."[5] For this reason, it is not good to mortify ourselves so much, and then have discredit for our deed. There have been many, and still are, who think that everything they do is worthless, unless they are in such great abstinence and fasting that everyone who knows them is talking about them. But frequently it happens that the more exterior delight and admiration they provoke from the approbation of men, proportionately less interior joy do they experience from God's prizing of them. In my opinion, they would please Jesus Christ much more, if, for love of him, in gratitude and praise of him, they accepted something, whatever God sen[t] at that time and place, with which to sustain their body in his service and to protect them from excessive converse with people, and subsequently gave themselves entirely and perfectly to the love and praise of [their] Lord Jesus Christ who wishes to be loved with endurance and served with constancy. In this way their holiness would be more apparent in God's eyes than in man's. For in every case, the better you are, and the less conversation you have with people, the greater is your joy in God's presence. Oh! what sort of greatness is it, to be worth praise and not to be praised? And what sort of misery it is to have the name and the outward garb of a holy life, and not to be so, but to conceal pride, anger or malice under the clothing of children of Christ. It is a disgusting [obscenity] to take pleasure and delight in the words of men, who can no more judge what we are in our souls than they can know what we think. For frequently they say that this man or woman is in the higher degree of spiritual life when he or she is in the lower; and the one whom they say is in the lower is in the higher. And so I consider it mere madness to be more happy or more miserable because someone is speaking well or ill about us. If we are intent on hiding ourselves from the talk and approbation of this world, God will reveal to us his approbation and hence our own joy. For that is his joy, when we are full of strength to stand against the secret and the blatant tempting of the devil, and when we seek nothing but honoring and approval from God, and want to love him absolutely. And that ought to be our longing, our prayer, and our intention, night and day, so that the fire of his love might set light to our heart, and the sweetness of his favor might be our comfort and our consolation in happiness and grief alike.

Now you have heard some part of how the Devil deceives [inconsistent and silly] men and women with his subtle [and wily] skills.[6] And if you intend to act according to good advice and to follow sacred teaching, as I think you will, you must destroy his traps, and burn all the ropes he would like to tie you up with, in the fire of love. Then all his malice will be converted into joy as far as you are concerned, and to greater chagrin for him. God allows him to tempt good men for their benefit, so that they can be crowned in a more exalted manner when, through his help, they have conquered an enemy so malign that frequently he destroys many people both in body and in soul.

In three respects the Devil has the authority to inhabit a person. In one respect, by damaging the goods which they possess through nature, as is the case with dumb people and others who are handicapped, darkening their attitudes. In a second respect, by depriving them of the gifts which are theirs through divine grace, and in this way he lives in sinful people, whom he has deceived through delight in the world and in their physical pleasures, so leading them to hell with him. In a third respect, he torments a person's body, as we read he did with Job. But recognize clearly that if he does not deceive you inwardly, you need not be afraid of what he can do outwardly, because he can do no more than God gives him permission to do.

Chapter 2

Because you have abandoned the comforts and the pleasures of this world and devoted yourself to the solitary life for the love of God, in order to endure distress and hardship in this life and subsequently to come to [rest and joy in heaven], I believe most sincerely that the consolation of Jesus Christ, and the sweetness of his love, with the fire of the Holy Spirit who cleanses all sin, shall be in you and with you, leading you and instructing you how you are to meditate, how you are to pray, and what you are to do, so that after a few years you shall certainly have more delight in being yourself and speaking with your beloved and your spouse, Jesus Christ, who is high in Heaven,[7] than in the possibility of being a lady[8] in command of the population of the whole earth a thousand times multiplied. People suppose that we live in suffering and in a life of[9] privation, but we have more pleasure and more real delight in one day than they have in worldly things throughout their entire lives. They see our bodies, but they do not see our hearts, where all our comfort lies. If they could see the heart, many of them would abandon all they have in order to follow us. So be heartened and emboldened and do not fear any discomfort or hardship, rather fix your whole desire on Jesus, so that your life may be good and quiet,[10] and there is nothing[11] in which you would be displeasing to him which you do not quickly put right.

The condition of life in which you live, in other words, solitude, is the most suitable of all for the revelation of the Holy Spirit. For example, it was when Saint John was on the Isle of Patmos that God revealed to him his secrets. It is the special goodness of God that he should encourage miraculously those who have no encouragement from the world. If they give their hearts entirely to him and desire nothing, and look for nothing except himself, then he gives himself in sweetness and delight, in the ardor of love, and in pleasure and music, and remains constantly with them in spirit so that his strength never leaves them. And should they any time begin to go astray through ignorance or weakness, at once he shows them the right path; and he teaches them everything they need. No man can arrive at such revelation and grace on the first day, but through long labor and diligence in loving Jesus Christ, as you will hear later.

Nevertheless, then he allows them to be tempted in various ways, both waking and sleeping. For at all times the more temptations, and the more severe they resist and overcome, the greater shall their happiness be[12] when they have escaped. Waking, they are sometimes tempted with evil thoughts, base desires, wicked pleasures, with pride, anger, malice, despair, spiritual presumption and many others. But their remedy is to be prayer, weeping, fasting, keeping vigil. These things, if done in moderation, dispel sin and corruption from the soul and make it pure to receive the love of Jesus Christ, who can only be loved in purity of heart.

Sometimes, as well, the Devil tempts men and women who are solitary and alone in a way which is ingenious and sly. He transforms himself into the appearance of an angel of light and materializes in front of them saying that he is one of God's angels come to encourage them, and in this way deceives silly people. But those who are discerning, and refuse to put their faith immediately in every spirit, but instead ask the advice of well-informed people, these he cannot dupe. On this topic, I have in my books the account of a recluse who was a good woman,[13] to whom the Evil Angel kept on appearing in the form of a good angel, saying that he had come to conduct her to heaven. She was absolutely delighted and thrilled at this. But just the same, she mentioned it in confession to her spiritual director, and he, being a sensible and cautious man, gave her this piece of advice: "When he comes," he said, "ask him to reveal our Lady, Saint Mary to you." She did this, [and] the Devil responded: "There's no need for you to see her; having me here ought to be quite enough for you." But she said that at all costs she must see her. It was clear to him that either he would have to do what she wanted, or she would have no respect for him at all. So at once he produced the most beautiful [figure of a] woman who could ever exist, in her opinion, and showed [it] to the recluse. And she fell on her knees, saying "Hail, Mary." And immediately everything disappeared, and because of the disgrace he never afterward approached her. I'm telling you this, not because I think that he is to be given permission to tempt you in this way, but because I want you to be cautious if any temptations of this kind come your way, when you are awake or asleep, so that you don't give credence to appearances too quickly, until you are certain of the truth.

More imperceptibly, he transforms himself into the shape of an angel of light, which all men universally are tempted by, when he conceals evil under the appearance of good; and this happens in two ways.[14] The first occurs when he entices us toward excessive material comfort and relaxation for the body and delicacy for our senses, claiming the necessity[15] of sustaining our bodily constitution, for these are the kinds of ideas he implants in us: Unless we eat well, and drink well, and sleep well, and lie in soft beds (lit: lie softly) and sit warmly, we are not able to serve God, nor persevere in the labor which we have begun. But his intention is to bring us to excessive pleasure-seeking. A second occurs when, in the appearance of spiritual benefit, he entices us to austere and excessively strenuous acts of self-discipline, in order to destroy our selves, remarking: "You know very well that he who undergoes most acts of self-mortification for God's love is to have most reward. Accordingly, eat only a small amount of food, food which is not nourishing, and drink even less; the weakest drink is good enough for you. Don't bother about sleep; wear a hair shirt and a coat of mail.[16] Everything which is self-inflicted pain for your body, do that, so that there is no one who exceeds you in self-mortification." The one addressing you like this is about to kill you with excessive austerity, just as he who made the other remarks was intent on killing you with too little. Accordingly, if we want to be properly regulated, we need to put ourselves in a good middle way, and in such a way that we can eliminate our vices, and keep our flesh under control, but nevertheless in such a style that it is robust in the service of Jesus Christ.

In the same way, our enemy will not allow us to relax when we are asleep; no, that is when he is busy tricking us in many ways. Sometimes with horrifying apparitions, to make our way of life seem scandalous and abhorrent to us. But at other times with attractive apparitions, lovely visions and things which seem edifying, to make us cheerful for no reason, and cause us to think that we are better than we are. At times he tells us that we are holy and good, to bring us into a state of pride; [at other times he will say that we are evil and corrupt us so as to cause us to fall into despair].[17] But he who is the provider of all things does not permit our sleep to be without any profit for us, as long as we dispose our lives to his wishes.

And be very sure of this: you will not commit sin in your sleep if when awake you always live without eating or drinking too much, and are without sinful thoughts. On the other hand, many has the devil deceived by means of dreams, when he has caused them to place their confidence in them. For he has revealed to them some that were true, and later on tricked them with one that was false. Accordingly, the sensible man's saying is that many troubles attend dreams; those who have trusted in them have been confounded.[18] For which reason, so that you are not deceived by them, I want you to know that there are six kinds of dreams.[19] Two occur which no one, devout or otherwise, can avoid: these arise from a too empty stomach, or an over-full one; under these conditions many worthless impressions are experienced by the sleeper, in various ways. The third comes from deceptive apparitions thrown up by our enemy. The fourth consists of prior obsessive preoccupation and subsequent delusion. And the fifth occurs through revelation of the Holy Spirit, which is brought about by many a method. The sixth comprises prior meditation concerning Christ or holy church, with revelation coming in consequence of this. In these numerous ways does the visual impression of the dream affect men when they are asleep. But with this proviso must we the more reluctantly place our confidence in any dream: there is no means for us to recognize instantly which dream is true, which is false, which comes from our enemy and which comes from the Holy Spirit. Indeed, wherever there are [so] many dreams there are going to be many worthless impressions. And many do they cause to go amiss, because they exhilarate the unwary and so deceive them.

Chapter 3

I know that your life is devoted to God's service. Therefore it is to your discredit if in spirit you are not as good as or better than you appear to by in the sight of men. To this end, direct your thoughts utterly to God, as you have by your outward appearance directed your body. For I don't want you to think that all those who bear the outward appearance of holiness are holy and not preoccupied by the world; nor that all who concern themselves with worldly affairs are sinful. But those alone are holy, whatever condition or rank they are in, who despise all worldly things, that is to say, who do not cherish the things of the world, but burn in the love of Jesus Christ, whose every desire is directed toward the joy of heaven, and who hate all sin, and never give up doing good, and feel in their heart a sweet savor of the love that never ends. And all the same, they reckon themselves to be the most despicable of all men, and consider themselves the most contemptible, most insignificant and most abject. This is the lifestyle of the holy: follow it, and be holy. And if you want to be in state of grace, along with the apostles, do not consider what you have given up, but what you despise. For those who follow Jesus Christ in voluntary poverty, and in humility, in love and in patience, give up exactly the same amount as those want to acquire who do not follow him. And consider how great and how good is the state of mind within you, with which you present your vows before him, because that is what he is looking for, and also[20] whether you are offering your prayers with great yearning love, and strive eagerly, with great fervor, to see him, seeking no earthly consolation except for the taste of heaven, and take your delight in the contemplation of it.

Marvellously does Jesus work in his lovers, whom he rescues from the appetites of flesh and blood by carrying them away through his tender love. He brings them to need no earthly thing, and causes them to ascend into enjoyment of him and to forget the worthless things and physical loves of the world, and to have no terror of any grief that may occur. To feel repugnance for excessive physical comfort, to suffer for his love, seem to them delightful; and to be solitary gives them great consolation, so that they are not hindered in their devotion.

Now you can perceive that many are worse than they seem, and many are better than they seem, especially among those who bear the outward appearance of holiness. And so endeavor, to the full extent of your ability, not to be worse than you seem to be. And if you are willing to act as I am instructing you in this brief *Form of Living* (Handbook of Life), I am confident through God's grace, that if people consider you good, you are bound to be much better.

Chapter 4

At the outset, turn yourself absolutely to your Lord Jesus Christ. That turning to Jesus is nothing other than a turning from all the acquisitiveness and the gratification and the preoccupations and the anxieties of worldly matters and physical craving and worthless love, so that your thinking, which was entirely downward, wallowing in the earth, while you were in the world, may now be entirely upward, like fire, searching out the highest part of heaven, right up to where your spouse is sitting in supreme bliss. Toward him you are turned when his grace illuminates your heart [so that it][21] relinquishes all corruptions and models itself on virtues and good qualities and all kinds of modesty and kindliness; and so that you may persevere and grow in the goodness which you have embarked on, without reluctance, grudging, or boredom with your way of life, you must have four things in your mind until you are in perfect love, since when you have arrived there your joy and desire will become one constant burning in Christ. The first is: the duration of your life here, which is so short that it is hardly there at all. For we live merely in a pinprick, which is the smallest thing that we can see,[22] and it is a fact that our life is less than a pinprick if we compare it with the life that lasts forever. A second thing to bear in mind is the uncertainty of our end, because we never know when we are going to die, nor where we are going to die, nor how, nor where we are going to go when we are dead, and the fact is, God wishes this to be a matter of uncertainty for us, because he wants us to be constantly ready to die. The third is, that we are bound to answer in the presence of the righteous judge for all the time that we have been here: how we have lived, what our occupation has been, and why, and what good we might have been doing when we have been idle.[23] On which subject the prophet remarked: "He has summoned the time as a witness against me,"[24] in other words, he has lent us this very day here to spend in good use, in self-mortification, and in the service of God. If we waste it in worldly affection and worthless things, we must be most severely censured and punished, because it is one of the greatest disasters that could occur if we do not exert ourselves courageously in the love of God, and do good to all those we can, while our short time lasts. And every moment that we do not have our thoughts on God, we can count as something we have lost.

The fourth thing to consider is that we should reflect on how great is the joy of those who persevere in God's love to their death, because they are to be brothers and companions with the angels and saints, loving and thanking, praising and seeing the King of Joy in the beauty and radiance of his majesty, that Vision which shall be reward and food and all the delights which any creature could conceive, (and more than any could describe)[25] for all his lovers unendingly. It is much easier to come to that bliss than to describe it. And besides, consider what agony and what grief and torment those are destined to have who do not love God above all other things which one can perceive in this world, but defile their bodies and souls in physical cravings and carnal desires of this life, in arrogance and acquisitiveness and other sins. They are born to be consumed in the fire of hell, with the devil whom they served for as long as God is in heaven with his servants—in other words: forevermore.

Chapter 5

I want you to be constantly climbing toward Jesus, and intensifying your love and your attendance on him. Don't do this in the way that silly people do: they begin at the most exalted level and descend to the most insignificant. I'm not saying this because I want you to stick to an unwise austerity which you may have embarked on, but rather because many who were ardent at the beginning, and adept in loving Jesus Christ, have harmed themselves by excessive self-denial and made themselves so weak that they are not able to love God as they should. That you should grow continually more and more in this same love is my earnest wish and my exhortation. I don't consider you to be of less merit if you are not practicing such very great austerities; but if you apply all your thoughts on how you may love your

Jesus Christ more than you have been doing, then I venture to say that your worth is increasing and not diminishing.

Chapter 6

With this objective,[26] in order for your mind and your body to be properly prepared, you must understand four things. The first is: what things corrupt an individual. The second: what purifies one. The third: what preserves one in purity. The fourth: what things induce one to subordinate the entire will to God's will. As to the first, you must realize that we commit sin in three respects to make ourselves corrupt, namely with our inner feelings, our speech and our actions.

The sins of the inner feelings are these: harmful thoughts, harmful pleasures, consent to sin, desire for harm, evil disposition, harmful suspicions, lack of spiritual dedication (if you allow your heart at any time to be idle, without being occupied in devotion to God's praises); gloomy fears, immoral affections, heresy, physical passion for any of your friends, or for anyone else whom you love, joy in any people's evil state (whether or not they dislike you); contempt for poor or bad men, giving special respect to the wealthy because of their money, disproportionate delight in any worldly frivolity of no value, despair about the world, impatience, perplexity (that is: uncertainty about what is to be done and what is not, since everyone ought to be confident of what he must do and what he must avoid); persistence in evil, disinclination to do good, annoyance at serving God, regret for not having done greater wrong, or not having responded to a particular urge or inclination of the flesh which one might have committed, vacillation of purpose, distress about acts of penance, hypocrisy, taking pleasure in pleasing people, being afraid of displeasing them, embarrassment about doing good deeds, delight in wicked actions, having idiosyncratic ideas, craving for positions of prestige or rank or to be considered better than others, or richer, or more beautiful, or to be more awe-inspiring, unjustified pride in any natural gifts or those of fortune or grace, embarrassment at having poor friends, arrogance about rich or socially superior relatives (because we are all equally noble in God's sight, unless our actions make us any better or worse than others), disdain of good advice and good instruction.

The sins of speech are these: swearing frequently, committing perjury, spreading wicked opinions about Christ or any of his saints, uttering his name irreverently, contradiction of and antagonism to truth, grumbling against God for any distress, harm or misfortune which may occur in the world, saying and hearing God's liturgy undevoutly and irreverently, malicious gossiping, flattering, lying, abusing people, calling down curses on them, giving them a bad name, squabbling, uttering menaces, stirring up discontent, treason, giving untrue evidence or wicked advice, being contemptuous, speaking disrespectfully, to convert good actions into evil ones so as to cause those to be considered evil who are performing them (we ought to envelop our neighbor's actions in the best, not the worst light); arousing anyone to anger, to reprimand in another what one does oneself, superficial conversation, a lot of chatting, bad language; to speak silly words or words which are not necessary; continually repeating[27] oneself and rephrasing expressions, protecting sin, shrieking with laughter, poking fun at anyone; to praise wicked actions, to sing more for the sake of being praised by people than to praise God.

The sins of action are these: greediness, sexual dissipation, drunkenness, taking or giving money for spiritual services, black magic,[28] disregard of holy days, sacrilege; to receive the body of Christ in a state of mortal sin—breaking of solemn vows, abandoning the faith, growing lax in God's service; to give example by bad actions; to hurt anyone in person, in property or in reputation; theft, mugging, usury, deception, suborning witnesses; listening to evil; to give things to vagabond entertainers;[29] to deprive your body of what is essential, or to abandon it to excess; to embark on something which is beyond our strength; habitual sin; frequently lapsing into sin; pretending to greater virtue than we possess so as to seem holier or more knowledgeable or wiser than we are; to hold a position which we are not qualified for, or that cannot be held without committing sin; immodest dancing;[30] to be the inventor of new fashions; to be rebellious to one's ruler; to oppress those subordinate to oneself; to sin by sight, hearing, smelling, touching, handling, swallowing, by bribes, procurement, signalling, soliciting, by written documents; to continue in the circumstances,[31] that is, the time, place, manner, number, person, living conditions, information, age (these make the sin greater or less); to want to sin before one is tempted; to compel someone to commit sin.

There are many further sins, these being of omission, in other words, of leaving the good undone, when people abandon the good deed which they should perform: not thinking of God, nor fearing nor praising[32] him nor thanking him for one's favors, not to do everything that one does for the love of God, not to be sorry for one's sin as one is obliged to, not to make oneself ready to receive grace, or, if one has accepted grace, not to deploy it as one ought or not to retain it, not to be converted by the inspiration of God, not to adapt one's will to God's will, not to give attention to one's prayers but to gabble on and never bother about anything except that they get said, to perform negligently something one is bound to by a vow, or an order, or has had imposed to perform as a penance, to drag out lengthily what is to be done immediately, not being glad for one's neighbor's advantages as if they were one's own, not being sorry for one's bad behavior, not resisting temptations, not forgiving those who have done one harm, not dealing as honorably with one's neighbor as one would have him do in return, and not returning one good deed for another wherever possible, not correcting those who sin in one's presence, not reconciling disputes, not instructing those who are ignorant, nor supporting those who are in sadness, or sickness, or poverty, or undergoing penance, or in prison.[33] These sins, and many others, make people corrupt.

The things which purify us of that corruption are three, to counteract those three modes of sinning. The first is: heartfelt contrition, to counteract the sins of the inward intentions. And for that it is essential to be perfect, so that you have no intention of ever sinning again, and are sorry for all your sins, and so that every form of satisfaction except what comes from God and lies in God may be expelled from your heart. The second is oral confession, to counteract the sins of speech, and this must be prompt without delay, frank without any excuses, complete without any separating, such as telling one sin to one priest and another to another: say everything you are conscious of to one, or the whole confession will be useless. The third is satisfaction, which itself has three aspects: fasting, prayer and acts of charity, which consist not only in giving food and drink to the poor, but in forgiving those who wrong you, and praying for them, and in instructing those who are about to pass away as to how they must act.

For the third aspect, you are to realize that purity has to be preserved: in the inner feelings, in speech and in action. Purity of the feelings is preserved by three factors. The first is alert and constant thought of God. The second is an endeavor to control your five senses so that all their wicked impulses may be excluded from your body. The third is respectable and useful occupation. In the same way purity of speech is preserved by three factors. One is that you should pause to think carefully before you speak at all. The second is that you should not be very talkative but sparing of comment, particularly during the time your heart is being made so resolute in the love of Jesus Christ that you are aware of gazing on him the whole time, whether you are speaking or not. But you cannot obtain a grace like that on the first day; only by long labor and great endeavor to love [and by] practice until the eye of your heart will be constantly inclined upward, will you arrive at it. The third, that [in] no [way] whatsoever for any reason—not even out of modesty—should you ever tell a lie, because every lie is a sin and is evil and is not God's will. You don't have to tell the whole truth all the time, only if you want to, but detest all lies. If you say something about yourself that sounds like self-praise, but if you are saying it to praise God and to help others, you are not acting imprudently, because you are telling the truth. But if you do want to keep something secret, don't tell anyone except just one of such a temperament that you can be confident that the matter would not be revealed except solely for the praise of God, from whom comes all goodness, and who creates some better than others, and gives them special grace, not merely for themselves but for all those in addition who wish to act well following their example.

Purity of action is preserved by three factors also. The first is attentive consideration of death, because as the wise man says, "Consider carefully your final end, and you will not sin."[34] A second is: Avoid all bad company which gives more of an example to love the world than God, earth than heaven, physical impurity than spiritual purity. The third is moderation and self-control in food and drink, making sure that these are done neither to excess nor to give less than reasonable nourishment for your body, because both over-indulgence and too restricted a regime operate to the same conclusion: neither is the will of God, yet many won't believe this, in spite of everything one might say. If you take your nourishment from such supplies as God provides for the day and the season, whatever it is (I'm not excluding any kind of food which Christian people are in the habit of eating) using self-restraint and moderation, you are acting well, because Christ and his apostles did the same. If you abstain from many of the foodstuffs available to mankind, not by despising the food which God has created to assist the human race, but because it seems to you that you have no need of them, you are acting well if you are aware that you have the strength for God's service and that it isn't ruining your digestion. The reason is that if you are going to have ruined it with over-great abstinence, your appetite for food will be taken away[35] and you will keep collapsing in fainting-fits as if you were on the verge of expiring; and be very sure of this, that action would have been a sin. Now if you are not able to recognize immediately whether your abstinence may be adverse to you or advantageous, [for this reason, while] you are still young I advise you to eat and drink the good or the bad, all just as it comes, so that you don't get misled. Then later on, when you have proved a great deal and conquered many temptations, and know yourself and God better than you [do now], then, if you should see that this is feasible, you can undertake greater abstinence, and all the time you are able to, perform secret acts of self-denial which there is no need for everyone to know about. Good behavior doesn't consist in fasting any more than in eating; rather, you are virtuous if everything is the same to you, scorn [as] praising, penury [as] riches, hunger and want as delights and dainties. If you accept these with praise for God, I consider you blessed and highly ranked in Jesus's eyes. People who visit you [praise][36] you because they observe your great abstinence and because they can see that you are an enclosed religious. But I can't praise you so readily just because of something external which I can see you doing, unless your will is entirely adapted to God's will. And do not give any weight either to their praise or to their criticism, and reckon it of no significance if they are speaking less well of you than they did, but do reckon it significant that you should be more ardent in loving God than you used to be. Now I'll give you one warning: I am certain that God has no perfect servant on this earth who hasn't got some enemies, because only total worthlessness has no enemy.

To induce us to bring our will into conformity with God's will there are three factors. One is the example set by holy men and women, who were diligent night and day in serving God and dreading and loving him:[37] if we take them as a model on earth, we are bound to be with them in heaven. The second is Our Lord's goodheartedness, despising no one but welcoming in all those who come toward his mercy: he is more intimate with them than brother or sister or any friend they feel they can most confide in. The third is the wonderful joy of the kingdom of heaven, which is greater than tongue can tell, or heart can think, or eye can see, or ear can hear.[38] It is so great that, just as nothing in hell could survive because of the great torment except that God's power does not permit them to die, so the joy of the vision of Jesus in his divinity is so great that they would die of joy, if it were not for his good nature, which wants his lovers to be forever living in bliss, even as his justice requires that all who have not loved him should be constantly living in fire, which is horrifying for anyone even to think of. So realize what it must be like to feel it; but those who refuse to consider it and do not feel terrified of it now will suffer it for all eternity.

Now you have heard how you can organize your life and direct it in accordance with God's will. But I am very well aware that you especially want to hear some particular details of the love of Jesus Christ and of the life of contemplation, which you have adopted in public notice. As far as I am given the grace and skill I want to instruct you.

Chapter 7

Amore Langueo. These two words are written in the Book of Love, which is called the *Song of Love* or *The Song of Songs.*[39] Someone who is very much in love often feels the urge to sing of his love because of the joy which he—or she—feels when they think of the one they love, especially if their beloved is faithful and affectionate. And the English for these two words is "I am languishing with love." Different people in the world have different gifts and graces from God, but the special gift of those who lead the solitary life is to love Jesus Christ. You'll say to me, "But everyone who keeps his commandments loves him." And that's true, of course, but not everyone who follows his commands follows his advice, and not everyone who acts by his advice is [equally] filled with the sweetness of his love and feels the fire of [love burning his] heart. Accordingly, the variety of love creates the variety of holiness and of recompense. In heaven, the angels which are most ardent in love are the closest to God.[40] Similarly, men and women who have most love for God, whether they live a life of austerity or not, are destined for the highest state of advancement in heaven; those who love him less, for the lower ranks. If you love him greatly, great joy and sweetness and ardor you will feel in loving him, which are your comfort and strength night and day. If your love for him is not ardent, then little is your delight. No one is able to feel for him in sweetness and joy unless they are pure and filled with his love, and you will attain to that with great effort in praying and meditating, experiencing such meditations as are entirely based on the love and praise of God. And when you are eating, always praise God in your mind with every mouthful you take, saying these words to yourself:

Praised be you, king,
and thanked be you, king,
and blessed be you, king,
        Jesu, all my joying,
of all your gifts most good;
who for me spilled your blood,
and died upon the rood;
        now give me grace to sing
        the song of your praising.[41]

And don't simply have this in your mind while you are eating but both before food and after: all the time except while you are praying or conversing. Alternatively, if you have other memorized prayers which you can get more sweetness from and more sense of devotion than from these which I'm teaching you, then you may keep [those] in your mind, since I'm sure that God will put such thoughts into your mind as he finds pleasing and you are suited for.[42] When you are praying, don't be concerned about how much you are reciting, but rather how well, so that the love[43] of your heart may always be directed upward, and your thought on what you are saying, as far as you are able. If you are in prayer and meditation all day, I know very well that you must inevitably develop a vast deal in loving Jesus Christ, and feel enormous pleasure, and all within a short space of time.

Chapter 8

Three degrees of love I wish to describe to you, because I would like you to reach the highest. The first degree is *insuperable*, the second *inseparable*, the third is *singular*. Your love is insuperable when nothing which is contrary to love of God can overcome it, but it is robust in the face of all temptations, and constant, whether you are in easy circumstances or in anxiety, in good health or in sickness, so that it seems to you that for the sake of retaining it perpetually you would not anger God [one single] time, not for all the world; and should things turn out otherwise, you would prefer to endure all the torment and sorrow that could possibly befall any creature before you would do what would displease him. In this mode your love shall be insuperable, which nothing can pull down—rather it goes darting upward. Blessed is he or she who is in this degree, yet even so those are more blessed who, having obtained this degree, might attain to the second, which in inseparable.

Inseparable is your love when all your heart and your thought and your strength are so wholly, so entirely and so perfectly fastened, fixed and confirmed in Jesus Christ that your thought never slips away from him, never being parted from him except for sleeping; and as soon as you wake up, your heart is on him, reciting *Hail Mary*, *Glory be to you, O Lord* or *Our Father*, or *Have Mercy on me, O God*[44] if you have been tempted in your sleep, or thinking about loving and praising him as you did when awake. When you are not able to forget him at any time, whatever you do or say, then your love is inseparable. Very great is the grace which those who are in this degree of love have, and it seems to me that you, who have nothing else to do except to love God, may reach it if anyone can get there.

The third degree is the highest and most wonderful to attain; that is called singular because it has no equal. Singular love is (the state) where all comfort and consolation are excluded from your heart except those of Jesus Christ alone. Other delight and other joy it does not desire, for in this degree the sweetness of him is so envigorating and enduring, his love so burning and cheering that he or she who is in this degree can as easily feel the fire of love burning in their soul as you can feel your finger burn if you put it in the fire.[45] But that fire, provided it is hot, is so delightful and so wonderful that I cannot describe it. Then your soul is loving Jesus, thinking Jesus, desiring Jesus, breathing[46] only in its desire for him, singing to him, catching fire from him, resting in him. Then the song of praising and of love has arrived.[47] Then your thought turns into song and into harmony. Then you feel compelled to sing the psalms which previously you recited; then you have to spend a long time over just a few psalms. Then death will seem to you sweeter than honey,[48] because then you are most certain to see him whom you love. Then you can boldly declare: "I am languishing with love"; then you can say "I am sleeping but my heart is awake."

In the first degree people can say, "I am languishing with love," or "I am longing with love," and in the second degree likewise, since "languishing" occurs when people are passing away in illness. And those who are in these two degrees pass away from all the acquisitiveness of this world, and from physical passion and the allure of sinful living[49] and place their mind and heart on the love of God; accordingly they can declare "I am languishing with love," and much more so those who are in the second degree than those who are in the first. But the soul which is in the third degree is like burning fire and like the nightingale which loves song and harmony and exhausts itself in its great love;[50] in this way the soul is [only] comforted by its praising and loving of God, and until death comes is singing spiritually to Jesus and in Jesus. And yet it is not [physically] calling out "Jesus" in speech—I'm not talking of that kind of singing, because both good and bad people practice that style of singing, whereas this kind of song no one possesses without being in this third degree of love, to which it is impossible to attain except in a great surge of love.[51] And so, if you want to know what kind of joy there is in that song, I am telling you that no one can know that except for the man or woman who feels it, has it and praises God with it in the form of song. One thing I will tell you: it comes from heaven and God gives it to whichever person he wishes to, but not without great prevenient grace. Whoever has it finds all the vocal talent and all the musicianship on earth nothing more than wailing and whining by comparison. In supreme repose will they remain, those who can obtain it. Layabouts[52] and comedians and those who carry on establishments with people coming and going early and late, night and day, or any who are involved willingly in sin they know to be such, or who derive gratification from any worldly object, these people are as far from it as heaven is from earth. In the first degree there are many; in the second degree there are very few; but in the third degree there are hardly any, because the greater the perfection, the fewer adherents it has. In the first degree people may be likened to stars, in the second, to the moon, in the third, to the sun; in this connection Saint Paul observes: "Either of the sun, or of the moon, or of the stars";[53] so it is with the lovers of God. In this third degree—if you can attain it—you will know more joy than I have [yet] described to you, and among other aspirations and songs[54] you [may in your] longing sing this in your heart to your Lord Jesus [when] you desire his coming and your leaving:

Cantus Amoris: Song of Love[55]

When will you come to comfort me and bring me out of care?
Give yourself to me, that I may see, having you forevermore.
Your love is ever sweetest and that love I adore.
My heart, when will it break for love? I'd languish then no more.
For love tight my heart takes: with joy from here I'd fare.
I stand in silent grieving: for the lovliest one I care;
[For him] my love-longing, which draws me to my day,
And this b(r)and of sweet burning preserves me alway
Till from palace and from his playing at long last I may
Have sight of my sweeting, who then goes not away.
In wealth then is our wa[l]king with no harm or night.
My love ever-lasting longs so for that sight.

Chapter 9

If you wish to be on good terms with God,[56] and have his grace direct your life, and come to the joy of love, then fix this name "Jesus" so firmly in your heart that it never leaves your thought. And when you speak to him using your customary name "Jesu," in your ear it will be joy, in your mouth honey, and in your heart melody, because it will seem joy to you to hear that name being pronounced, sweetness to speak it, cheer and singing to think it. If you think of the name "Jesus" continually and cling to it devotedly, then it will cleanse you from sin and set your heart aflame; it will enlighten your soul, remove turbulence and eliminate lethargy; it will give the wound of love and fill the soul to overflowing with love; it will chase off the devil and eliminate terror, open heaven and create a mystic. Have "Jesu" in your mind, because it expels all wickedness and delusion from his lover; and greet Mary frequently, both day and night. Great will be the love and joy you feel if you are willing to act in accordance with this instruction. There is no need for you to be very eager for a lot of books: Hold on to love in heart and deed and you've got everything which we can talk or write about. For fulfillment of the law is love: on that everything depends.

Chapter 10

But at this point you may question me with the words: "You talk a lot about love: tell me what love is and where it is and how I am to love God properly, and how I can recognize that I love him, and in what situation I am best enabled to love him."[57] These are hard questions for a weak and merely human man like me to [resolve], but all the same I shan't just for that reason avoid showing you my line of argument and where it seems to me the answers could lie, because I am confident of having the assistance of Jesus, who is the fount of love, of peace and of sweetness.

The first question was: "What is love?" and I reply: love is an ardent yearning for God, with a wonderful delight and security. God is light and burning. Light illuminates our reason; burning ignites our yearning so that we can desire nothing except him. Love is one life, coupling together the one loving and the one beloved. Meekness makes us sweet to God, purity joins us to God, and love makes us one with God. Love is the beauty of all virtues. Love is a device through which God loves us and we God and each of us one another. Love is the desire of the heart, constantly thinking about what it loves; and when it has what it loves, then it rejoices, and nothing can possibly make it mournful. [Love is a yearning between two people, with constancy of feeling;] love is a stirring of the soul to love God for himself and all other things for God; this same love, when it is established in God, destroys all immoderate love for any thing which is not good. But all mortal sin is immoderate love for a thing which does not exist—hence love drives out all mortal sin.[58] Love is a virtue which is the most proper affection for the soul of man. Truth may exist without love, but it cannot be of any use without it. Love is the perfection of scholarship, the strength of prophecy, the fruit of truth, the [spiritual strength] of the sacraments, the confirming of intellect and knowledge, the wealth of the poor, the life of the dying. Notice how good love is. If we endure being killed, if we give everything we have to support beggars, if we know as much as all men in the world put together can know, without love nothing is decreed for all these but misery and torture. If you want to enquire how good this man or that woman is, ask how much he or she loves, and that no one can tell; [there]fore I consider it just stupidity to judge someone's motives, which no one knows except God. Love is a virtuous turning away from all earthly things, and is united to God without separation, and inflamed with the fire of the Holy Spirit, far removed from defilement, far from depravity, subject to no vice in this life, high above all the urges of the flesh, constantly prepared and avid for the contemplation of God, in all things unconquered, the sum of all good aspirations, the culmination of all morality, the purpose of God's commandments, the demise of sins, the animating of moral principles, strength while combat lasts, the crown of conquerors, [weaponry] for holy meditations; without it no one can please God; with it, no one commits sins, because if we love God with our entire emotions, nothing remains in us through which we might be subservient to sin. Real love purifies the soul and sets it free from the torment of hell and from wicked subservience to sin, and from horrifying companionship with devils; and from a son of the fiend it creates a son of God, a part-inheritor of the heritage of heaven. We must strive to clothe ourselves in love, as iron or as charcoal do in fire, as the air does in the sun, and as the wool does in the dye. The charcoal is so imbued with fire that the whole is fire; [the air so clothes itself in the sun that the whole is light;] the wool so essentially adopts the dye that it [totally] matches it.[59] In this fashion a real lover of Christ is to act: his or her heart is to burn in love to such an extent that it will be turned into a fire of love, and be, so to speak, entirely fire, and he or she will so shine in virtues that no part of Christ's lover will be darkened by degenerate behaviour.

The second question was: "Where is love?" and I respond: Love is in a person's heart and will, not in his hand nor in his mouth; which means: not in his actions but in his soul. Now many people speak well and behave well and yet do not love God, such as hypocrites, who endure great self-disciplinary suffering, and appear devout in people's opinion, but because they court adulation and the respect and popularity of mere mortals, they have lost their reward, and in God's view they are the sons of the devil and ravening wolves. However, if a person behaves with generosity and consideration to others, adopts simple poverty, and performs acts of self-discipline, this is a sign that he or she does love God; yet it is not through those actions that they are loving God, but by abandoning the world solely for the love of God and by directing all their attention to God, and loving all people as themselves, and doing all the good deeds which they are able to with the intention of pleasing Jesus Christ and arriving at the tranquil repose of heaven. Then they are loving God, and that love is in their soul, and consequently their actions reveal this externally.[60] If you want to speak of goodness and you perform good actions, people assume that you love God. For this reason, be very careful that your thought is God-centered, or else you will condemn yourself and deceive others. No act which I perform externally is proof that I love God, since a wicked man could perform as great physical self-denial, keeping vigil and fasting just as much as I do. How then can I believe that I love or conduct myself better than someone else because of things which everyone can do? It is a fact that no one except God knows whether my heart is loving my God, [so no one knows enough to inform me if I love God][61] because of anything they can observe me doing. Accordingly, love really is in the motivation not in the action, except [as] an index of love;[62] and so if a man says he loves God and refuses to perform in action what lies within him in such a way as to reveal love, then tell him he is lying. Love refuses to be idle: over and over again, it keeps on doing good of some kind or other. If it gives up working, you can be sure that it is growing cold and will disappear altogether.

The third question was: How am I really to love God? And I respond: Real love is loving him with all your strength valiantly, with all your heart attentively, with all your soul devotedly and sweetly. Valiantly one cannot love him without being valiant. Someone is valiant if they are humble, because all spiritual strength comes from humility. Where does the Holy Spirit settle? On the soul which is humble. It is humility which controls us and maintains us in all our temptations to prevent them from conquering us. But the devil does trick many who are unassuming, with afflictions and insults and slander; but if you are exasperated by any great affliction in this world, or because of any expression that people use about you, or because of anything people say to you, then you are not humble, and you cannot love God valiantly in that manner. This is because love is as valiant as death, which kills everything on earth, and hard as hell which in no way spares the dead at all; moreover, a person who loves God perfectly doesn't distress himself whatever disgrace or acute difficulty he may endure, but desires and longs to be worthy to endure pain and torture for Christ's love, and he is highly pleased when people rebuke him and speak badly about him. Just as a dead man [doesn't] reply, no matter what people do or say, so anyone who loves God perfectly is not moved by any words which someone might say. The case is that a man or woman who cannot endure pain and affliction for love of their friends doesn't know how to love, since anyone who loves doesn't find that any problem. Arrogant men or women don't love valiantly, because they are so weak that they collapse at every stirring of the wind of temptation. They are on the lookout for a higher rank than Christ's because they insist on having their wishes carried out, whether this is legal or illegal, whereas Christ wants nothing to be done except justly and without injury to other people. But anyone who is really patient will want not to have their own way in this world, so that they can have it more fully in the next. In no respect can the devil be more quickly conquered than in patience.[63] This the devil deeply loathes, because he is able to keep vigil and fast and endure agony more than any other creature is capable of doing; but patience and love he cannot tolerate.

And in addition you have got to love God intelligently, and you cannot do that unless you are intelligent. You are intelligent in being poor, without any yearning for the things of this world, and in despising yourself for the love of Jesus Christ, and expending all your intelligence and all your strength in his service. Yet some who seem most intelligent are the greatest idiots, because they waste all their intellect in acquisitiveness and frenzied activity on the world's behalf. If you saw a man, with precious gems sufficient to buy a kingdom with, handing them over in return for an apple, as a child would, you might justly claim that he wasn't intelligent but a great idiot. In exactly the same way, if we choose, we have precious gems: poverty, self-denial and spiritual labor, with which we can buy the kingdom of heaven, because if you love poverty, and despise the wealth and pleasures of this world, and consider yourself insignificant and poor, and reckon you have nothing in your account except sin, in return for such poverty you are to receive riches without limit. And if you grieve for your sins and for the fact that you are so long in exile from your country, and if you abandon the comforts of this life, in return for this grief you will have the joy of heaven. And if you are hard at work, and subdue your body reasonably and sensibly in keeping vigils, and fasts, and in prayer and meditation, and endure heat and cold, hunger and thirst, deprivation and intense discomfort, for the love of Jesus Christ, for all this toil you will come to eternal repose, and sit on a seat of joy accompanied by angels. But there are cases where people don't love intelligently but like children who love an apple more than a castle. A lot do this: they forfeit the joy of heaven for a little physical gratification of their bodily urges, which is not worth a plum. Now you can recognize that whoever is willing to love intelligently must love something enduring in an enduring way, and things which pass away must merely be loved in passing, so that the heart may be fixed and fastened on nothing besides God.

To continue: if you wish to love Jesus properly, you are to love him not only valiantly and intelligently but also devotedly and sweetly. Love is sweet when your body is chaste and your heart pure. Love is devoted when you offer your prayers and your meditations to God with spiritual joy and a burning heart in the fervor of the Holy Spirit, so that you feel as if your soul is, as it were, drunk with delight and with the consolation of Jesus's sweetness, and your heart yearns so much for God's help that you feel you can never be parted from him. And then you arrive at such rest and peace in your soul, and tranquility without distracting thoughts of frivolities [or] of depravity, as if you were in silence and asleep and put into Noah's ship, so that nothing can hinder you in devotion and the burning of sweet love.[64] From the time you have obtained this [love], all your [life] until death comes will be joy and comfort, and [you are] really Christ's lover, and he resides in you, in a home furnished in peace.[65]

The fourth question was: how you might recognize that you were in a state of love and charity. My response is that no one in the world knows whether they are in a state of charity unless through some privilege or special grace that God may have given to any man or woman, which no one else could take as a pattern.[66] Holy men and women believe that they have faith and hope and love, and in so doing they are acting as well as they can, and they trust most confidently that they will be saved. They don't know this at present, because if they did know, their merit would be the less. Solomon, moreover, confirms that there are just men of intelligence, and their actions are in the hand of God, and it is no contradiction of this that one does not know whether one is deserving of hatred or of love, but everything remains uncertain until another world.[67] Even though this is so, anyone who were to obtain the grace to attain to the third degree of love which is known as singular, would in fact recognize that he or she was in a state of love; yet that person's knowing is of such a sort that he would never be able to carry himself any more loftily nor be in less of a state of activity of loving God, but the more certain he is of love, so much the more will he be occupied in loving and fearing him who has made him of such a kind, and accorded him that favor. And anyone who is as high as that will not reckon himself more worthy than the most sinful man who walks the earth.

What is more, there are seven criteria for knowing whether a man is in charity. The first is when all craving to acquire worldly things has been obliterated in him. For wherever there is acquisitiveness, there is no love for Christ; thus, if a man has no acquisitive desire, the signs are that he has love. The second is burning longing for heaven. The case is that when people have relished anything at all of that taste, the more they have, the more they crave; and anyone who has felt nothing requires nothing. Accordingly, when anyone is so greatly dedicated to the love of heaven that he is not able to find any joy in this life, he has evidence that he is in charity. The third is, if his language is changed: someone who was [accustomed] to talk of the world now speaks of God and of the life which lasts forever. The fourth is activity of spiritual benefit, such as occurs if any men or women give themselves entirely to the service of God and have nothing to do with worldly affairs. The fifth sign is when the thing that is intrinsically difficult seems easy to do; this is caused by love. For as [Cassiodorus][68] observes, "Deep affection is what brings the[69] impossible to be obviously possible." The sixth is boldness of mind to endure all agonies and afflictions which occur; without this, all the rest is quite insufficient, because it will prevent a just person from being distressed whatever happens to him, in that a man or woman who is just hates nothing except sin, loves nothing except God; [for God's sake] he is not afraid except of angering God. The seventh is exultation in the soul whenever one is in a time of great trial, uttering praises to God in every anxiety which one undergoes: this demonstrates clearly that one loves God [very much], when no grief can bring one down. Now there are many who love God[70] while they are in comfort, but in hardship they grumble and fall into such deep depression that it is almost impossible for anyone to console them, and so they give a false impression of God, quarrelling and struggling against his decrees. It is useless worship that is induced by any worldly prosperity, but that worship which no extremes of grief can eliminate is of supreme value.

The fifth request was: in what situation people are best enabled to love God. My response: in [whatever] situation that happens to allow people to be in greatest physical and spiritual repose and to be least preoccupied with any demands or concerns of this world; the reason is that the thought of the love of Jesus Christ, and of the [day] which lasts perpetually, requires external repose so that it may not be distracted by comings and goings and preoccupation with things of this world,[71] and requires greater interior silence from the dangers of materialism and trivialities and worldly ideas. In particular, all those who love the life of contemplation seek repose in body and soul, the reason being, as a great doctor of the church has explained,[72] that those who remain constantly in one place, not dashing about, but firmly established in the sweetness of the love of Christ, are indeed "the throne" of God. And I have loved to sit, not as a penance, nor as a freakish eccentricity because I wanted people to talk about me, nor for any such motive, but simply because I knew that I loved God more effectively, and the consolation of love lasted longer [with me] than walking or standing or kneeling. This is because when sitting I am most relaxed, and my heart is most inclined upward. But it could be the case that it is not the best thing just for that reason for someone else to sit, as I've been [accustomed to] doing, unless he or she were directed to it by the Spirit, as I was.

Chapter 11

(This chapter, although probably by Rolle, is not part of the original *Form of Living* and has perhaps been added from another, lost, treatise; it occurs here in MS C but is not given in Lt.)[73]

There are seven gifts of the Holy Spirit in men and women who are destined for the joy of heaven and who conduct their lives justly in this world.[74] They are these: wisdom, understanding, counsel, strength, knowledge, piety and the fear of God. Let us begin with counsel, because there is greatest need for that at the beginning of our actions, so that we don't regret them later. With these seven gifts the Holy Spirit touches different people in different ways. *Counsel* means abandoning the wealth and pleasures of the world and of all things which one may become [trammeled][75] with in thought or activity, and, by that abandoning, to be attracted to interior contemplation of God. Understanding is: to recognize what is to be done and what avoided, and to give what is to be given to those who are in need and not to others who are not in any hardship. Wisdom is forgetting worldly things and reflecting on heaven with discernment in everything one does.[76] In this gift there radiates the experience of contemplation which, [as] Saint Augustine declares, is "a spiritual act of corporeal emotion through the joy of an uplifting of the mind."[77] Strength is endurance in completing a good intention so that it is not given up, either through hard times or happy ones. Piety consists in individuals being submissive and not contradicting holy scripture when it castigates their sins, whether they understand it or not; but with all their strength let them cleanse the defilement of sin in themselves and in others. Knowledge is what makes a person confident in hope, not allowing himself to go back on his right course, but repenting of his sin; and that person should amass property solely for the glory of God, and more for the benefit of other people than for his own advantage. The fear of God consists in preventing us from returning to our sin through any evil enticement; and it is then that fear, holy fear, is perfected in us when we are afraid of angering God by the smallest sin which we may be aware of, and run from it as from poison.

Chapter 12

There are two lifestyles adopted by Christian people. One is called the active life, because it consists mainly in physical activity; a second, contemplative life, because it consists mainly in spiritual sweetness. Active life is largely exterior, and it is more laborious and more perilous because of the temptations which there are in the world. Contemplative life is largely interior and for that reason it is more enduring and secure, more delightful, more lovely, more rewarding, because it rejoices in God's love, and relishes the life which lasts forever, in the course of this present life, provided it is properly conducted. And that feeling of joy in the love of Jesus surpasses all other good deeds in the world because it is so difficult to attain to, since the weakness of our bodies and the many temptations which we are surrounded by [are a hindrance to] us night and day. All other things are easy to attain in comparison with this, because this no one can ever merit; on the contrary, it is only granted, through the goodness of God, to those who really devote themselves to contemplation and to quiet for the sake of loving Christ. Two things are requisite for men or women who embark on the active life. One [is] to instruct their household in the fear and love of God and provide them with their requirements, and fulfill God's commandments completely themselves, doing to their neighbor what they wish their neighbor to do to themselves. The second is that they perform, as far as they are able, the seven works of mercy, which are: to feed the hungry, to give the thirsty drink, to clothe the naked, to give shelter to those who have no housing, to visit the sick, to give assistance to those who are in prison,[78] and to bury the dead. All who have the means and ability cannot be let off with one or two of these; rather, they are obliged to do them all if they want to have the blessing at doomsday which Jesus is to give to all those who perform them; otherwise they may fear the curse which all those who refused to perform them, while having the material goods to perform them with, must receive.

Contemplative life has two grades, a lower and a higher. The lower grade consists [in] meditating the holy scriptures, which are God's word, and in other thoughts, beneficial and sweet, which by God's grace one experiences concerning the love of Jesus Christ; and also in praising God in psalms and hymns, or in prayers. The higher grade of contemplation is beholding and longing for the things of heaven, and rejoicing in the Holy Spirit, which is frequently experienced, even [though] in the form it takes people are not praying with their voices, but just thinking of God and of the beauty of the angels and holy souls. So I can declare that contemplation is a wonderful enjoying of the love of God, and this joy is [a way of] worshipping God which cannot be described. And that amazing worship happens within the soul, and because of the overflowing joy and sweetness, it rises up to the mouth, so that the heart and the voice combine in unison, and body and soul rejoice in the living God.

A man or woman who has the vocation to the contemplative life is first inspired by God to abandon this world and all the frivolities and materialism and the debased physical urges of it. Afterward, he takes them away on their own and speaks to their heart and, as the prophet pronounces, "he gives them to suck of the sweetness of the beginning of love," and then he motivates them to devote themselves to holy prayers, meditations, and tears.[79] Later, when they have experienced many temptations, and when the impure assault of thoughts which are trivial, and of frivolous matters, which will overwhelm those who are not able to destroy them, are retreating, then he does cause them to assemble their heart within themselves and fix [it] solely on him; and he opens the gates of heaven to the eye of their souls, so that the eye itself [may look] into heaven. And then the fire of love is really ablaze[80] in their heart, burning there, making it cleansed of all earthly contamination; and from that time onward they are contemplatives, enraptured in love, because contemplation is a vision, and they gaze inside heaven with their spiritual eye. But you must be aware that no one has a perfect view of heaven while they are living here in the body, but as soon as they die, they are brought into God's presence, and see him face to face, eye to eye, and live with him unendingly. For it was him they looked for, and him they longed to have, and him they loved with all their strength.

Well now, Margaret,[81] I have briefly outlined for you a "Pattern for Life,"[82] and described how you can reach perfection, and love the One whom you have given yourself to. If it helps you and is useful to you, thank God, and pray for me. May the grace of Jesus Christ be with you and keep you. *Amen.*

Here ends the Form of Living.

Appendix: The Lyrics

It is difficult to decide which lyrics attributed to him are by Rolle himself, and which by his "school." The four lyrics in two of his prose works (*ED* and *Form*) are certainly his, although they incorporate some borrowed material, but are far less regular in form than the seven short lyrical pieces which occur in four manuscripts and which in two of the four are ascribed to Rolle. In CUL MS Dd v.64 III(MS C) there are two sets of lyrics; of these, the first is written as prose, and the second, written in verse lines and immediately following the first, has a colophon after the penultimate item which reads *Explicit cantica divini amoris secundum Ricardum Hampole.* Hope Allen assumed, probably correctly, that the colophon covers only the second set of lyrics; no claim is made for Rolle's authorship of the first set, written as prose. Of the second set, *A Song of Mercy* and *A Salutation to Jesus* occur in no other extant manuscript. *The Nature of Love* and *Thy Joy Be in the Love of Jesus*, however, are also found in the Lincoln Thornton MS (MS T), where they are joined together, with *The Nature of Love*, as Allen titles it, following as part of the same piece; the scribe of MS C indicates that he knows, perhaps prefers, this arrangement,[1] and it is also that presented by the scribe of MS Longleat 29. I have followed this format in the translation.

Similarly, alternative arrangments of material also occur in the Lambeth MS 853 (MS L), Longleat 29 (MS Lt), and MS CUL Dd v.64 (MS C). MS L contains, without author attribution, the lyric "Love Is Life" (which Allen titles *A Song of the Love of Jesus*) with another lyric, "Jesu, Son of God" (Allen's *A Song of Love Longing to Jesus*) inserted between lines 68 and 69. MS Lt, which unambiguously ascribes the lyrics to Rolle, along with the prose works, has the same insertion of "Jesu, Son of God" as MS L, but whereas the amalgamated lyric in MS L is written as one long poem, in MS Lt the inserted "Jesu, Son of God" is marked off as a separate poem by being preceded and followed by "Amen," thus making a third separate poem of the last section, which begins "I sigh and sob," and forms lines 69–96 of the poem "Love Is Life" in MS C. MS C does not insert "Jesu, Son of God" but has this, immediately preceding "Love Is Life," as a separate poem. I have followed Allen's titles, and arranged "Jesu, Son of God" in the order of MS C (i.e. preceding "Love Is Life"), but have marked off lines 69–96 of "Love Is Life" as a separate part; in MS Lt, of course, it is a completely separate lyric. Following a suggestion of Vincent Gillespie ("Mystic's Foot: Rolle and Affectivity," in *The Medieval Mystical Tradition in England* II, Dartington 1982, p.222), I further divide at line 28, "If I love." The arrangement in MS Lt may well be authorial, since Lt has been shown to have descended from authoritative copies of Rolle's other works. MS Lt also contains another lyric, "Jesu sweet, now will I sing," which it ascribes to Rolle; this is based on two lyrics which occur in the collection of lyrics in BL MS Harley 2253, one of which is headed *Dulcis Jesu Memoria*, the title of a pseudo-Bernardian hymn on which it is indeed based; Rolle may have used this prayer in his devotions, and perhaps even written additional stanzas, but I have not included it here since it is unlikely he wrote the bulk of it. Dr. Ogilvie-Thomson's discussion of "Love Is Life" is in *Review of English Studies* N.S.10 (1959) s.n. Sarah Wilson.

Rolle did not aim to produce lyric brilliance, nor do his lyrics seem to be attempts to capture his mystic *canor;* they are prayer pieces, part of the purgatorial discipline which includes prayer, meditation and reading. Their style, syntax and diction are simple in the extreme. I have tried to match Rolle's rhymes as closely as I could; where I resort to assonance, it must be remembered that Rolle used exact rhyme. Indeed, he is far more confident of his rhyme than of his rhythm. The internal rhymes do not follow the monorhymed quatrain form of the end-rhymes, but frequently move into couplets, (e.g. in stanza 4 of *Exhortation*), and I have attempted to indicate this in my translation. I have also attempted to follow Rolle's use of monosyllabic nouns and verbs, wherever possible.

Sources: Allen, *EW*, pp. 39–53; Horstman, *YW* I, pp. 74–82. The non-Rollean lyrics are printed by Horstman in *YW* I, pp. 71–3. See also Allen, *WA*, pp. 287–311.

Lyrics

Exhortation

All sins you must gainsay through practice of free will,
And yearn to walk in the way which is without evil;

Slide not from that high state which you aspire to still:
It leads to the King's own gate where you can play your fill.

Here if you live sparely, there wealth you yourself win.
No wonder if you be in sorrow for your sin.
Some say that they can see yet blind are they within:
Unless they're now set free then death shall them ruin.

Death dashes all down bare: no one can that withstand,
And makes many ill fare, which they don't comprehend.
I know none whom he'll spare; after all men he'll send.
Therefore from sin be clear: you do not know your end.

Now may we watch a-tremble: in dread so low we lie.
The trump blows to assemble, the Judge is close us by;
The King comes with all his host to fell his enemy,
The proud with all their boast he now condemns to die.

It rings now in my ear: "Rise, dead, to be chastised";
The devil can't come near him who here Christ appeased.
The wicked in their fear for Hell's fire now are seized;
The King has cast the spear: he suits such enterprise.

That day joy shall begin for all who in pain decline;
Our flesh great bliss will win, radiant as sunshine;
Our place is heaven within—I long to sit in mine—
Love Christ and hate all sin, and so earn yours in time.

Song of Mercy

Mercy is most in my mind, for mercy 'tis that I most praise.
Mercy, considerate and kind, from all my troubles may me raise;
Alas! so long I have been blind, walked astray in all my ways.
Mercy I dearly wish to find to lead me in my last days.
Mercy, lead me at the last when I out of this world must wend:
Crying to you, I trust most fast that you will save me from the fiend.

Mercy is true as any steel when rightly it's besought.
Seek Mercy, you who would it feel, for it will ne'er fall short.
Mercy, the vision which will heal, for which I have it most in thought.
Mercy pleases me so well, for through that Mercy I was bought;
I do not know what I may say to Mercy, who is always good:
"Grammerci! you with Mercy pay and it's my solace and my food."

APPENDIX: THE LYRICS

Mercy I am glad to honor, it is so sweet in my own sight;
It lies within my Creator who made us of his own great might.
Mercy is my whole succor to lead me to the land of might,
And take me to the royal tower where I can see my God so bright.
God of all, my Lord and King, I ask you, Jesu: be my friend,
So that I may your Mercy sing in your bliss without an end.

Mercy is so high aloft no sin may take it by surprise.
To your mercy my heart is moved for in it all my pleasure lies.
Lord, let it not be removed when you appoint your great Assize.
With Mercy may my soul be soothed when I shall come to your Justice;
To the Judge I am to come but do not know my day.
Mercy, part and total sum: in it I trust and for it pray.

A Song of Love Longing to Jesus

Jesus, son of God, Lord of Majesty,
Send to my heart the will you to desire solely.
Seize from me all love for this land so you my love may be;
Take my heart into your hand: set me in stability.

Jesu, the Maiden's son, who with your love me bought,
Pierce my soul with your spear which greatest love to all has brought.
In longing, lead me to your light, firmly fix on you my thought;
With your sweetness fill my heart; my cares away be caught.

Jesu my God, my King, neglect not my desire:
My mind, make it most meek, detesting pride and ire.
Your wish is my desiring, with love now kindle fire
That I in sweet praising with angels make my prayer.

Wound my heart entire, control it at your command;
On enjoyment that endures firm make me fix my mind.
May I your love secure; with grace my thoughts expand
Clean me from things impure, let me to you ascend.

Root it in my heart, that memory of your pain;
In sickness or unhurt, your love be ever mine.
My joy in you I see: receive my soul again.
My love all growing be, so it may ne'er decline.

My song is in sighing, while I live in this way:
My life is in longing, which binds me night and day,

Till I come to my King, where dwell with him I may,
And see his fair shining, in life that lasts for aye.

Longing on me descended, for love which I can't leave,
Love has me quite ended, yet grief it will relieve;
Since my heart was branded, in Christ's sweet love alive,
All woe from me has wended, here no more to arrive.

I sit and sing of love-longing that in my heart has bred:
Jesu, my King and my joying, why can't I to you be led?
I estimate in great estate with joy I would be fed;
Jesu, me bring to your dwelling, through blood which you have shed.

Adjudged on cross to cling, the angel's fairest food,
Most dire they did him ding, when he in bonds there stood:
His back raw with beating, and spilt his blessed blood;
The thorn then crowned the King, who was nailed upon the rood.

White was his naked breast and red his bloody side,
Wan was his fairest face, his wounds both deep and wide;
The Jews would not evade torturing him in pride;
As streams in full cascade his blood gushed in a tide.

Blinded were his dearest eyes, bloody his flesh with wounds,
His lovely life was laid full low, and sorrow now him surrounds;
Death and life begin their strife; which will him master more?
When angels' bread was condemned and dead to save our souls from sore.

Life was slain and rose again: now frolicking may we fare;
And death is brought to little or nought and cast into endless care.
May he who you bought have all your thought to lead you by his lore:
Give all your soul to Christ your goal and love him evermore.

A Song of the Love of Jesus

Love is life which lasts for aye, if with Christ it's impressed,
When weal nor woe ne'er change it may, as is written in words wisest;
The night is turned into the day, your travail into rest;
If you will love just as I say, you can be with the best.

Love is thought, with great desire, of God's fair loving;
Love I liken to a fire extinguished by no thing.

APPENDIX: THE LYRICS

Love will cleanse us of our sin, love our cure shall bring;
Love the King's own heart may win, love of joy may sing.

The throne of Love is lifted high, right up to Heaven its span;
On earth it acts most secretly and makes men pale and wan,
Yet the bed of bliss it goes most nigh, I tell you, for I can:
Though the way may seem heavy, Love couples God and man.

Love is hotter than the ember, love will none defame;
Who might the flame of love endure, if it were ever the same?
Love us conceals and sets apart, raises to Heaven's plane;
Love ravishes Christ into our heart, but quite unlike lust's shame.

Learn to love, if you would live when you from here must pass.
All your thought to him you give: it keeps you from distress.
See your heart of him ne'er cloy, though troubles you oppress;
This way you'll keep him, in joy, and love the one timeless.

Jesu, who to me life lent, into your love me bring:
To you take my whole intent, for you be all my longing.
Woe would away from me be sent, done would be all my wanting
If but my soul hear and consent to the song of your praising.

Your love is everlasting, which to us you impart;
Make me in it burning, may its heat ne'er depart;
Take my mind in your holding, and steady it every part,
That I may not be yielding to love this world's false art.

Part II

If I love any earthly thing that panders to my will,
And secures my joy and pleasing if it may on me prevail,
I must then dread my parting, as loathsome and evil,
For all my wealth is but weeping when pain my soul must spoil.

The joy which men have seen may be likened to hay,
Which now is fair and green, and then withers away.
And this world, I maintain, is like this till Doom's-day,
In travail and ruin: escape it no one may.

If you love with all your thought and hate the filth of sin,
Give to Christ the heart he bought: with joy he will you win;
As Christ your soul has sought, whose love will not give in,
So shall you to bliss be brought, and heaven dwell within.

The style of love is this, where it is tried and true:
Constant to stay in steadiness and change for no one new.
Each life which love can find, before the heart it knew,
Turns from grief to nature kind and with joy lives in virtue.

Love Christ then, I entreat, as I can you tell,
And with angels take your seat; such joy see you don't sell.
On earth hate now no plight, save what might love dispel;
Greater than death is love's own might, love is as hard as hell.

Love is a light burden, love gladdens young and old,
Love is without all pain, as lovers have me told;
Love is a holy wine, which makes men brave and bold.
Love shall no jot decline once we in heart it hold.

Love is the sweetest thing that man on earth has known;
Love is God's own darling; love binds by blood and bone.
In love be our liking, I know not a better home;
For me and my loving, by love we're both made one.

But earthly lovers fare as flowers do in May,
And will endure no more than does one single day.
And sorrow then most sore for their lust, their pride, their play,
When they are tossed to care, to pain that lasts for aye.

When earth and air shall burn, then may they quake and dread,
For up must rise all men and answer for each deed;
If they are caught in sin, as now their lives they lead,
Hell's fire they must sit in and darkness have as meed.

Rich men their hands must wring, wicked deeds repenting duly;
In flame of fire both knight and king in sorrow and shame must lie.
If you will love, then may you sing, to Christ in melody;
The love of him overcomes each thing; in love let's live and die.

Part III

I sigh and sob both day and night for One so bright of hue.
There is no thing my heart ease might save love that's ever new.
Whoever had him in his sight, or in his heart him knew,
His mourning would turn to delight, his longing to joy true.

In mirth he lives both night and day whose love is that sweet Child:
Jesu it is, in truth I say, meekest of all and mild.

Wrath would from him go away, though he were never so wild,
Each who in heart loved him that day, from evil would he shield.

Of Jesu then most must I speak, who can my griefs delete.
My heart I feel could simply break when I think of that Sweet;
In love he has laced up my thought; this shall I never forget:
Most dearly, yes, he has me bought with bloody hands and feet.

For love my heart is forced to burst that Fair One to behold.
Love is fair once it is fast, and never will grow cold.
Love deprives us our night's rest, through grace it makes us bold.
Of all actions love is the best, as holy men have told.

No wonder I should sighing be, and now by sorrow am beset:
Jesu was nailed upon the tree; bloodily they him beat;
Consider him with deep pity, how tenderly he wept;
This suffered he for you, truly, if sin alone you'd let.

There is no tongue on earth may tell of all love's sweetness;
Who steadfastly in love can dwell, his joy is endless.
God forbid he go to Hell who loves and longing is,
Or that his enemies him should kill, or make his love be less.

Jesu is love which lasts for ay: for him is our longing.
Jesu the night turns into day, the ebbing to flooding.
Jesu, think on us all for aye, for you we take as King.
Jesu, give us grace, as you well may, to love you without ending.

A Salutation to Jesus

Hail Jesu, my Creator, of sorrowing the cure;
Hail Jesu, my Savior, for me suffering torture;
Hail Jesu, help and succor, to you love I assure;
Hail Jesu, blessed flower of maiden mother pure.

Hail Jesu, leader to light, in soul you are most sweet;
Your love shines both day and night, which strengthens me on this street.
Lend me longing for your sight, and give me grace to weep;
For you, Jesu, have the might my sorrows away to sweep.

Jesu, with grace my heart inspire, to bliss may it me bring:
On you I place all my desire, you are my love-longing;
Your love is burning like the fire which ever up will spring;

Far from me put pride and anger: for them I've no loving.

Hail Jesu, prize for which I pray, Lord of Majesty.
You are joy which lasts for aye, all delight you are to see.
Give me grace, as you well may, your lover now to be.
My longing will never go away, till I come to your knee.

Jesu, to love may I be keen, you are my heavenly good.
Alas, my God, like a ruffian, is nailèd on the rood:
His tender veins begin to burst, all running with blood;
Hands and feet with nails are fast: this changes all my mood.

Jesu, my King, to me is dear, who with his blood me bought:
Spread with spittle is his flesh clear, to death by beating brought;
For me he suffered pains severe: I am the wretch he wrought.
Therefore they press my heart most near; of them forget I nought.

Jesu, fortune of every fight, grace grant me to succeed,
That I may love you right, and have you as my meed.
Your love is firm through each tempting, there always at our need:
As you through grace are my yearning, in to your light me lead.

Thy Joy Be

Be it your joy to intend to serve your God alway;
The wealth the world misspends, see how it slips away;
Try now this to comprehend: with you it lasts for ay,
And your care shall mend, your pain turn into play.

On Christ now set your thought, hating all wrath and pride,
And think how he you bought with wounds so deep and wide.
When you that Man have sought, well-being will betide;
Of riches care right nought, so he from Hell you hide.

They turn their day to night, who love this earthly sin,
And slain are in that flight where we our life shall win;
Those who love not aright and ever anew begin
They lose the land of light and Hell sit deep within.

Do as I you persuade, lift heart in adoration;
Say to him who was dead "Christ, you are my salvation."
Sin sinks down like lead, falls far from destination;
Therefore steady your steed, since spurring will not hasten.

APPENDIX: THE LYRICS

Learn to love your King whose love will ever last;
Keep him in your musing, and fasten his love so fast
That no worldly thinking by quibbling it outcast;
Your song and your sweeting he will be at the last.

In Christ be your solace, let his love give you cheer:
With joy follow his trace, and seek to sit him near;
Ever seeking his face you will make your soul clear;
High he appoints your place who in love persevere.

Keep his commandments ten; hold back from mortal sin;
Forsake the games of men, that you his love may win.
Your heart from him shall burn, your love never decline.
Longing will you liven Heaven to dwell within.

Think now on his meekness, how poorly he was born;
Behold his bloody flesh: his head is pricked by thorn.
Your love must not grow less; he saved you, all forlorn.
To serve him in sweetness, to that we have all sworn.

Make firm your heart to flee from all your worldly care,
Till you in rest may be; save now your soul most bare.
His love take unto you and love him more and more,
His face that you may see when you shall from here fare.

In time of temptation of love you have great need
To steady you stably and give grace to succeed;
Live forever with your King, in his love to feed;
Very little is my knowing to write of his fair head.

Love him well with all your might, while you are living here,
And look well to your sight, to you be none else dear.
Say to him day and night: "When may I draw you near?
Lead me up to your light, your melody to hear."

To that life be taken where you may be ever living;
Give him your love as token that you would with him sing;
Joy in your breast has woken when you are him loving;
Your soul then has he fed, in sweetest love burning.

(*All Vanities Forsake*)

All empty things forsake if you his love will feel;
Your heart to him donate: he can keep it so well.

Your mirth no man may slake, God's joy it is you feel.
Your thought never let quake, your love never dispel.

From sin's great bitterness your way now fast you set;
This world's low wickedness may it not with you meet;
This earthly fussiness, which brings men such regret,
Will make your love much less, if that is your target.

All of us love some thing, thinking with reason's skill,
In it thus delighting when it comes to us still;
So do Christ's own bidding and love him well, by his will,
Whose love has no ending in joy without evil.

Those who love bodily are likened to the swine,
In filth let themselves lie, their fairness undermined.
Their love departs poorly, plunged where they sore repine.
More sweet is love holy, which never will decline.

If you love, while you may, the King of Majesty,
Your woe departs away, happiness hies to you,
Your night turns into day, may your bliss ever be.
When you are as I say, I beg you: think of me.

Our thoughts now let us set:[2] together in Heaven to dwell,
For there the good are met whom Christ holds back from Hell.
When we our sins regret then great news we may tell:
That we from far have fetched the love none shall dispel.

The world, cast it behind, say, "Sweet Jesu, consent
Me fast in love to bind; give me grace to lament;
By your love make me kind: I am with love ardent
That I your love may find: such good my grief must stint.

"With love wound me within, and to your light me lead.
Now make me pure from sin, that death I may not dread.
As you to save mankind suffered your sides to bleed,
Give me the grace to win the sight of you as meed."

His love is tried and true, for those who him adore.
Since first that I it knew, recovered I am from care.
I found it ever new to teach me God's own lore,
And now I need not rue that I have suffered sore.

In love keep heart on high: try the Devil's wiles to end;
Your day's diversity all sadness will suspend.
When death approaches nigh, and you must from here wend,
You shall see him with eye, and come to Christ, your friend.

Make firm yourself to feast in Christ your desiring;
And choose him as the best, he is your wedded King;
For joy your heart shall burst to have such a sweeting;
I think it worst of all to love one other thing.

His love is life to all who living well must be;
Lead him through your portal: let him not from you flee.
Full soon he will you call, your seat is kept with glee,
And have you in his hall, forever his face to see.

This meed for you I name, to rouse your mind to fire,
And make your love the same, in truth, as your own sire:
Each who to love might aim, if he be love's denier,
To suff'ring turns his game; he asked for such poor hire.

Sin that is so sour, give it in you no scope,
Of love take you the flower, so you can play with hope;
Sweeter is the savor than of field or wood-slope.
Seat him as your succor: as leech of limb to cope.

Take Jesu in your thinking, his love he will you send;
Your love and your liking, to him you must both lend.
Take good care of praying: that you can always mend,
So shall you love your King in Joy without all end.

Ghostly Gladness[3]

Ghostly gladness in Jesu, and joy in heart, with sweetness in soul of the scent of heaven in hope, is health unto healing; and my life lives in love, and lightheartedness laps over my thoughts. I dread nothing which can work woes for me, so much do I wit of well-being. It would be no wonder if death were dear, so that I could see him whom I seek. But now it lingers far from me and I must live here till he will release me. Listen and learn of this lore, and you shall not dislike it. Love makes me murmur and joy brings me into jesting. Look you lead your life in lightheartedness; hopelessness, hold it far apart; sorriness, let it not sit with you; but in gladness of God evermore give forth glee. Amen.

Here conclude the songs of holy love of Richard of Hampole.

Notes

Introduction

1. *Officium de Sancto Ricardo de Hampole*, ed. G.G. Perry, in *The English Prose Treatises of Richard Rolle de Hampole*, EETS OS 20 (rev. ed. 1921), Lectio prima, p.xxv; also in R. Woolley, *The Officium and The Miracula of Richard Rolle of Hampole* (London: 1919).
2. *Officium*, Lectio octava, p.xxxvi; trans. in F. Comper, *The Life of Richard Rolle* (1933), p.302.
3. Comper, pp.301–2; Perry, Lectio prima, p.xxv.
4. Allen, *WA*, p.526.
5. Comper, p.307; Perry, Lectio octava, pp.xxxiv–xxxv.
6. Perry, Lectio octava, p.xxxvi.
7. Allen, *WA*, p.508.
8. Comper, pp.310ff.
9. Allen, *WA*, p.507.
10. Allen, *WA*, p.516.
11. Allen, *WA*, p.523.
12. Allen, *WA*, pp.521–2.
13. *Judica Me Deus*, A, ed. J.P. Daly (Salzburg: 1984), p.2.
14. *Incendium Amoris*, Chap.12; *Melos Amoris*, Chap.4 and Chap.36.
15. Allen, *WA*, Chap. XVI, pp.430–526; Comper, Part I; G. Hodgson, *The Sanity of Mysticism: A Study of Richard Rolle* (1926).
16. Allen, *WA*, pp.39–43, on Vienna MS National Bibliothek 4483.
17. E.g. del Mastro, *The Fire of Love and the Mending of Life*, p.11, citing Comper, pp.3–4.
18. Allen, *WA*, pp.449–52.
19. Allen, *WA*, pp.452–58.
20. Allen, *WA*, pp.453.
21. Allen, *WA*, p.433.
22. Allen, *WA*, p.435.

NOTES

23. Allen, *WA*, pp.444–449.
24. Allen, *WA*, p.459.
25. E. Colledge, *The Mediaeval Mystics of England* (1962), p.51.
26. Allen, *WA*, p.443.
27. Allen, *WA*, p.19, citing M. Noetinger, in *The Month* 147 (Jan 1926).
28. Allen, *WA*, p.458.
29. CUL MS Dd.v.64; Allen, *WA*, p.37.
30. Allen, *WA*, p.459.
31. Del Mastro, p.16.
32. *Incendium Amoris*, Chap.11; *Judica Me* B 1, ed. Daly, p.18.
33. Allen, *WA*, p.459.
34. *Comment on the Canticles*, ed. Boenig (1984), pp.106–7.
35. Clifton Wolters, *The Fire of Love* (1972), p.15.
36. Allen, *WA*, p.465.
37. *Contra Amatores Mundi*, ed. and trans. Theiner (1968), p.179.
38. Perry, p.xxxiv.
39. Daly, p.2.
40. Daly, p.2.
41. Daly, p.2.
42. Allen, *WA*, p.121, translates "mouldy bread"; corrected by E.F.J. Arnould, *The Melos Amoris of Richard Rolle of Hampoule* (Oxford, 1957), Foreword, p.viii.
43. Daly, p.liii.
44. Allen, *WA*, p.55 and p.59.
45. Allen, *WA*, p.517.
46. Perry, pp.xxxiv–xxxvi; Comper, pp.307–8.
47. Allen, *WA*, p.55.
48. See note 42.
49. Allen, *WA*, pp.517ff.
50. Chap. 1.
51. Allen, *WA*, pp.502,503.
52. R.M. Clay, *The Hermits and Anchorites of England* (1914), cited in Allen, *WA*, p.502.
53. Allen, *WA*, p.506.
54. Allen, *WA*, p.508.
55. Allen, *WA*, p.501.
56. Allen, *WA*, p.456.
57. Allen, *WA*, p.505.
58. Allen, *WA*, pp.490–500.
59. E.J.F. Arnould, *Melos Amoris*, pp.210–238.
60. N. Marzac, *Richard Rolle de Hampole* 1300–1349 (1968), pp.24f.
61. W. Riehle, *The Middle English Mystics* (1981), pp.7 and 171.
62. M. Noetinger, "The Biography of Richard Rolle," *The Month* 147 (1926), pp.22–30.
63. John Clark, "Richard Rolle: A Theological Re-assessment," *Downside Review* 101 (1983), p.132. Clark thinks it unlikely that Rolle was at the Sorbonne; del Mastro, pp.12–13, is sceptical.
64. Allen, *WA*, p.513; p.493. The question of Rolle's priesthood is raised by

Noetinger (n.62) and is based on a reference in *Melos* to his "receiving the Saviour's Blood," which only priests then did. See Wolters, *The Fire of Love*, p.33, fn.2.

65. Allen, *WA*, p.520.

66. Allen, *WA*, pp.518–19.

67. *Incendium Amoris*, Chap.15.

68. Margaret Jennings, "Richard Rolle and the Three Degrees of Love," *Downside Review* 93 (1975), pp.193–200. Jennings shows that neither Rolle's *calor, dulcor, canor*, nor his *insuperable, inseparable, singular* schemes can be shown to correspond to *purgatio, illuminatio* and *unio*.

69. A systematic study of medieval English and German mystical imagery, especially in relation to patristic and biblical sources is given in Wolfgang Riehle, *The Middle English Mystics* (1981).

70. Riehle, pp.104ff.

71. Riehle, p.104.

72. Riehle, p.104.

73. Hilton, *Scale of Perfection*, Book I, Chap.26; *Cloud of Unknowing*, Chap. 45.

74. Allen, *WA*, p.5.

75. E.g. Phyllis Hodgson, *Three Fourteenth-Century Mystics* (1967).

76. Riehle, p.1.

77. *Incendium Amoris*, Prologue and Chap. 15.

78. Riehle, p.1.

79. Riehle, p.5.

80. R.W. Chambers, "On the Continuity of English Prose from Alfred to More and his School," in *Harpsfield's Life of More*, ed. E.V. Hitchcock, EETS 186 (1932), p. ci and also p. cviii, fn.2.

81. Del Mastro, p.25.

82. Allen, *WA*, p.249.

83. Allen, *WA*, p.249.

84. G. Liegey, "Richard Rolle's Carmen Prosaicum, an Edition and Commentary," *Medieval Studies* 19 (1957), pp.15–36, esp. 23–24.

85. G. Shepherd, *Alliterative Poetry in Late Medieval England*, Proceedings of the British Academy, Vol. LVI (1970), p.17.

86. Liegey, in "The 'Canticum Amoris' of Richard Rolle," *Traditio* 12 (1966), pp.369–91.

87. Allen, *WA*, p.288.

88. Riehle, p.5.

89. See J. Gilmour, "Notes on the Vocabulary of Richard Rolle," *Notes and Queries* 201 (1956), pp.94–95.

90. Shepherd, p.16.

91. Jennings, pp.198f.

92. Allen, *WA*, p.203.

93. Allen, *EW*, p.xvii; *WA*, p.90. But contrast Liegey, *Traditio* 12, pp.372f.

94. Liegey, *Traditio* 12, p.373.

95. The dating assigned by Allen in *WA* is currently being reconsidered. See J.P.H. Clark, "Richard Rolle as a Biblical Commentator," *The Downside Review* (1986), pp.165–213.

96. Outlined in Boenig, *Richard Rolle, Biblical Commentaries* (1984), pp.3–13.
97. Cited in Allen, *WA*, p.120.
98. D. Everett, "The Middle English Prose Psalter of Richard Rolle of Hampole," *Modern Language Review* 17 (1922), pp.217–227 and 337–50.
99. Allen, *WA*, p.196.
100. N.F. Blake, "Middle English Prose and its Audience," *Anglia* 90 (1972), pp.446–7 and fn.16.
101. Allen, *WA*, p.108, citing *Judica B;* cf. Vandenbroucke, *Le Chant de l'Amour*, Paris (1971), p.94.
102. Daly, p.liii.
103. Daly, p.viii.
104. Ed. and trans. P. Theiner, University of California, (1968), Chap.5, p.168.
105. V. Gillespie, "Mystic's Foot: Rolle and Affectivity," in *The Medieval Mystical Tradition in England*, 2, Papers read at Dartington Hall, July 1982, ed. Marion Glasscoe (Exeter: Univ. Press, 1982), p.218.
106. Allen, *WA*, p.288 and p.118; cf. also R.M. Wilson, "Three Middle English Mystics," *Essays and Studies* n.s.9 (1956), p.94.
107. Shepherd, p.18.
108. E.g. by Vandenbroucke, p.58 and Shepherd, p.18.
109. Liegey, "Carmen Prosaicum," pp.18–19, p.21; Allen, *WA*, pp.79–80.
110. Allen, *WA*, pp.79–80. But also see L. Smedick, *Med. Studs.*, 41 (1979), p.405 n.3, for a different view.
111. Liegey, "Carmen Prosaicum," p.15.
112. Liegey, "Carmen Prosaicum," p.23.
113. Alford, "Biblical *Imitatio* in the Writings of Richard Rolle," *ELH* 40 (1973), pp.1–23.
114. Allen, *WA*, p.164, pp.491f.
115. *Melos Amoris*, Intro., p.lxviii; Allen, *WA*, p.120.
116. Nicholas Watson, in a private communication received after this was written, suggests that in fact *Melos* immediately precedes *Emendatio Vitae.*
117. Allen, *WA*, pp.109–10 and fn.1.
118. Daly, p.111.
119. Allen, *EW*, p.xxvi; Arnould, *Melos Amoris*, p.lxvi and fn.7.
120. Allen, *WA*, p.141.
121. Alford, p.10.
122. Vandenbroucke, *Le Chant de l'Amour*, p.59.
123. Vandenbroucke, pp.59–60.
124. Clark, *Downside Rev.* 101, pp.119, 117.
125. Daly, *Judica B 1*, p.93.
126. Daly, p.xxii.
127. *The Prayers and Meditations of St Anselm*, trans. and Intro. by Sr. Benedicta Ward, S.L.G. (1973); R.W. Southern, Foreword, p.10.
128. Colledge, p.22.
129. Colledge, p.23.
130. Liegey, "Carmen Prosaicum," p.29.
131. Vandenbrouke, p.72.
132. Colledge, p.27.

133. Riehle, p.25.
134. Colledge, p.25.
135. Colledge, p.27. Also Riehle, p.152.
136. R.W. Chambers, pp.xlv–clxxiv and p.xciii.
137. Colledge, pp.41–43.
138. Chambers, p.xciii.
139. Colledge, p.52.
140. Ed. W.M. Thompson, EETS OS 241 (1958), p.35.
141. Horstman, *YW* II, p.258.
142. Perhaps Rolle's verse should be printed as eight short lines, rather than four (irregular) long lines; it would then resemble, presumably fortuitously, the scaldic verse of the Vikings, which also used internal rhyme (but within the short lines of three stresses and six syllables) and alliteration linking pairs of short lines (see C. Fell, ed. and trans., *Egils Saga* (London: Dent, 1975), pp.xxiii–iv). Rolle's verse is far less regular than the highly exacting techniques of scaldic verse, but seems to be based on a similar blend of syllabic and stress patterns. For his Latin verse he seems to have borrowed the native English alliterative technique, apparently his own innovation; see Liegey, "Canticum Amoris," p.379.
143. G.V. Smithers, in *Early Middle English Verse and Prose*, ed. J.A.W. Bennett and G.V. Smithers (Oxford: Clarendon Press, 1968), p.224.
144. Chambers, p.xcvi.
145. Allen, *WA*, pp.521–2.
146. As in B.L.MS 37049, or the verse rendering of the first half of *The Form of Living* in B.L.MS Cotton Tib.E.vii. ff.85v–90r.
147. Richard Kiekhefer, *Unquiet Souls: the Fourteenth-Century Saints and their Religious Milieu* (Chicago: University Press, 1985).

The Psalter: Prologue

1. No source has been found for this section of the Prologue; Rolle has translated the first two sentences from his own *Latin Psalter*.
2. Augustine is the source for this section.
3. *Indeed this radiant book . . . purest softness:* Based on Cassiodorus, from whom derives the expression "angels, whom we cannot hear," which contradicts Rolle's own consciousness of angelic song; Rolle translates the rhetorical patterning of Cassiodorus by a closely corresponding pattern of verb inflections and word order in his Middle English.
4. *Psalterium*, Greek ψαλτήριον "a stringed instrument played by twanging," from ψάλλειν," to twang (*OED*). The Hebrew is *nebel.* Like the dulcimer, the psaltery originated in the Middle East, where it survives as the *ganun.* It generated many descendents as it moved West: the *kantele* of Finland and the *zither* of the Austrian Tyrol among them. The psaltery was plucked, the dulcimer is "basically a psaltery struck with hammers. The psaltery reached Europe in the twelfth century through the Crusades; the dulcimer may not have arrived until the fourteenth century. . . . The two instruments had evolved their separate identities in the East before their arrival in Europe" (David Munrow, *Instruments of the Middle Ages and Renaissance* [Oxford, 1976], p.23).

NOTES

5. In fact, the sound board of the psaltery is underneath the instrument and normally rests on the player's lap as he or she plays, although it could also be played leaning up against the chest (Munrow, p.23). Rolle seems to be thinking of the sound as it is emitted by the strings, which allegorize the finely tuned personality.

6. This designation of a tripartite scheme for the 150 psalms seems to bear some similarity to the threefold mystic way of *purgatio*, *illuminatio* and *unio*. The actual interpretations, derived essentially from Peter Lombard, are not predominantly mystical and are consistent with the view expressed here, that the theme of the last triad is a future eternity with God rather than a knowledge of him here in mystic rapture. But Rolle almost at once qualifies this by referring to "mystic contemplation of the highest degree."

7. Rolle's own translation of Psalm 150 is "Let every spirit praise the Lord," on which his interpretation rests; I use here the commonly accepted translation.

8. That is, those in the world as distinct from the enclosed religious.

9. Rolle addresses the individual who will be meditating from his psalter by using the pronoun "thou," indicating the kind of intimacy which I have tried to convey by the expression "my reader."

10. Based on Peter Lombard, source of many of Rolle's interpretations in both English and Latin Psalters, but expanded by Rolle, as the Psalter commentaries also are. Rolle takes the Lombard's technical terms "subject matter," "intention" and "method of instruction," and the definition of the "title," "Book of Hymns," which derive from the scholastic method of the University of Paris. The minute distinctions "topics" in structuring scholastic works can be seen in Chaucer's *Parson's Tale;* Rolle avoids such scholarly extremes and makes the borrowings his own by adding emotive expressions like "rejoicing and tenderness in the soul," establishing an intimacy of tone.

11. It was traditional to "excuse" one's writing because of simplicity of expression or choice of language medium. Rolle's account of his translation method of "following the letter" resembles that of King Alfred in the preface to his translation of Gregory's *Pastoral Care*, and is also conventional. In fact, Rolle follows the letter rather than the sense, and often produces unidiomatic English as a result (e.g. Psalm 61:2). Rolle's premonition was correct: The work did fall into the wrong hands and was much expanded by heretical Lollard material.

The Psalter: Psalm 3

12. Rolle wrote "in God of him," signaling to the learner of Latin the function of *eius* at the end of the clause; this is a gloss rather than a translation.

13. *Saturated with sleep:* The Latin really means "drugged with sleep" and is corrected in the new Latin version (1945) to "lie down and go to sleep."

The Psalter: Psalm 12

14. The yearning for death expressed here occurs throughout Rolle's work; here he generalizes the death wish, assuming it to be common to all mystics. One original addition in his Latin Psalter indicates that the "last degree of per-

fection" consists in desiring to die and be with Christ. Death, claims Rolle in *Incendium Amoris* (Chap. 16) would be like heavenly music to him.

15. This should perhaps read "burning in love for you" ("thee," for MS *me*), a reflection of Rolle's own experience of "burning fire," *calor*.

16. Puns: *hele* in Middle English means both "health" and "salvation"; to Rolle Jesus means "Savior," and the allusion echoes his own devotion to the Holy Name.

17. Rolle assumes that his "song" is a universal mystic experience, but significantly also regards the daily round as a "song of praise."

The Psalter: Psalm 56

18. Peter Lombard saw in this psalm of David fleeing from Saul a type of Christ; Rolle's interpretation is based on the soul, and largely original.

19. I have reproduced, for interest, the literal grammar of Rolle's rendering, which exactly follows the Latin syntax except that in this instance Rolle (or a scribe) has added the verb "to be"—in the wrong number; normally Rolle follows Latin idiom in omitting the copula. This shows clearly how he was using the Psalms as a Latin Primer, but it produces peculiar English, which for the most part I have tried to normalize.

20. Rolle is right in regarding the harp as the nearest equivalent to the ancient *cithara*, a triangular instrument like a lyre, and very different from the medieval *gittern*, which shares the name of the ancient instrument and was the precursor of the modern *guitar*. Medieval musicians discussing in Latin the theory of music use the term "cythara" for the harp, which was so brilliantly used in secular entertainment (Munrow, p.22); Vincenzo Galilei observed in 1581 that the harp of Ireland was the ancient cithara with many strings (Munrow, p.74).

21. Rolle's Latin Psalter uses rhyme at this point, in an attempt to echo the *jubilus;* this equivalent attempt in English, like so much of Rolle's English verse, is very weak by comparison.

22. An exact translation of Peter Lombard; both Rolle and his source avoid repetition where the poetic language of the Psalms involves repeating phrases or imitating passages from other psalms.

The Psalter: Psalm 61:2

23. Not derived from Peter Lombard nor from Rolle's *Psalter* but closely paralleling the *Jesu Dulcis Memoria;* it is repeated (in Latin) in Chapter 46 of *Incendium Amoris*, and this, in turn, is echoed in the lyric in *Ego Dormio* in the lines, "A marvel then to see . . . make it your lover be." This instance of rhyme, together with those in Psalm 3 and Psalm 56, have been held to prove that Rolle is the author of the English Psalter; there are no other instances in the work.

24. *Weal:* "happiness."

25. Probably an error for "love of his praising."

26. I have given a literal rendering of both psalm translation and verselet in this extract from Psalm 61 which concludes Hope Allen's selection. Psalm 61:2 illustrates, apart from the rhyme, the literal translation from the Latin, not sup-

plying the verb, and translating *nam et* by the unidiomatic "for and," and also Rolle's use of the old word *hele* "healing," or "salvation" in the translation, but his preference, as elsewhere, for French *salvation* in the commentary, thus enabling himself to pun on the senses "healer" and "savior"; in a similar way, he uses "buyer" for "redeemer."

The Psalter: Psalm 102:1–5

27. Rolle here has the unidiomatic "the holy name of him," otherwise this first verse is very close to the Authorized Version translation.

28. Rolle uses the word "buys."

29. A nonce-word, meaning "pitying," formed on the rare verb *to mercy*, "to have compassion."

30. I have not found a source for this observation; traditionally the eagle's proverbial long life was said to derive from its renewal of vigor after moulting. Rolle could well have seen the osprey, as a passage migrant, and the white-tailed sea eagle as a regular winter visitor in Yorkshire (information from Dr. Ian Dawson of the Royal Society for the Protection of Birds). The golden eagle could have been still more common in Rolle's Yorkshire.

The Psalter: Psalm 103:11–24

31. The last letter of the Hebrew alphabet, and originally of the Greek alphabet. The letter signifies the end of time. In the northern poem *Cursor Mundi* (11.12199–12208) Christ as a boy asks his schoolmaster to explain "*taw*," promising then to expound *alpha*.

The Psalter: Psalm 150

32. Rolle's list of instruments has been accommodated to the instruments common in medieval Europe; these in their turn had often come from the Near East, most recently through the Crusades.

Trumpet: Not the sixteenth-century valve trumpet, descendents of which are in use in orchestras today, but the six-foot long *trump* or *buisine*, capable of only six notes, but of extreme resonance; it was used in fanfares at feasts, for dancing and for battle, but less, presumably, in churches. (See Munrow, p.19.)

Psaltery: It is unlikely that this would be audible beside the *trump;* in manuscript illuminations, psalteries are usually played by ladies and angels. See note 4, above.

Harp: See note 20, above. The harp was played with great verve in the Middle Ages, especially by Celtic harpists, and was "struck" with specially long and tapered fingernails; the method of playing must have seemed similar to that of the psaltery, plucked with a quill, and often, it seems, struck with the same implement. In size, playing technique, and sound the medieval harp must have been very different from the modern concert harp. Earlier so-called harps (that of the Anglo-Saxon Sutton Hoo Ship Cenotaph, for example) were lyres; the

lyre was superseded in Europe by the *harp* (eleventh century) and by the *crowd* (Munrow, pp.22–23).
Tabor: A cylindrical drum played with one stick with two drum heads; it was held if it were small, and attached to the waist if larger, and, like the trump, was associated with royalty and nobility, for use at feasts and ceremonies (Munrow, pp.32–33).
Crowd: Better known by its Welsh name, *crwth:* The bowed lyre, which survived in Wales until recent times, and, in its earlier form without fingerboard, still survived in the early twentieth century in Estonia as the *tallharpa*, which was stopped with the fingernails. The early *crowd* (11th century) had only three or four strings, but by Rolle's time six-stringed forms were known (Munrow, pp.29–30). The Latin really means "in the dance" rather than "in/on the crowd," of course.
Strings: Rolle probably has in mind the early *fiddle*, and the three-stringed *rebec*, but presumably not the *gittern* and *citole*, which were plucked.
Organs: Both portative organs and church organs were well-known by Rolle's time. Rolle's French contemporary, the priest Machaut, called the organ the "king of instruments." Rolle's description would fit the "great organ" of medieval churches, which was often enormous, or the positive ("Chair/choir") organ, which was between the two in size.
Cymbals: Medieval cymbals were two bell-shaped discs which were banged together horizontally rather than vertically. Because of their similarity in shape to bells, *cymbals* were corrupted by popular etymology to "chime-bells," and since cymbals could not have played much part in church music, medieval commentators may well have understood the 150th Psalm to refer to the "cup-bells" of contemporary music, tuned and hung on a wooden frame, which seem, in any case, to have developed from cymbals; they were struck with a hammer. Cymbals are depicted in manuscripts, usually played by angels, probably because cymbals figure in the psalms. Because it is not clear whether Rolle means bells or cymbals, I use both *chimes* and *cymbals* in the translation. (See Munrow, pp.34–35.)

33. In medieval times it was usual to regard the entire Psalter as the work of David.

The Ten Commandments

1. *Desire and Delight* ends with the same puzzling etc. in the Thornton MS; perhaps it simply means "continue meditating on this." The Hatton MS of *Ten Commandments* is fuller, but the additional material is perhaps not by Rolle; possibly Thornton was aware of the existence of a longer version, and so wrote *etc.*, but did not actually make any abridgment himself. There is a preponderance of French words in *The Commandments*, which may possibly indicate that it was translated from a French *Manuel*. The number of French loans here seems to be greater than in his other early work in English, but this need not mean that Rolle is not the author of *Commandments;* in tone and emphasis it seems very typical of him.

NOTES

Meditations on the Passion: The Shorter Meditations

1. These Latin prayers come from the Matins of the Hours of the Cross, which were composed in the early fourteenth century; they were therefore an up-to-date devotion when Rolle was writing. Like the Latin tracts which Rolle translated as *Judica Me Deus*, like his use of James of Milan's *Stimulus Amoris* (c. 1300) in these *Meditations*, and his quotations in *The Form of Living* and *Emendatio Vitae* of Hugh of Strasbourg's *Compendium*, they show Rolle in touch with developments in the contemporary church.

2. I have corrected this by the reading in the *Longer Meditations*.

3. The manuscript reads *inne;* my reading is a guess.

4. *Denounced:* The original reads *forcryed* which is not in the dictionaries. Old French *crier* was used in the sense "raise the hue and cry against" (*MED*, 3(b)).

5. *Driven:* MS *hyed*, probably for *hued* (OFr *hüer*), "raise outcry against someone" (MED, *hue* (c)), but *hyed* can mean "made to hasten."

6. Isaiah 53:3.

7. Rolle wrote "and watched all night" but seems to have mistaken his construction: *wooke* ("watched") should be a verbal noun to match "flogging" and "punching." Such grammatical confusions are not uncommon in Rolle's early work in English.

8. *Vapor: Reke* in the manuscript might mean the rush of the crowd, or the sweat or the dust which it gives off.

9. Rolle writes with similar approval of the ordinary Christians, those who are not perfect, but in their simplicity do their best, in *Judica Me Deus*, where he contrasts them again with the learned and wealthy clerics, whose sole concern is physical satisfaction and wealth.

10. The next three paragraphs, on the sufferings of Our Lady, are based on the *Stimulus Amoris* (c. 1300) of James of Milan.

11. Horstman would emend to "was set *on* your son's suffering," as in MS T of the *LM* but the sense does not seem to fit the context: *set,OED* sense 37 "set one's heart on" is hardly appropriate here.

12. Written over an erasure in the manuscript.

13. In this poetic conceit Our Lady is semi-jocularly said to keep her grief for herself without sharing it. The conceit depends for its effect on the class distinction which Rolle is careful to establish throughout the *Meditations* between himself as a beggar and Christ and his mother as members of the family from the great house on the manorial estate. The tone here is a blend of wheedling intimacy and self-conscious reserve. When at the Dalton's house, Rolle seems to have been lacking in self-assurance and social graces.

14. Written over erasure and perhaps a scribal modernization.

15. It must have been a passage such as this which Julian of Norwich had been reading when she desired from God the gift of three wounds: true contrition, true compassion and a genuine ("wylfulle") longing for God (Shorter version of *Showings*, Chap. ii).

16. Written over erasure.

17. This must refer to the sweat of Christ's agony at the scourging, referred

to above, rather than the bloody sweat at Gethsemane or the water which followed the sword at the crucifixion.

18. The original reads "compassyoun of that dere passyon," a pun which Rolle also uses in his comment on Psalm 68:25.

19. The full version of this lyric appears in MS Dd.v.64 III which also contains Rolle's own lyrics. This lyric, however, appears among the first group of lyrical pieces in the manuscript, and seems not to be covered by the colophon ascribing the second set to Rolle. It appears third among the four lyrics in the first group, and is, like the other three, poetically superior to Rolle's own lyrics, despite its tone of affective piety. It begins: "My truest treasure so traitorly was taken" and the verse quoted here reads as follows in that version: "My dearworthy darling, so dolefully dight/So straitly upright stretched on the cross (*rode*, which alliterates better than *cros* in Rolle's version)/For your great meekness, your mercy, your might/Cure all my evils with the remedy of your blood.

20. By contrast, this poem, in lightly alliterative verse, may be by Rolle, as Hope Allen thinks. It is written as prose in the manuscript, and is evidence of a long tradition of lay vernacular devotion to the passion of Christ, which Rolle continues in these *Meditations*.

21. Written over erasure.

22. Synaesthesia; this conflation of various bodily senses in compound metaphor for a spiritual or moral state is common in Rolle's writing, especially in the Latin *Melos Amoris*.

23. Corrected by a second hand in the manuscript from "your love of divinity."

24. Written over erasure.

25. The MS reads *owt castyng* and a correction has been made to *owt casten* by comparison with the *LM* for translation, although the error may be Rolle's own, rather than a scribe's; he uses verbal nouns in passive as well as active senses.

26. Rolle's own gifts of heat, sweetness and song would be considered such "signs."

27. Mark 15:31.

28. Lamentations 1:12.

29. *So hard* is overlined, as if some correction were required.

30. MS reads *sette*, which Horstman emends to "said"; I take *sette* in the sense "lay something burdensome upon; impose, inflict a penalty upon" (*OED*,s.v. *set*, sense 44).

31. This is a pun: One meaning of "thief" in Middle English is "evil man, villain, scoundrel," a term of general reproach (OED,s.v. *thief*, sense 2); Rolle sees himself as a worthless wretch, but associates himself with the thief on the cross too, in the modern sense of the term, since he has misappropriated Christ's treasury of merit and grace.

32. The MS reading is corrected here, from *seldom seth* ("seldom sees") to *seldsene*, which I assume a scribe misread as *seld sees;* I have translated an assumed original: *for seldsene is ony man that ne is.*

33. MS reads *rody*, "redness"; Horstman emends to *rode*, *rude* "rosy complexion, face."

34. Luke 2:39.

35. This expression is familiar from Marlowe's use of it in *Dr. Faustus: So-*

lamen miseris socios habuisse doloris (II i 42); it was previously quoted (in English) in Barclay's *Ship of Fools* II 236 and Lyly's *Euphues* (see Tilley, *A Dictionary of the Proverbs in England in the Sixteenth and Seventeenth Centuries* [Ann Arbor, 1950]). Apparently the author of the Latin original is unknown; à Kempis used the quotation in the fifteenth century, and Chaucer in the fourteenth (*Troilus and Criseyde* I 708, *Canon's Yeoman's Tale* 746f); it was also quoted by Dominicus de Gravina, c. 1350. Rolle's use antedates all these. See Skeat, *Early English Proverbs*, p. 63, n.152.

36. Written over erasure.

37. Jerusalem, as in Dante's *Divine Comedy*, was considered to be at the centre of the world.

38. Written over an erasure in the MS.

39. *That* has been written over something erased; the scribe was very punctilious in removing his errors.

40. The MS reads "earth" for sun, an obvious error.

41. MS *closyng* can mean the act of closing, a means of closing (gate), or space which is enclosed, enclosure. Rolle's use antedates all senses recorded in *MED;* I assume the last is meant.

42. The original has *whe*, an interjection of surprise or to demand attention, like modern "hey," "here now," "help," "oh look." In the later occurrence (see note 47) the word is almost equivalent to *ME wa,wei*, "woe, misery me."

43. Horstman and Allen regard this sentence as corrupt; I see no need to emend.

44. Here there is a difficulty: The MS reads *and so dyen whan thi wylle is.* I assume that he is punning on *dye* and *die;* he has spoken of his soul as a sheep, marked with the red of Christ's blood, so that he can be recognized as part of the flock of Christ; cured now of his disease, his fleece treated and softened, he can now be completely imbued with Christ's love like dyed wool, as in the image of dyeing in *The Form*, Chap. 10.

45. Horstman emends the MS *that thou it ryghte*, "that you should direct it," because this does not rhyme with *be lyghted*, and corrects *to be ryghted*, as in *LM*. There is an extended pun in this section on *light:* alight, enlighten, lighten (load), set light to, and *right:* righteousness, justice (i.e. punishment).

46. Horstman adds (*styred*) "to thee" (*of thi grace*) as in *LM*, but it is probably not necessary.

47. Here the original again has the colloquial interjection *whe!*

48. MS reads *syght*, carelessly.

49. MS has *the* (def. article?) but *thi* seems to be intended.

50. MS has past tense *lokyd*, "looked," but the historic present dominates most of this section.

51. Horstman suggests that *sight* should read *sigh:* "permit . . . one single sigh."

52. Horstman would prefer to read *wete*, "wet," but *water* is right (*OED* s.v. *water*, sense 17d).

RICHARD ROLLE: THE ENGLISH WRITINGS

Meditations on the Passion: The Longer Meditations

1. *Pleasure . . . enjoyment:* Puzzlingly, Rolle here uses the words *lust . . . liking*, an ancient alliterative collocation which he normally uses in the (later) pejorative senses of "sensuality" and "sexual pleasure." Here he seems to use them in the neutral sense "enjoyment." The phrase was still current in Malory's time, over 120 years after Rolle died.

2. MSS O and T read *put out*, for which C *not at* might be an auditory error in dictation, except that U has *putte out not* (presumably by conflation).

3. The phrase *that is my ioie* is omitted in MSS O, T and U and has apparently been displaced into the preceding line in C; if genuine, it cannot belong where it occurs, after "to yours," and perhaps belongs here.

4. MS C *oon of the grettest synnes* has the modern idiom, but the expression was originally *oon the grettest*, "the most extreme instance of," which is far stronger; Rolle probably wrote this, indicating that he saw Judas' betrayal as the supreme instance and type of all human betrayal, not merely a typical example of a capital sin.

5. There is a miniature allegory here: The lord claims back the runaway serf, who is his own bonded slave, and forces him back to his accustomed toil; this is a figure of Christ claiming the lost soul and impelling it to show its remorse by undergoing penitential hardship.

6. This sentence is not in OTU, which must therefore be related manuscripts, if the sentence is original; the Good Samaritan allusion seems genuine enough to have been Rolle's and not a later addition.

7. St. Augustine, *Confessions*, IV,12.

8. This is a common conceit, found in Meditation 9 ascribed to St. Anselm and imitated in later works such as *Ancrene Riwle* in Middle English.

9. This concept of the soul as an image of Christ, inherited from Augustine, was to be especially developed by Hilton in Book I of *The Scale of Perfection* and referred to by Julian of Norwich. It is rare, however, in Rolle. The immanence of God appears in Rolle's conceptual imagery in the form of heat and taste and sound imagery, rather than in visual and pictorial images.

10. MSS O,T, and U read *hertly, lord (and) continuely hit to preie*, "sincerely (and) continually to pray for it."

11. MSS C and O read *better*, but MS T has the curious form *bightter*, which may be an error for *brighter;* the reading of MS U. Perhaps the original had the northern word *bigger*, "more powerful, richer." Hope Allen preferred *better*.

12. Medieval books were written with ink blended from lampblack and resin, which was dark brown or black when first written. Red ink was used for quotations from biblical or scholastic authorities in Latin, for running titles, and other important directives, such as chapter headings, paragraph signs and notations; these might be written in red entirely, or touched with a red blob, or underlined with it. This was called rubrishing, and was often done by the main scribe. If valuable enough, a book might then be finished off by an illuminator, who supplied miniatures, full-page illustrations, and historiated or flourished initials for section headings. Christ is so important and authoritative a "book" that he is rubrished throughout.

13. MSS C and U read "all your outer blood," *vtter blood.* This being before

the circulation of the blood was discovered, the understanding seems to be that the exterior blood has bled away, leaving only the blood within the viscera. MS O reads *vntyr blood*, "entire blood"; in the fifteenth century *utter* came to mean "complete, entire" and *utter*-"outer" was then confused with *utter*-"entire," hence the synonym "entire" in MS O.

14. MSS T and U supply the correction to MS C, as does *Shorter Med.*; C has "the emperor of hell is now hound crowned"; "emperor" may be a scribal addition in C since it is not in T,U nor *SM*, but it follows the line of Rolle's thought, and I have let it stand.

15. Leprosy was an exotic disease for the Greeks and Romans, but it became endemic in Europe during the Dark and Middle Ages, lingering until after the fifteenth century in Scotland and Scandinavia. Rolle would very likely have seen, or even ministered to lepers, who were isolated from the community, living by begging at the town gates, sleeping in a lazar-house on the outskirts of town, and ringing a bell or sounding a clapper to warn off the unwary public. Medical textbooks of the time contained detailed descriptions of the disease, which was thought to be incurable, except by divine intervention. The image derives from Isaiah (Is 53:3) as pseudo-Bonaventure's *The Privity of the Passion* records, although it has been reinforced from Psalm 22:6–8 because of the application of the latter to Christ.

16. Perhaps an allusion to James of Milan's *Stimulus Amoris*, which Rolle quotes from in *SM*, cf. *SM*, n.10.

17. As in the Mystery Plays which were subsequently acted in Rolle's home region of York, the cross is here supposed to have been drilled for the crucifixion prior to Christ's arrival at Calvary, but his size was overestimated (in one tradition because torture and consequent loss of body fluid had actually altered his size), and his smaller frame had to be stretched, as on the torture rack, to fit the prepared holes. The germ of this idea is present in the translation of pseudo-Bonaventure, *The Privity of the Passion*, whence it was possibly derived, independently, by Rolle and the *Northern Passion* 11.1603ff (EETS 145, pp.186–90), which may have inspired the York Mystery Plays, Play xxxv, 11.105–48.

18. Parchment was the usual material for book manufacture in Rolle's time, paper appearing during the fourteenth century, to become more common in the fifteenth. Parchment was made from the skins of sheep that were soaked in corrosive (e.g. lime) to loosen and dissolve the hairs, and then the skins were scraped and stretched on timber tenter-frames to dry, flatten and bleach them in sunlight. After this they were pumiced and stretched again before being brushed with powdered chalk, and folded for use. This image matches Rolle's previous allusion to Christ as a rubrished book. It may derive from Rolle's university experience at Oxford; perhaps such sights of drying parchment were more common in the university towns and near monasteries. Most leather was cured for use as footwear, saddlery, clothing, drinking vessels and containers, and only the best manuscripts were made of vellum. Tanners' yards were malodorous and banished to city suburbs, where the gentlefolk and higher clerics would be unlikely to see them. Rolle writes for those more in touch with the working population, perhaps. This image seems "metaphysical" to us, but it is paralleled by a similar conceit in a Middle English translation of pseudo-Bonaventure, *The Privity of the Passion*, and is echoed in the Longer Version of Julian

of Norwich's *Showings*, in which she sees Christ's desiccated body like a cloth drying in the wind.

19. The *SM* here reads *savor* rather than *fervor* and seems preferable in context. Allen prefers *LM* reading here because it typifies Rolle's *calor*.

20. The expression is not one of the seven words from the cross and is not mentioned in the pseudo-Bonaventure translation *The Privity of the Passion*, nor does it occur in the *Meditation on the Passion and the Three Arrows of Doomsday*, once attributed to Rolle. The phrase of course comes from *Lamentations* 1:12 (see *SM*, and *SM* note 28) and was traditionally interpreted as Christ's expression of grief; it occurs in the York Crucifixion as Christ is first raised on the cross.

21. See *SM*, note 35.

22. Other variant readings are *kele*, "cool" in MSS O and U, and *kepe*, "protect" in MS T.

23. Mt 27:46; Mk 15:34; based on Ps 22:1 (Vulgate Ps 21:1).

24. All four MSS of the *LM* are in error here. The scribe of the archetype jumped from *al thi (bodily) woo* to *al thin other wo*, thus omitting the observation that the culmination of Christ's agony, surpassing even his grief for his mother, was the loss of the souls of his torturers. I have emended from the *SM*.

25. See *SM* for a similar reference to the splitting of the Temple. The Gospel accounts speak of the Temple *veil* rending: Mt 27:51; Mk 15:38.

26. The *SM* here reads *rode*, "cross." In post seventeenth-century usage the term *crucifix* has been erroneously applied to the image of the cross with the figure of Christ on it; the word originally meant "the crucified one," and I take it that that is the sense here, although the reading of *SM* is puzzling, in that case.

Ghostly Gladness

1. For convenience of reference, I retain the title of Hope Allen's edition, but have modified the opening lines and supplied new alliteration, because the word *ghost* has undergone semantic change from its original sense, "breath of life," equivalent of Latin *spiritus*, the moral and thinking part of the personality, which has now replaced *ghost* in this sense. A more literal version of this prose lyric is given in the Appendix, p. 195.

2. After this piece, the Cambridge MS reads, "Here conclude the songs of holy love of Richard of Hampole," and then adds "Thy Joy Be" under the note: "one more of the same Richard." It is probable that this colophon only covers the six lyrics and one prose lyric immediately preceding ("Love Is Life" being reckoned as one lyric in this MS), and not the lyrics written as prose in the preceding section; the rider covers "Thy Joy Be" as certainly attributed to Rolle.

The Bee and the Stork

1. Rolle's preoccupation with activity contrasts with the later mystics, and his association of mystic experience with tangible experience is explicitly refuted in *Cloud of Unknowing*, Chapter 57.

2. *History of the Animals* ix. 27, a different section from that which provided

the source of lines 1–5; the opening derives from *Hist.Anim.* ix. 40. Rolle, or his intermediate source, has rearranged the material in a systematic way.

3. Wormwood is the old name for the plant *artemesia absinthium*, used in the manufacture of absinthe and vermouth (the same word as *wormwood*). Its leaves were once used as medicine and tonic, and to dispel moths and fleas from clothes and worms from the body (hence the folk-etymology of "worm-wood" from vermouth). It later became a metaphor in religious writings for the bitterness of sin and its punishment, but Rolle is thinking of the literal contrast in taste between sweet things and bitter.

4. *Hist.Anim.*ix.8., but the moralizing comes from Gregory, *Moralia* xxxi, Chap.39.

5. The "*strucyo*" is clearly the ostrich, described in Job 39:13–18, and alluded to as sign of devastation in Jeremiah 50:39. It is strange that Rolle should translate the word as *stork*, since, as passage migrants, storks have always been known in the British Isles, and a pair is on record as having nested in Edinburgh in the early fifteenth century. The bird Rolle means is perhaps the Great Bustard, which bred on the Yorkshire Wolds until 1835, one of the "greate fowle" of the English table at banquets. This bird does resemble an ostrich in gait, and is large, but it can, reluctantly, fly strongly. It still survives in Spain, and in Austria, and east to the Russian Steppe. The old word for bustard was *ou(s)tarde*, which might be responsible for some confusion; the error seems to emanate from some manuscripts of the *Ancrene Riwle*, Part iii (Trans. Salu, p.59), where some manuscripts read *struchion*, the old word for ostrich, while others read *stork;* Hope Allen finds evidence that Rolle knew *Ancrene Riwle*, and could have found his material there; if so, he knew his English devotional writers better than his ornithology. It looks as if *struchion* was "localized" as *oustarde* by some scribe of *Ancrene Riwle*, and later miscopied as *storke*, or perhaps the confusion arose because the stork, with the swan, peacock and bustard were "greate fowle" for the table.

The Latin for "ostrich" is *(camelo)struthio.* As Hope Allen points out (*MLR* 24 (1929),12–13) the fifteenth century homilist (?Dr. Lichfield) who quoted from *Ancrene Riwle* had the correct reading, "ostrich," in the copy of *AR* which he used. Much of the information in this note is derived from colleagues at Hatfield Polytechnic, Herts., England, and from Dr. Ian Dawson of the R.S.P.B., who also notes an unreferenced statement that ostriches may have been kept in English zoos from the twelfth century on.

Desire and Delight

1. The Longleat MS has *desyre;* the Thornton MS has *gernyng*, "yearning," which is a northern word, but does not alliterate and is probably wrong.

2. "Holy" is omitted in Longleat, probably correctly since it is not expanded in either version.

3. Lt *effectuous* would mean "urgent, pressing"; Hope Allen suggests *affectuous*, "earnest, affectionate," as in the final line of the second paragraph; "affections *and* thoughts" in MS Thornton is wrong.

4. Rolle's word here is *tagillyng;* it caused the scribes much difficulty. The

word seems to mean "entanglement," and to be related to the Scots *taigle*, "impede, detain"; its only recorded occurrence in Middle English is in Rolle, who uses it several times.

5. Rolle's expression is "mekely has styrrynge in," which is very close to one of the favorite phrases of *The Cloud* author who writes in the Prologue, for example, of "inward stering after the prive sperit of God"—an "inward prompting of grace."

6. *Sensuality:* Rolle calls it "the nether (lower) party of my saule" in his commentary on Psalm 6:6. This lower nature of the soul is concerned with appetite and instinct; in Richard of St. Victor's *Benjamin Minor* it is said to serve the affection or "will." Rolle knew other works by Richard of St. Victor, and may have known this, which was later to be translated by the author of *The Cloud of Unknowing*.

7. MS Thornton ends with "etc.," which led Hope Allen to call this an extract, but the Longleat MS ends in the same place, and the work is probably complete, despite the failure to explore the epithet *faste*, "firm," in the way that "wonderful," "elevated" and "pure" have been; *faste* has only been given a one-sentence definition. But it is unwise to expect symmetry of structure in Rolle; he utilizes the scholastic method for clarity in explaining, but never allows its rigidity to stifle his emotion. I have left the scribe's *explicit* here so that the modern reader can sample the format of these pieces as contemporaries experienced them.

Ego Dormio

1. Song of Songs 5:2. The imagery of the first paragraph is based on 2 Corinthians 11:2.

2. Rolle assumes a derivation from the root *sărāph*, "to burn"; there is some dispute as to whether the word used for a type of serpent in the Pentateuch, *sārăph*, may or may not be connected. The *seraphim* of Isaiah 6:2 may have been originally conceived as lightning or fiery flying serpents. The association of seraphim with fire has a venerable liturgical history. Rolle inevitably places contemplatives with the seraphim because of their experience of "the fire of love"; Gregory also has this schema for the orders of contemplatives, but Dante puts St. Francis among the seraphim. Depictions of the nine orders were common on windows, roodscreens and frescoes in parish churches.

3. Gregory first defined three grades of contemplatives. The threefold mystic way probably derived from the pseudo-Dionysius the Areopagite, and was developed especially by St. Bonaventure. Richard of St. Victor has a fourfold gradation, and Rolle applies the names of the first three of these to the threefold scheme of Gregory in his other three epistles.

4. Scribes always muddle numbers, and usually exaggerate. Here some manuscripts read "seven hundred" (e.g. Longleat), and some read "seven thousand"; MS C reads "seven hundred thousand."

5. MS C reads "five," which may be another instance of scribal emphasis, or could be an allusion to the loaves of the miracle of the feeding of the five thousand. This devotion to the Holy Name occurs in all three English letters; in *ED*

and *Commandment* it is part of the practice of the second degree; it is mentioned there in *The Form* too, but there a more refined devotion to Jesus also takes place in the highest grade.

6. Rolle uses the word *mantel.* This was a sleeveless garment worn over the tunic or kirtle, and under the cloak. It was really a kind of coat, necessary for indoor wear in draughty castles and wattle and daub cots alike.

7. The term here is *kirtle,* a tunic worn, at different lengths, by both sexes, usually as an outer garment, although men might wear it under armor, and ladies would wear it over the smock, and wear on top of it the sleeveless and often open-sided *mantel.* Out of doors, a cloak or shawl would be worn over everything else.

8. This is the title given in the margin of MS C. The first three stanzas are derived from two Latin meditations: *Respice in faciem Christi*, and *Candet Nudatum Pectus.* The latter is ascribed to Anselm, but here in *ED* they appear through an intermediary version of Rolle's own in *Incendium Amoris*, Cap.27. Stanzas 5–7 derive from *Incendium* Cap.42. The version of *Candet nudatum Pectus* Rolle used was a Middle English translation, extant in Bodley MS 42: "White was his naked breast and red with blood his side/ Bloody was his fair face, his wounds so deep and wide/ Stiff were his arms outspread upon the rood/ In five places on his body streams ran with blood."

9. *First in ring:* The allusion is to the *caroles*, ring dances like "ring o' roses," where a leader within the ring sang the verses of a long narrative song, while those forming the ring by joining hands would move in a clockwise circle to their left as they sang the refrain. In *The Form*, Chap.6. This and the following two stanzas derive from *Incendium* Cap.42, which reads: "*amor . . . coream ducit.*"

10. The lyric *Cantus Amoris* which follows contains similar lines in stanza 2, probably derived from *Jesu Dulcis Memoria.*

11. This echoes Rolle's experience of the "opening of heaven" nearly three years after he embarked on his eremetical life. This was not just the experience of a novice, but, to judge from this passage, a constant feature of his mystic experience.

12. What Rolle craved was quiet, rather than seclusion for its own sake. He probably had to rely on patrons all his life as a solitary, and therefore could not be wholly apart from the world. Like St. Gregory, whose example he looked to, he had to cultivate inner peace amid the world's affairs. Many hermits supported themselves by maintaining roads, ferries, bridges, hospitals or chapels precisely so that they could achieve independence from others, but in the very tasks they maintained themselves by, they lost their quiet.

13. "Langyng" and the Latin *languor, langueo* are favorite expressions in Rolle, occurring in *Incendium* (Caps.32,42), in *Melos*, and in Chap. 8 of *The Form;* see also *The Song of Love Longing* in the Appendix.

14. Based on *Jesu Dulcis Memoria;* the *Cantus Amoris* in Chap.8 of the *The Form* contains lines similar to these.

15. This line is obscure: It has some feudal connection, continuing the images of "tower" and "hall," and must refer to some kind of tester or banner over the seating at a feast, rather than a funeral hatchment over a tomb. Comper (p.232) associates the image with John 14:2.

16. MS C concludes: "Here ends the treatise of Richard Hermit of Hampole

written to a certain nun of Yedingham." This colophon has no authority, and it is even possible that this epistle was written to Margaret Kirkby; Dr. Ogilvie-Thomson has suggested that it may have been written to Margaret before her clothing as a nun (*An Edition of the English Works in MS Longleat 29*, Ph.D. diss., Oxford, 1980, p.451.

The Commandment

1. The opening is translated from Hugh of Strasbourg's *Compendium theologicae veritatis*.

2. I have kept the word "stirring" since it is one of Rolle's favorites and copied by the later mystics; see *Desire and Delight*, n.5.

3. These titles come from Richard of St. Victor, *The Four Grades of Violent Love*. In Chapter 8 of *De Diligendo Deo* St. Bernard also has four degrees of love. But Rolle has accommodated these to Gregory's tripartite scheme, see *Ego Dormio*, n.3.

4. The directive to love Christ in place of a human lover, and to find physical qualities in him which one seeks in human lovers is an old motif by Rolle's time; it occurs in Part VII of *Ancrene Riwle:*

> "If (your love) is to be given," Christ says, "where better may you bestow it than on me? Am I not the most beautiful of creatures? Am I not the richest of kings? Am I not the most noble in birth? Am I not the wisest of men? Am I not the most gracious of rich men? Am I not the most generous of creatures?"

5. There seems to be a pun here on *good* in the two senses of "goodness" and "goods, property." Throughout this paragraph Rolle seems to be drawing on the passage in *Ancrene Riwle* cited in the previous note.

6. This suggests a very untried spirituality; perhaps Rolle is not writing for the same recipient as that of *ED*, or perhaps he intends a more general audience among the addressee's community of sisters to be included as well.

7. Rolle's practical advice echoes that of *Ancrene Riwle*, which he seems to have read. It is followed, in its turn, by many later mystics.

8. Rolle's praise of early rising occurs also in his comment on Psalm 118:147: "It is a disgrace if the sunbeams find people lazing in their beds" [HEA].

9. *Swaddled:* "swedeled"; the actual practice of wrapping babies for their first three months in tightly wound strips of cloth was universal in most parts of the world until after the Middle Ages. Doctors in the eighteenth and nineteenth centuries were still deploring it. Presumably "like a pauper's child" refers to the quality of the cloth rather than the practice. The idea was to make the limbs grow straighter. The notion of seeking Christ and not finding him until one looks in the crib and finds him swaddled there occurs in Rolle's *Comment on the Canticles* in the often extracted "Encomium Nominis Jesu." Rolle's obsession with the waste of money on clothes had real point in the Middle Ages, when wealth was displayed on the wearer's back as a reinforcement of the social hierarchy.

10. Rolle has in mind the magnificent decorated tombs of the early fourteenth century, especially in the North, as he meditates on Christ's observation "whited sepulchres" (Mt 23:27).

11. In Chapter 40 of *Incendium* Rolle explains that he no longer weeps as he did when love was new, because of the great sweetness he knows now.

12. This is similar to, and may well be derived from, a thirteenth-century lyric on the *contemptus mundi* theme: "Where are they who were before us?" which contains the line: "and in the twinkling of an eye they were gone" (Carleton Brown, *Thirteenth Century Lyrics*, no.48, from MS Digby 86, fols.126v–127); both probably echo Job 14:2.

13. The Hebrew *Jeshua*, *Jehoshua* means "Yahweh is salvation."

14. Based on Peter of Ravenna (4th century A.D.) and echoed in Rolle's *Ego Dormio* and *The Form*. In his comment on Psalm 90:14, Rolle adds the personal observation, not taken from Peter Lombard, that "Jesu" has power to make devils flee and to purify the thought [HEA].

The Form of Living

1. There is a similar comment in Chapter 5 of *Emendatio Vitae:* "When the devil sees one man from a thousand to be perfectly converted to God . . . he prepares a thousand frauds to harm him and a thousand arts to attack him, so that the man may turn away from the love of God to the love of the world" (trans. del Mastro, *The Fire of Love and the Mending of Life*, N.Y.,1981).

2. 1 Kings 19:7: "Get up and eat, or the journey will be too long for you" (Jerusalem Bible).

3. Psalm 59:9 (Vulgate 58:10): "Fortitudinem meam ad te custodiam."

4. Rolle has probably culled this quotation from a florilegium, a collection of the sayings of the fathers and doctors; he may have had a similar source for his references to Augustine, Cassian, Cassiodorus and Bonaventure; such a source would explain his lack of attribution of the quotations from Richard of St. Victor on the three grades of love, and his failure to cite the names of the authors whom he quotes in Chapter 12 of *Emendatio Vitae.*

5. This is not St. Bernard, but from the *Epistola ad Fratres de Monte Dei*, attributed to him in the Middle Ages, but by William of St-Thierry.

6. Here Longleat reads "(deceives) inconsistent and silly men and women" while MS C, in place of the two adjectives describing the people, has a second adjective referring to the devil's skills, *whaynt*. The sense in MS C is not certain; perhaps *whaynt* is a northern spelling of *quaynt*, "clever, wily," which has not been understood in the southern text, where two compensatory adjectives (applied to "men and women") are supplied instead. I have compromised by translating the readings of both manuscripts.

7. Longleat has the reading: "speaking of your beloved, your spouse Jesus."

8. MS C adds "(a lady) here."

9. MS C adds "(a life of) great (privation)."

10. MS C has an unusual form *wheme* = Middle English *queme*, "agreeable, fair," but *OED* records a form similar to Rolle's for 1883, current then in the sense "quiet," and quotes from the *Almondbury and Huddersfield Glossary:* "*weam* or *weme* 'quiet': 'a weme woman in a house is a jewel.' " Rolle was possibly using a colloquial word, if this is his original form; one MS reads "to wheme," probably misunderstanding the unfamiliar word as "whom," but most other manuscripts read "pleasing to God," probably a gloss of the usual sense "agreeable."

11. MS C reads "see to it that (there is nothing)."

12. MS C reads "(the more) shall they rejoice in his love"; I follow Longleat.

13. From Cassian, Collat.xvi, Cap.11 [HEA].

14. *Compendium theologicae veritatis*, ii. cap.66.

15. MS C, MS Rawlinson C.285, read "underneath"; Lt and related MSS read *undre need*, a correction proposed by Horstman and adopted by Hope Allen.

16. The hair shirt was often worn next to the skin as a form of penance; to judge from the number of individuals who took the surname of "hair shirt weaver" this habit was not uncommon. Others wore a coat of mail next to the skin, which would be uncomfortable and give danger of hypothermia as the metal would conduct out body heat. Here the mail coat is to be worn over the hair shirt, at the devil's prompting, so that the pressure on the prickly material would cause intolerable itching and soreness, especially in hot weather. One hundred and eighty years before Rolle was writing, Thomas à Becket was discovered to be wearing breeches as well as shirt of hair when his monks laid him out for burial after his murder. FitzStephen's biography records that the corpse was found to be covered with lice (which the *South English Legendary* writer has converted into worms), which must have made the hair shirt even more penitential. Rolle sanely observes in his comment on Psalm 34:15 that he finds no record that Christ ever wore the hair shirt.

17. This clause is present in most MSS; the omission in MS C was probably caused by homoeoarchy:*at times . . . at other times*, the second instance being omitted because the scribe thought he had already copied it.

18. Ecclesiastes 5:2.

19. These are derived from St. Gregory, *Moralia in Job*, viii,cap.24,42–3; and *Liber ad Sororem de Modo Bene Vivendi*, cap.68 [HEA].

20. I have rearranged the syntax here; in Hope Allen's punctuation there is no main clause in what I have translated as the second of two co-ordinate subordinate clauses dependent on "consider."

21. This is the reading of MS Rawlinson C 285; the rest, apart from MS C, read "illuminates to (i.e. so as to) relinquish"; C reads "and relinquishes."

22. Literally the text reads "that can exist," but since Rolle lived before the concept of atoms and molecules, I have modified the expression for the modern reader without introducing concepts Rolle could not have entertained.

23. Rolle is not thinking of worldly occupations here, of course. His society was interdependent, so that one man's lack of employment would mean his neighbor's loss of the man's skills, as well as the starvation of his family. Such deprivation was not unknown, with the conversion of agricultural land to sheep-runs, especially on monastic estates, but usually the feudal system would guarantee some kind of employment because labor was valuable to the lord of the manor (although perhaps less so in Rolle's youth, when there was a high population in rural areas—soon to be cut by disastrous harvests and land shortage—than after Rolle's death, when the plague killed so many agricultural laborers). But Rolle is thinking here of "good works," both societal and spiritual. Medieval preachers taught that idleness was a grave danger to the soul; *accidia*, "lassitude, boredom or disaffection," was the besetting sin of the cloister. Rolle seems to have reckoned it was equally prevalent among solitaries, whom he constantly urges to be ever active.

24. Cf. Lamentations 1:15: "He has summoned the time as a witness against me." In Authorized Version "summoned an assembly against. . . . "

25. This is the familiar medieval "inexpressibility *topos*," a rhetorical device inherited from Graeco-Roman forensic rhetoric, and even used by St. Paul.

26. Much of this chapter resembles the briefer account in Chapter 4 of *Emendatio Vitae;* both sections derive from Hugh of Strasbourg's late thirteenth century compilation *Compendium theologicae veritatis* (iii, caps. 30–33); Rolle translates closely and adds little except to explain; his explanations appear in brackets.

27. Hope Allen connects the verbal noun *rusyng* here with *roose* (ON *hrósa*), "boast," rather than a vb. *ruse*, "to double back." The Latin of *Comp. theol. verit.* reads *iactantia*, "ostentation, bragging," from *iacto*, "bandy about in discussion."

28. Cf. *Ten Commandments*, pp.87–88 above, commandment I.

29. The Latin reads: *joculatoribus dare.*

30. Rolle's text reads "to lead carols," translating *choreizare*. The *carole* was a round-dance, see *Ego Dormio*, n. 9. The *carole* was often about love-affairs, hence, presumably, this clerical stricture, coupled with the fact that dancing was often performed in the local churchyard, as Rolle's contemporary Robert Mannyng describes in his version of the familiar tale of the dancers of Colbek, who sang in the churchyard all night and were rooted to the spot in punishment. The modern Christmas carol is a clerical parody of the *carole* made popular by the fifteenth-century friars.

31. The Latin reads: "by kisses, bribes, journeys, signs, lies, letters, *omitting important circumstances*," i.e. in the confessional, during shrift. MSS C and Lt read *receyve;* others have *reteyne*, "keep back."

32. The Latin reads *amare*, hence "loving." but the MS C reads *lovand.*

33. Rolle omitted from the list in his source references to not performing one's Easter duties, not honoring one's parents, not examining one's conscience, and avoiding churches and preaching; these would not apply to Margaret.

34. Ecclesiasticus 7:40.

35. This looks like an early identification of *anorexia nervosa*. The wisdom of this advice matches that of the author of *Ancrene Riwle* who, while advocating a far more stringent regime than Rolle's, yet allows the anchoresses to eat as many vegetables as they wish. Rolle is concerned that Margaret may overdo the fasting; it could be that this is what caused her seizures.

36. MS C reads *luf*, "love," but Lt has "praise," from a reading *lof.*

37. Or: "praising him."

38. 1 Corinthians 2:9.

39. Otherwise: *The Song of Solomon*, or *Canticle of Canticles*. Rolle wrote a Latin commentary on the first two verses of *Canticum*, and the imagery of this work seems to have colored much of his mystical experience, as well as his written style. Song of Songs 2:5.

40. Cf. the section of *Ego Dormio* on angels, above, pp.133–34.

41. This lyric is probably but not provably Rolle's. It is also found in the *Lay Folk's Mass Book*, where it is a devotion to be used at the Elevation at Mass. Hope Allen thinks that the *LFMB* borrowed the prayer from Rolle; it is a thirteenth-century, later revised, translation of a twelfth-century Anglo-Norman work,

which seems to have been made in the York diocese, see EETS (OS)71, Introd., pp.xi-liii; pp.40–41; 286–87.

42. This sentiment is echoed in *Emendatio Vitae*, cap.8: "Certainly, I think that those meditations in you which God himself pours into your soul through himself will be more pleasing to God and will accomplish more for you (sc. than my own meditations)," trans. del Mastro, p.72.

43. MS Lt reads *eigh*, "eye," and twelve MSS read *loue;* MS C has *lofe*, which could stand for either "praise" or "love."

44. The prayers Rolle prescribes were those which every confirmed adult was expected to know: *Ave Maria*, *Pater Noster*, *Gloria Patri* (not the salutation mentioned here), and the *Credo*, all in Latin, were the required knowledge even of illiterate peasants. *Miserere me Deus*, Psalm 50:1 (Vulgate) was the "neck verse": Anyone who could recite this was reckoned a cleric, and could plead "benefit of clergy," thus being subject to ecclesiastical, and not civil law courts; the former had no power to impose a death sentence, hence Psalm 50 could literally "save one's neck." These prayers are the most basic requirement of a young, not very intellectual religious. The recluses for whom *Ancrene Riwle* was prescribed had more elaborate prayers, with concessions for those who could not read.

45. Rolle insisted that his "fire" was real; he was defended in this by the late fourteenth-century hermit, Thomas Basset, against certain detractors. Others gave cautions to those who expected this "fire" to be "as hot as bodily fire" (Hilton, *Scale* I, chap.26), and the *Cloud* author terms a "feigned physical, not spiritual activity" the claim to have "breasts inflamed with unnatural heat caused by misgoverning the body" (*Cloud of Unknowing*, chap.45).

46. MS C reads *anedande;* Lt has *ondynge*, "panting"; the form *anelede*, "hurried" (*anelande* is prob. meant in MS C) occurs in *Sir Gawain and the Green Knight;* the expression seems to mean here: "solely aspiring, panting in desire for him," cf. *Emendatio Vitae*, Chap.xi: "He (sc. the soul) desires Him alone, namely Christ. He pants in a single desire, for Him. He sighs for Him, from Him he is kindled; in Him, burning, he rests" (trans. del Mastro).

47. Rolle means his own gift of *canor*.

48. A partial allusion to *dulcor*.

49. MS C reads *lyfe*, which is probably correct; otherwise, read *lufe*, "love."

50. The nightingale was a traditional type of the lover by Rolle's time and had been celebrated in religious allegory as well as secular song and *lai* by Rolle's time. His meaning here is not clear, since "fail" is not recorded in the sense "die" until after Rolle's time (it does not have this sense in *MED*), yet in both *Melos* and *Incendium* Rolle compares himself to the nightingale with the association of the nightingale singing until death: "continuing continuously until death in song" (*Melos*); "For in the beginning of my conversion and of my singular purpose, I thought that I wished to be made like the little bird that languished beyond love for his Beloved, but by languishing also rejoiced, by reaching in himself what he loves, and in rejoicing sings, and by singing languishes, but in sweetness and ardor. For the nightingale is carried away the whole night to indulge in singing and melody, so that it may please him to whom it is joined" (*Incendium*).

The nightingale, *luscinia megarhynchos*, is within the northern limit of its range in Yorkshire, where it bred frequently in the nineteenth cent. (there are no earlier records), and was especially common round Doncaster, the very region in which Hampole and its convent lay (T.H. Nelson, *The Birds of Yorkshire* (1907), p.48). It is a shy bird, preferring woodland undergrowth; the ornithological details make it a most apt symbol for a recluse or hermit, of course.

51. Rolle's devotion to the Holy Name derives from his early conversion, when he resisted a diabolical temptation in female form by invoking Christ: "O Jesus, how precious is your blood" (Lesson VII, Office). *Incendium* cap.15 explicitly associates the gift of *canor* with the love of Jesus: "I judge that this gift (of song) is given to no one because of merit, but to whomever Christ shall will. Nevertheless, I think that no one would receive it unless he loved the name of Jesus especially, and also honoured it, so much that never, except in sleep, would he allow it to fade from his memory" (trans. del Mastro). Despite the caution Rolle gives here that he does not mean mere mouthing of the name Jesus, Hilton had to explain the importance of devotion to Jesus in terms of its meaning, "spiritual health," and refutes the claim Rolle made in his *Canticles* that one cannot be saved without finding sweetness in devotion to the Holy Name (*Scale* I, Chap.44); "therefore all who love his name will be glorified . . . and indeed they will be glorified because they love your name. Truly, if they did not love it, they would be unable to be glorified . . . he who does not love will be eternally destitute of glory. Hence many worldly wretches who think they rejoice with Christ yet do not love the name Jesus will sorrow without end. . . . Therefore they will not see glory who did not love the name Jesus that makes all things glorious" (*Comment on the Canticles*, trans. Boenig, *Elizabethan and Renaissance Studies* 92:13 (Salzburg, 1984), pp.102–3. Rolle later curbed these youthful transports; actually Rolle and Hilton were not far apart in their thinking: In *Scale* I, Chap.46 Hilton advises the use of the name Jesus in meditation, and the *Cloud* author allows its use as a mantra (*Cloud*, Chap.48).

52. *Layabouts:* Rolle uses the word *gangrels*, which must have been colloquial in his time: *MED* cites only this passage, while *OED*, giving meaning "vagabond, lanky person," has sixteenth-century examples as its earliest citations.

53. 1 Corinthians 15:41: "The sun has its brightness, the moon a different brightness, and the stars a different brightness, and the stars differ from each other in brightness."

54. *Aspirations and songs:* or, "songs of affection."

55. This piece appears as prose in MS Lt; despite its title *cantus* in MS C it is less lyrical than Rolle's other "songs." The meaning is obscure; I have repunctuated; Hope Allen's punctuation would give a translation for lines 6–10 as follows: "love-longing is the most delightful in its teaching, the bond of sweet burning leads me to (the life of) day, for it keeps me away from palace and playing until I can obtain a vision of my beloved, who/which never departs." In line 8, *haldes* can mean "protects" or "holds back"; I prefer the former, seeing the lines as an allusion to an allegory: Waiting alone, the speaker attends like a servant in the palace, standing beside one of the braziers (the fire of love), until the prince arrives from his affairs of state or his recreation, and looks for his beloved; once he comes, he will never leave her side, walking (MS Lt) or waking (MS C etc.) with her. The scene echoes Song of Songs 1:4,12; 3:2; 5:7. The first two lines are based on the lyric in *Ego Dormio*.

56. This chapter was often excerpted; some of it is based on St. Bernard's Fifteen Sermons on the Canticles, parts on Rolle's own *Comment on the Canticles:* "We untiringly burn to seek the sweetness of eternal refreshment, internally and supernally singing delights in the mellifluous sweetness of spiritual fervour"; "Because the mind, inebriated by the divine cup strives to break out before the greatness of spiritual joy into the voice of God's praise, it is raised to the highest, singing and rejoicing in heavenly melody. . . . we fly rejoicing, snatched away to Christ unto a song of joy, shadowed by the heat of eternal light. . . . we are gratified not rarely but continually." (trans. Boenig, pp.124;131–2).

57. In MS Lt all five queries are indirect questions; in MS C the first two are direct questions; it is tempting to regard this involvement in dialogue as original: it certainly creates a more intimate and colloquial tone. It is probably, however, scribal rewriting, perhaps prompted by the direct questioning of the instructor in later mystical works, e.g. in Chap. 68 of *The Cloud of Unknowing*. Wiclif answers the same questions in an English tract (also translated into Latin). The first half of Rolle's exposition ("The first question . . . heritage of heaven") comes ultimately from Julianus Pomerius (formerly ascribed to St. Prosper of Aquitaine), *De Vita Contemplativa*, quoted in Hugh of Strasbourg's *Com.theol.verit.*v. cap.23.

58. The thought-processes here are ultimately derived from Augustine.

59. The similes of charcoal, air and wool derive from St. Bernard, *De Diligendo Deo*,cap.x, who probably took them from Augustine, *City of God* XI, ch.10. (A nature is called simple because it cannot lose attribute) "there is no difference between what it *is* and what it has, as there is, for example, between a vessel and the liquid it contains, a body and its colour, the atmosphere and its light or heat, the soul and its wisdom. None of these is what it contains" (trans. Henry Bettenson, Harmondsworth, 1972). But if this is the ultimate source, Bernard has distorted it. The allusion is also made in Richard of St. Victor, *Benjamin Minor* v, Chap.11, whence Rolle may have taken it.

60. I have altered the pronoun from "he" in the original to the colloquial indefinite "they," a practice Rolle himself often adopts in *The Form*. Rolle's own unease with the masculine pronoun in the context of a letter to a woman is shown by his switch to "you" in the following sentence.

61. This clause is not in most manuscripts, but is present in Lt, and seems necessary to the sense. Its loss can be accounted for in a hyparchetype in the MS C tradition by assuming eye-skip from *bot God* to *loue God* in the following clause.

62. *Motivation:* Rolle used the word *will*, an ultimately Augustinian emphasis inherited by Rolle, probably from Richard of St. Victor, whose source may have been Anselm [HEA].

63. An echo of Satan's words to St. Machary in *Lives of the Fathers* iii [HEA].

64. This and the following sentence are adapted from Bonaventure, *De Triplici Via*, vii [HEA].

65. Cf.Ps 75:3 (Vulg.): "And his place is in peace: and his abode in Sion" (Douay).

66. There is a similar discussion in Chapter 10 of *Emendatio Vitae*, where, however, the warnings that the just can still be tempted and sin are stronger, including a confession of weakness by Rolle himself. Nevertheless, he includes

the observation: "In this condition (of a cleansed conscience) a man can know that he is in the state of love, even in that love which can never be lost. He does not, nevertheless, live without great fear—not lest he incur torment, but lest he should offend his most dearly Beloved" (trans. del Mastro).

67. Wisdom 3:1: "The souls of the just are in the hands of God, and the torment of death shall not touch them" (Douay), blended with Eccl 9:1: "Here are upright men and wise; and every task of theirs is in God's keeping, nor can any tell whether they have earned his love, or his displeasure!" [Knox].

68. The ascription to Cassiodorus occurs in MS Lt; MS C has Augustine, who greatly influenced Cassiodorus; Augustine has an observation in Sermon 70 to the effect that "love makes all things harsh and enormous become straightaway easier and nearly non-existent."

69. MS C reads "the thing that is distant close to hand and the impossible . . ."

70. Lt has "praise" rather than "love" (MS C *lufes*) here.

71. Such "comings and goings" (Rolle wrote "comers and goers") caused Rolle to remove from his first cell at John de Dalton's because of the disturbance between June and November when the produce from the outlying farms was brought in for storage.

72. There is doubt as to who Rolle means here (perhaps he himself did not have a name for a quote he had found in a collection of similar material); both Augustine and Albertus Magnus were suggested by Noetinger.

73. The additional chapter may have been supplied to bring the total number of chapters to twelve, as in *Emendatio Vitae.*

74. Rolle lists the seven gifts in his comment on Psalm 11:7 in the same order. The qualities derive from Isaiah 11:2–3: "The spirit of the Lord shall rest upon him, the spirit of wisdom and of understanding, the spirit of counsel and of fortitude, the spirit of knowledge and of godliness; and he shall be filled with the spirit of the fear of the Lord" (Douay). *Piety: pyte* in MS; both "pity" and "piety" derive from *pietas.*

75. The word is *tagild* in the best manuscripts; see *Desire and Delight*, n.4.

76. Cf. Rolle's comment on Psalm 48:3: "Wisdom is appropriate to the things of God" [HEA].

77. *Joy:* This reflects Rolle's favorite word for mystic ecstasy, *jubilus.* He defines contemplation in Chapter 12 of *Emendatio Vitae* in a similar way, but without ascribing the definition to Augustine: "Certain men say that contemplation is nothing other than that knowledge of hidden future things, or the freedom from all the occupations of the world, or the study of divine writings. Others say that contemplation is the free and sharp-sighted exploration of wisdom, raised with wonder. Still others say that contemplation is a book, the penetrating observation of the soul opened wide in every direction for the discerning of virtues. Still others say, and well, that contemplation is rejoicing in holy things. And others say, and say best, that contemplation is the death of carnal affections through joy, by the raising of the spirit" (trans. del Mastro., p.85). The quotation has no traced parallel in Augustine.

78. This corporal work of mercy had real point in Rolle's time when prisoners were not fed or clothed except through charity.

79. Hosea 2:14: "For this reason I shall give her to suck (Douay:allure her;

Knox:lead her out), behold, I shall lead her into solitude and I shall speak to her heart."

80. MS C has *ligges*, "lies," echoed by *lieth* in most manuscripts; Lt reads *lightheth*, "is alight"; it seems likely that Rolle wrote *on leye*, "aflame, ablaze."

81. This address to Margaret does not occur in all manuscripts. In some, the final paragraph is omitted, in some the name does not occur, or appears as Margery, or is adapted to suit a male reader. The original recipient was undoubtedly Margaret Kirkby, whom Richard cured of seizures with the promise that the condition would not recur in his lifetime, as recounted in Lession 8 of the Office drawn up for Rolle's canonization.

82. I have retained the usual title "Form of Living," but give here a reminder of its actual meaning.

Notes to Appendix

1. In MS C the scribe indicates that *Al vanitese forsake* should follow *Thy joy Be;* because he has already copied the former, when he comes to the end of *Thy joy Be*, he writes *Al vanitese forsake . . . ut supra.* The Thornton and Longleat scribes correctly linked the two parts of the lyric, and in the right order; in MS C *Ghostly Gladness* is interposed between the two reversed parts.

2. *Thoughts:* The original reads "heads" and may perhaps be an allusion to the occasion when Margaret rested her head on Rolle's breast as she leaned out of her cell window, on the occasion when he cured her; described in Lesson 8 of the *Office of Richard Rolle*, presumably based on her own reminiscences.

3. A less literal version of this is given above, pp. 125–26. This version is included to show as much as possible of the alliteration.

Suggestions for Further Reading

Rolle's Works: English

Allen, Hope Emily, ed. *English Writings of Richard Rolle, Hermit of Hampole.* Oxford: Clarendon Press, 1963; repr. St. Clair Shores, Michigan: Scholarly Press, 1971. [Extracts from *Psalter* and *Meditations*, fewer lyrics than in Comper, the rest complete, but lacking *The Commandments;* in Middle English.]

Bramley, H.R., ed. *The Psalter or Psalms of David and Certain Canticles.* Oxford: Clarendon Press, 1884.

Colledge, E. *The Mediaeval Mystics of England.* New York: Scribner, 1961. [Contains a modern rendering of *Ego Dormio* and useful introduction on English spirituality.]

Comper, Frances. *The Life of Richard Rolle, Together with an Edition of his English Lyrics.* London and Toronto: J.M. Dent and Sons, 1928; repr. N.Y.: Barnes and Noble, 1969.

Harrell, J.C., ed. *Selected Writings of Richard Rolle.* London: SPCK, 1963. [Selections include *Desire and Delight*, *Seven Gifts of Holy Ghost* (*Form*, Chap.11) and extracts from *Meditations.*]

Heseltine, G.C., trans. *Selected Works of Richard Rolle, Hermit.* London: Longmans Green and Co., 1930. [Contains translation of *Commandment*, *Form*, *Shorter Meditation* (complete), *Ten Commandments*, *Ego Dormio*, short pieces, including *Oleum Effusum* in English from the Thornton MS, a modern rendering of Misyn's *Emendatio* translation, and some canticles (not all by Rolle) from the *Psalter.*]

Hodgson, G., trans. *The Form of Perfect Living and Other Prose Treatises of Richard Rolle of Hampole.* London: Thomas Baker, 1910.

—. *Some Minor Works of Richard Rolle.* London, John M. Watkins, 1923.

Horstman, Carl, ed. *Yorkshire Writers: Richard Rolle of Hampole, An English Father of the Church, and His Followers.* London: Swan Sonnenschein and Co., Vol.I, 1895; Vol.II, 1896. [Contains many works no longer attributed to Rolle; in Middle English.]

Lindkvist, Harald, ed. *Richard Rolle's "Meditatio de Passione Domini."* Skrifter utgifna af Kungl. Humanistika Vetenskaps, 19, Uppsala, 1917. [Uppsala MS of Long Version of Meditations; in Middle English.]

Madigan, M.F., ed. *The Passio Domini Theme in the Works of Richard Rolle: His Personal Contribution in Its Religious, Cultural and Literary Context.* Elizabethan and Renaissance Studies 79. Salzburg: 1978. [Long, full introduction, and transcription of BL MS Cotton Titus C.19.]

Ogilvie-Thomson, S. (ed.), *Richard Rolle: Prose and Verse, from MS. Longleat* 29, EETS (OS) 293 (1988).

Perry, George, ed. *English Prose Treatises of Richard Rolle of Hampole*, EETS OS 20, 1866, repr.1921; repr. N.Y.: Kraus, 1973. [Besides short pieces, and wrongly ascribed matter, contains *Office* in Latin.]

Rolle's Works: Latin

Arnould, E.J.F., ed. *The Melos Amoris of Richard Rolle of Hampole.* Oxford: Basil Blackwell, 1957. [Latin only.]

Boenig, R., trans. *Richard Rolle: Biblical Commentaries: Short Exposition of Ps.20, Treatise on the Twentieth Psalm, Comment on the First Verses of the Canticle of Canticles, Commentary on the Apocalypse.* Elizabethan and Renaissance Studies 92:13. Salzburg: 1984.

Comper, F. *The Fire of Love or Melody of Love and The Mending of Life or Rule of Living.* London: Methuen, 1914. [Modernizations of Misyn's fifteenth-century translations, Introduction by Evelyn Underhill.]

Daly, J.P., ed. *An Edition of the "Judica Me Deus" of Richard Rolle.* Elizabethan and Renaissance Studies 92:14. Salzburg: 1984. [with translation]

Deanesly, Margaret, ed. *The Incendium Amoris of Richard Rolle of Hampole.* Manchester: University Press, 1915; repr. Folcroft, PA.: 1974.

Harford, Dundas, trans. *The Mending of Life.* London: H.R. Allenson, 1913. [with introduction]

Harvey, Ralph, ed. *The Fire of Love and the Mending of Life or The Rule of Living of Richard Rolle*, EETS OS 106, 1896; repr. N.Y.: Kraus 1973. [Misyn's fifteenth-century translation of Rolle's *Incendium* and *Emendatio;* in Middle English.]

Marzac, Nicole, *Richard Rolle de Hampole (1300–1349): Vie et oeuvres suivies du tractatus Super Apocalypsim.* Paris: J. Vrin. [Parallel text of Latin and French translations, plus biographical introduction.]

Mastro, M.L. del, trans. *The Fire of Love and the Mending of Life.* Garden City, N.Y.: Image Books, 1981. [Translated from the original Latin.]

Noetinger, M. *Le Feu de l'amour, Le Modele de la Vie Parfaite, Le Pater.* Tours: 1928. [French translation]

Theiner, P., ed. and trans. *The Contra Amatores Mundi of Richard Rolle of Hampole.* Univ. of California Publications, English Studies 33. Berkeley and Los Angeles: 1968.

Vandenbroucke, Francois, ed. *Le Chant d'Amour (Melos Amoris).* Trans. Les Moniales de Wisques from the Latin Text of E.J.F. Arnould's edition. Paris: Les Editions du Cerf, 1971. [French and Latin texts in parallel; excellent introduction]

Wolters, Clifton, trans. *The Fire of Love.* Harmondsworth: Penguin, 1972.

Woolley, Reginald, ed. *The Officium and the Miracula of Richard Rolle of Hampole.* London: 1919.

Studies Relating to Rolle

Alford, J.A. "Richard Rolle and Related Works," in *Middle English Prose:* A Critical Guide to Major Authors and Genres, ed. A.S.G. Edwards, New Brunswick: Rutgers University Press, 1984.

Allen, Hope Emily. *Writings Ascribed to Richard Rolle, Hermit of Hampole and Materials for his Biography.* The Modern Language Association of American, Monograph Series 3, N.Y.: D. Heath and Co., 1927.

Clark, J.P.H. "Richard Rolle: A Theological Re-assessment," *Downside Review* 101 (April, 1983): 108–139.

———. "Richard Rolle as a Biblical Commentator," *The Downside Review* (1986), pp.165–213.

Clay, R.M. *Hermits and Anchorites of England.* London: Methuen, 1914.

Coleman, T.W. *English Mystics of the Fourteenth Century.* Westport, Conn.: Greenwood Press, 1938.

Deanesly, Margaret. *The Lollard Bible and Other Medieval Biblical Versions.* Cambridge: University Press, 1920; repr. 1966.

Hodgson, G. *The Sanity of Mysticism.* London: 1926.

Hodgson, Phyllis. *Three Fourteenth-Century English Mystics.* London: Longmans, 1967.

Knowles, David. *The English Mystics.* London: Burns, Oates and Washbourne, 1927.

———. *The English Mystical Tradition.* N.Y.: Harper, 1967.

Knowlton, Mary Arthur. *The Influence of Richard Rolle and Julian of Norwich on the Middle English Lyrics.* The Hague: Mouton, 1973.

Lagorio, V. and R. Bradley. *The Fourteenth-Century English Mystics. A Comprehensive and Annotated Bibliography.* N.Y.: Garland, 1981.

Pepler, C. *The English Religious Heritage.* Saint Louis: Herder, 1958.

Renaudin, Paul. *Quatre Mystiques Anglais.* Paris: Eds. Montaigne, 1954.

Riehle, Wolfgang. *The Middle English Mystics.* Trans. Bernard Standring. London: Routledge and Kegan Paul, 1981.

Sitwell, Gerard. *Spiritual Writers of the Middle Ages.* N.Y.: Hawthorne Books, 1961.

Thornton, Martin. *English Spirituality.* London: SPCK, [illegible]3.

Tuma, G.W. *The Fourteenth-Century Mystics: A Comprehensive Analysis.* Elizabethan and Renaissance Studies 61 and 62. Salzburg: 1977.

Walsh, J. *Pre-Reformation English Spirituality.* London: 1965.

Other Middle English Spiritual Writings

Blake, N.F. *Middle English Religious Prose.* York Medieval Texts. London: Edward Arnold, 1972.

Butler-Bowdon, W. *The Book of Margery Kempe*. The World's Classics, Oxford: University Press, 1954. [Modernized].

Colledge, Edmund and J. Walsh, eds. *A Book of Showings to the Anchoress Julian of Norwich*, Pontifical Institute of Mediaeval Studies, 2 vols., Toronto: Universa Press, 1978.

Hodgson, Phyllis, ed. *The Cloud of Unknowing and Related Treatises*. Analecta Cartusiana 3. Salzburg: 1982.

Mastro, M.L. del, trans. *The Stairway of Perfection*. Garden City, N.Y.: Doubleday and Co., 1979.

Salu, M.B., trans. *The Ancrene Riwle*, with an Introduction by Dom Gerard Sitwell, and a preface by J.R.R. Tolkien. London: Burns and Oates, 1955. [Modern translation]

Sherley-Price, Leo, trans. *The Ladder of Perfection*. Harmondsworth: Penguin, 1957.

Thompson, W.M., ed. *De Wohunge of Ure Lauerd*, EETS OS 241, 1958.

Underhill, Evelyn. *The Scale of Perfection*. London: John M. Watkins, 1923. [Based on Harley MS 6579, with introduction]

Ward, Sr. Benedicta. *The Prayers and Meditations of Saint Anselm*, with a foreword by R.W. Southern. Harmondsworth: Penguin, 1973. [Translation]

Index to Introduction

Index to Texts

INDEX TO TEXTS

Other Volumes in this Series

Julian of Norwich • SHOWINGS
Jacob Boehme • THE WAY TO CHRIST
Nahman of Bratslav • THE TALES
Gregory of Nyssa • THE LIFE OF MOSES
Bonaventure • THE SOUL'S JOURNEY INTO GOD, THE TREE OF LIFE, and THE LIFE OF ST. FRANCIS
William Law • A SERIOUS CALL TO DEVOUT AND HOLY LIFE, and THE SPIRIT OF LOVE
Abraham Isaac Kook • THE LIGHTS OF PENITENCE, LIGHTS OF HOLINESS, THE MORAL PRINCIPLES, ESSAYS, and POEMS
Ibn 'Ata' Illah • THE BOOK OF WISDOM and Kwaja Abdullah Ansari • INTIMATE CONVERSATIONS
Johann Arndt • TRUE CHRISTIANITY
Richard of St. Victor • THE TWELVE PATRIARCHS, THE MYSTICAL ARK, and BOOK THREE OF THE TRINITY
Origen • AN EXHORTATION TO MARTYRDOM, PRAYER AND SELECTED WORKS
Catherine of Genoa • PURGATION AND PURGATORY, THE SPIRITUAL DIALOGUE
Native North American Spirituality of the Eastern Woodlands • SACRED MYTHS, DREAMS, VISIONS, SPEECHES, HEALING FORMULAS, RITUALS AND CEREMONIALS
Teresa of Avila • THE INTERIOR CASTLE
Apocalyptic Spirituality • TREATISES AND LETTERS OF LACTANTIUS, ADSO OF MONTIER-EN-DER, JOACHIM OF FIORE, THE FRANCISCAN SPIRITUALS, SAVONAROLA
Athanasius • THE LIFE OF ANTONY, A LETTER TO MARCELLINUS
Catherine of Siena • THE DIALOGUE
Sharafuddin Maneri • THE HUNDRED LETTERS
Martin Luther • THEOLOGIA GERMANICA
Native Mesoamerican Spirituality • ANCIENT MYTHS, DISCOURSES, STORIES, DOCTRINES, HYMNS, POEMS FROM THE AZTEC, YUCATEC, QUICHE-MAYA AND OTHER SACRED TRADITIONS
Symeon the New Theologian • THE DISCOURSES
Ibn Al'-Aribī • THE BEZELS OF WISDOM
Hadewijch • THE COMPLETE WORKS
Philo of Alexandria • THE CONTEMPLATIVE LIFE, THE GIANTS, AND SELECTIONS
George Herbert • THE COUNTRY PARSON, THE TEMPLE
Unknown • THE CLOUD OF UNKNOWING
John and Charles Wesley • SELECTED WRITINGS AND HYMNS
Meister Eckhart • THE ESSENTIAL SERMONS, COMMENTARIES, TREATISES AND DEFENSE
Francisco de Osuna • THE THIRD SPIRITUAL ALPHABET
Jacopone da Todi • THE LAUDS
Fakhruddin 'Iraqi • DIVINE FLASHES
Menahem Nahum of Chernobyl • THE LIGHT OF THE EYES

Early Dominicans • SELECTED WRITINGS
John Climacus • THE LADDER OF DIVINE ASCENT
Francis and Clare • THE COMPLETE WORKS
Gregory Palamas • THE TRIADS
Pietists • SELECTED WRITINGS
The Shakers • TWO CENTURIES OF SPIRITUAL REFLECTION
Zohar • THE BOOK OF ENLIGHTENMENT
Luis de León • THE NAMES OF CHRIST
Quaker Spirituality • SELECTED WRITINGS
Emanuel Swedenborg • THE UNIVERSAL HUMAN AND SOUL-BODY INTERACTION
Augustine of Hippo • SELECTED WRITINGS
Safed Spirituality • RULES OF MYSTICAL PIETY, THE BEGINNING OF WISDOM
Maximus Confessor • SELECTED WRITINGS
John Cassian • CONFERENCES
Johannes Tauler • SERMONS
John Ruusbroec • THE SPIRITUAL ESPOUSALS AND OTHER WORKS
Ibn 'Abbād of Ronda • LETTERS ON THE SŪFĪ PATH
Angelus Silesius • THE CHERUBINIC WANDERER
The Early Kabbalah •
Meister Eckhart • TEACHER AND PREACHER
John of the Cross • SELECTED WRITINGS
Pseudo-Dionysius • THE COMPLETE WORKS
Bernard of Clairvaux • SELECTED WORKS
Devotio Moderna • BASIC WRITINGS
The Pursuit of Wisdom • AND OTHER WORKS BY THE AUTHOR OF THE CLOUD OF UNKNOWING